AF573935

JULIA CALFEE
SPIRITS AND GHOSTS
Journeys through Mongolia

Edited and with an Introduction by Antonin Kratochvil

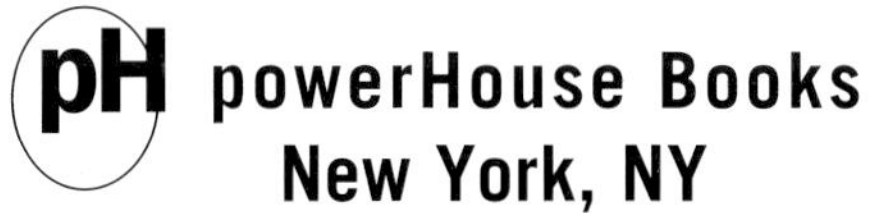
powerHouse Books
New York, NY

To the SPIRITS
who protected and accompanied me on my journeys;
may they continue to do so

...And here were forests ancient as the hills,
Enfolding sunny spots of greenery.

But oh! that deep romantic chasm which slanted
Down the green hill athwart a cedarn cover!
A savage place! as holy and enchanted...

—Samuel Taylor Coleridge, *Kubla Khan*

MONGOLIA: a country many of us have little on. Mention it to the majority and you'd be lucky if even the names Genghis or Kublai are spoken. At a stretch, it may bring back a memory of a color spread in a travel magazine long ago, or similarly force an account of the decorative costumes worn by the herdsmen of the Gobi, but for the most part, nothing. For many, "Mongolia" is just a word, and a space sitting between a former and a present superpower, in that of Russia and China. Little is known of this vast land, less stirs the mind of this relic that once was, and today hardly a thought can be cast to the enigma that is Mongolia.

My travels in photography have taken me to two Mongolias. In 1993 I journeyed to the country itself to shoot an essay on Ulaanbaatar's street children. Ulaanbaatar is Mongolia's capital, and the street children are the casualties of its collapse. Back then what hit me was the vacuum the country was reeling from. When the Soviet Union finally withered, the roots that had stretched into Mongolia withered too. The vacuum was the cooperatives and factories, installed to power its centrally-run economy, which had turned fallow and become broken-down through neglect. The vacuum was the urban expansion, its socialist-realism housing, and modern infrastructure that instead of exemplifying the success of its political philosophy embodied the stereotypical Orwellian nightmare: pollution, poverty, and more important, the loss of identity for a people whose ancestors once held the reins of the world's greatest empire. My images were saying the same thing, capturing the vagabond kids that inhabited the sewers. This was the vacuum, and the social experiment gone wrong; here was the place I journeyed to that first time; it was the first Mongolia.

I'd seen this societal free fall before; I'd lived it in the Czech Republic. The injection of ideology into the minds and habits of people, and then when it failed...nothing, just a hollowed-out colony, and just a group of living ghosts.

If my grasp of Mongolia wasn't enough, the actions of its people left no doubt: outsiders looking in were unwelcome! There were warnings. Prior to my arrival in Ulaanbaatar, a BBC cameraman had been severely beaten—he'd been looking in for too long. In some cultures shame goes hand in hand with appearance—like hope, it is let slide. Not so the Mongolians. There was suspicion everywhere, with scrutiny and disbelief aimed toward any stranger. If you weren't photographing reindeer and their keepers, throat singers, or dinosaur theme parks, you were looking in, at them, spying on their misery, and mocking their pride. I was fortunate to get the material I'd come for, and more fortunate to leave unscathed, if not a little uneasy from the ghosts inside their abandoned world.

In 1997 I met Julia Calfee. We'd been put together as student and teacher at a documentary photography workshop. Julia stood out from all the other students because of the images she'd brought. They were of Mongolia—a rarity for any photographer. The handful of brightly-colored shots I saw did little in the way of photography but the subject was unique. That summer a transformation took place: the conformity and structure that had restrained the message and aesthetic so evident in Julia's work turned into a passion for shooting gritty, off-the-cuff pictures. Added to this was an appreciation for working in black-and-white. This was the way I saw the world, and somehow it had rubbed off. I'm not sure how it happened, or why so quickly. I'd like to think it was my instruction, although there seems to be more to it. By the end of the workshop Julia had completely understood, and made the leap.

At the end of that summer she set out for the place in her pictures with a new understanding. With every homecoming, momentum gathered. Her understanding through experience was showing in the way she worked, and the Ziploc bags full of shot film proved it. The pictures were improving, but to see in this country completely she needed to go beyond its exotic facade. Twice more she went, and each time I called on her to look deeper. It worked. Her arrival a year later from the wilds of the country's plains, traveling beside a shaman, showed that this journey had pushed the project into another dimension. This time she had brought with her a country I'd only read about, unlike my images of its victims, and unlike *National Geographic*; Julia Calfee had revealed the supernatural and the shamans who bridge the void between the worlds of the living and that of the spirits. For me, it was the other Mongolia.

The land that sat amongst the contact sheets was mystical. Dark tents with candle-lit offerings tell of the Mongols' beliefs in the past that so governs their present. Animals, and nature blending into an energy so primitive it fills the soul entirely. In black-and-white the images had form and feeling, and were free from all color and its literal effects. Julia had found a road into Xanadu, but that wasn't enough. Mongolia was made up of many parts, each needing representation if the project was to address the questions that would bring truth as its final answer. To me, it seemed obvious that the division within Mongolia had come, on one side, in the subject matter I'd shot over half a decade before, and in this portal that Julia had returned back from. To compare the contrasts would go some ways to tying together the ancient with the present, the loss and the damage, and of course the spirits and the ghosts.

It has been a five-year commitment to this book. In that time I've watched its progress meander, and change moving quicker at times than at others, but never stopping. Julia never wavered, but kept on and pushed through. She remained uninhibited in her efforts and opened up to her subjects at every instance with every instinct. In putting the body of work together she has had to witness the jails, the dilapidation, and the cities, which in the culture of these nomads represent hell on earth—that was my job, to help her see this, to help her examine the human fallout and measure its tragedy, and to teach her to walk amongst ghosts.

As photography goes, especially photojournalism, her style is very contemporary, mixing blurs and shifting focus through the objects in her images, persuading you of a message or drawing out an emotion. And yet, with all this, the images remain direct, taking aim, giving the impression you exist in what sits open in front of you. The people within her pictures have been handled respectfully, as have those without any. Never has she lain in wait for a facial expression to illustrate a predetermined attitude such as anger, madness, or hostility. Julia is honest that way, shooting only the reality—not the agenda. But it is the landscapes where I think the unique shines amongst the unique. The cityscapes, the slender passages through low mountains, and not least of all, the desolate steppe. The landscapes speak from the manner in which they've been taken, uncluttered so that the emphasis is on little else but the land. In a way their emptiness allows the viewer to transpose what the other images in the book have inspired—it could be the sweeping hordes of Mongol soldiers, or a hunting party of bowmen and their enormous camps, moving with the seasons, the food supply, or the war to come. These landscapes move you to imagine this, and that the *Monkh Khoh Tenger* (Eternal Blue Heaven), which once reigned over the earth protecting the Mongol people, is hearing their wishes and receiving their communions. In SPIRITS AND GHOSTS, the landscapes symbolize the mystic.

This book is the work of a novice. It is the result of an awakening of a dormant talent. In traveling through Mongolia she has opened up, discovering perhaps as much about herself as the country itself. I was fortunate to travel along, like I said, in the contact sheets and amongst each frame, with every new twist and turn. I followed. I was a guide from my home in New York, steering her desire to its natural conclusion—the two of us were both doing something never done before, traveling together only in different ways.

—Antonin Kratochvil
January, 2003

JOURNEYS THROUGH MONGOLIA

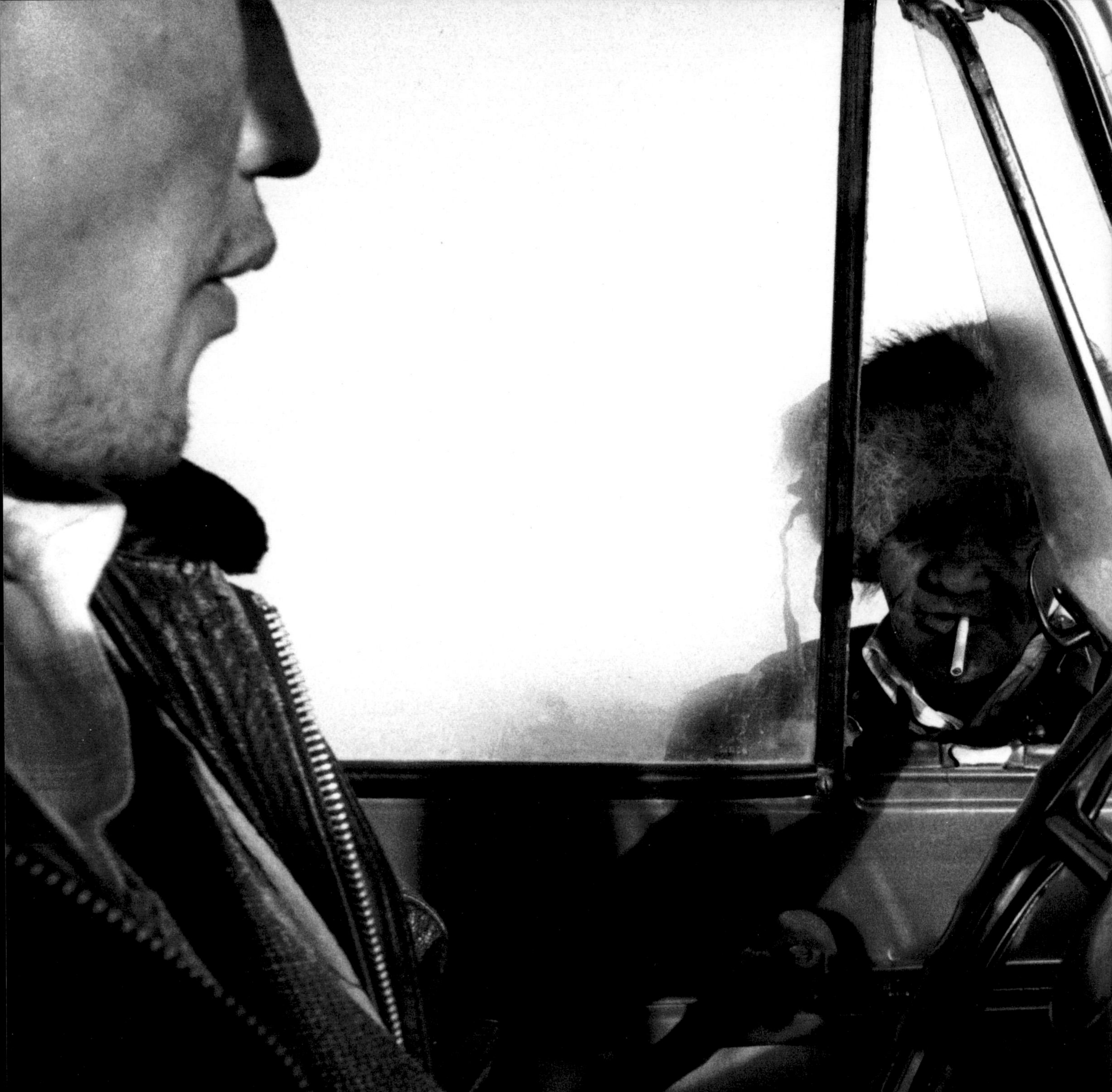

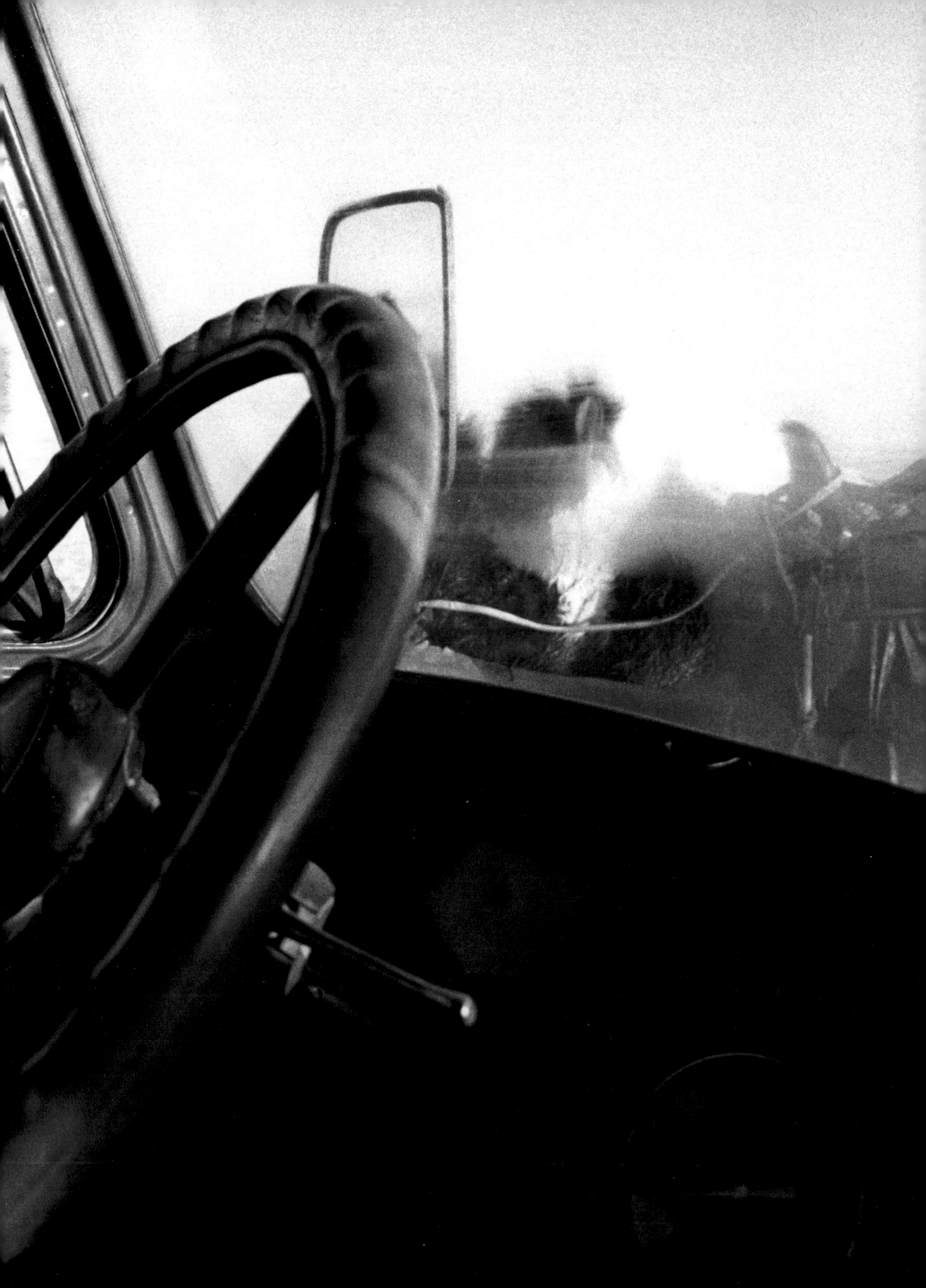

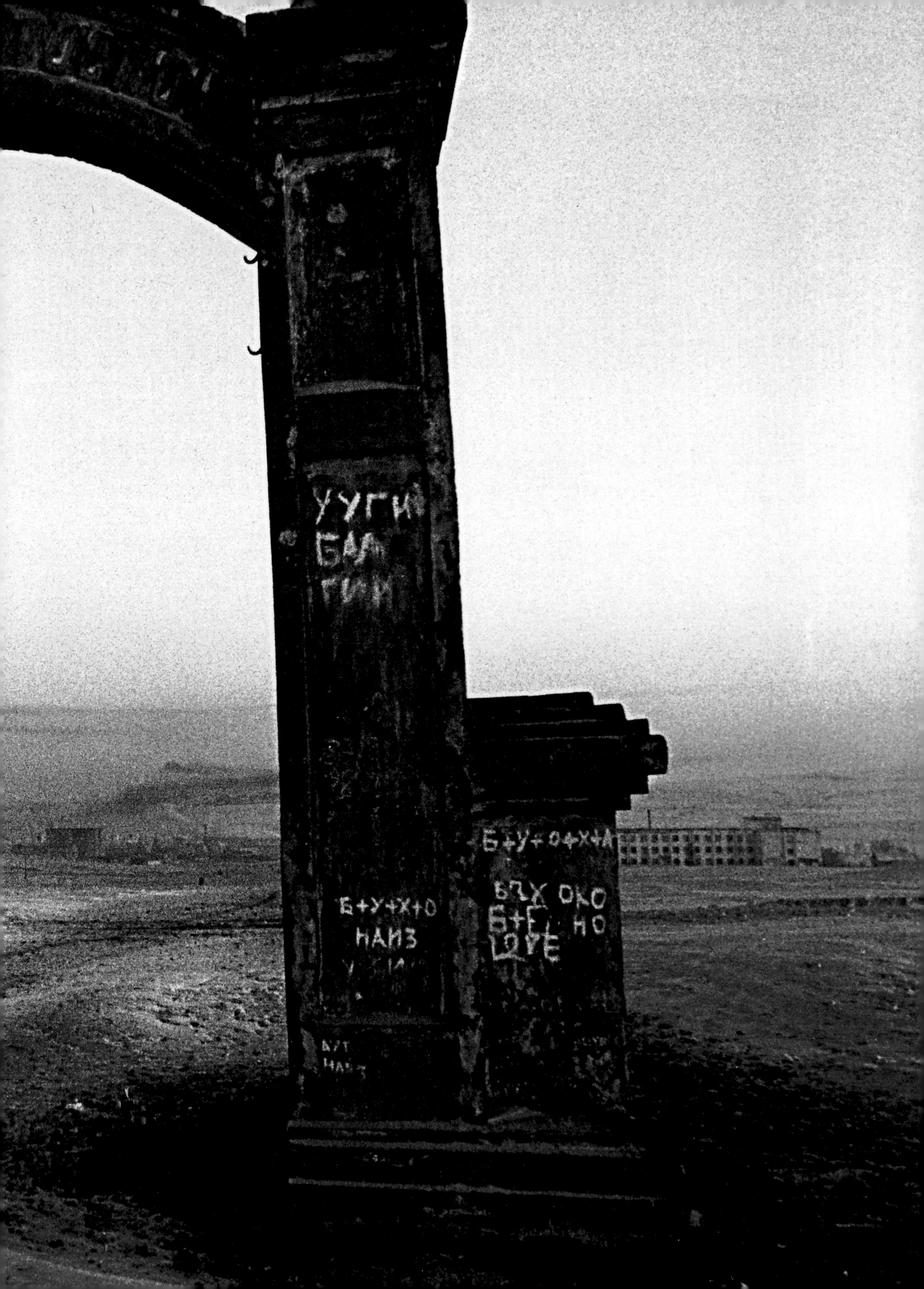
УУГИ
Б+У+Х+О
НАЙЗ
Б+У+О+Х+А
LOVE

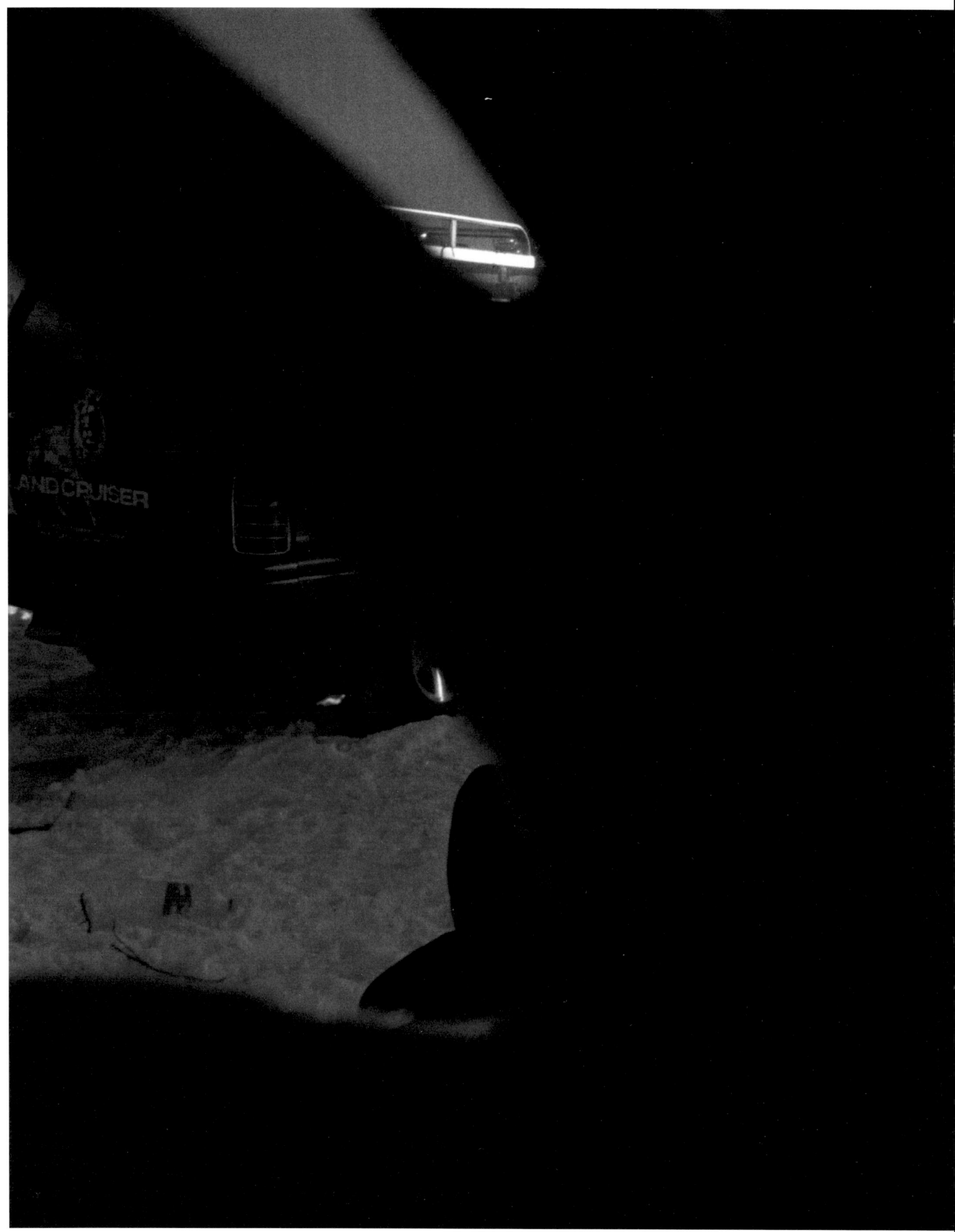
ANDCRUISER

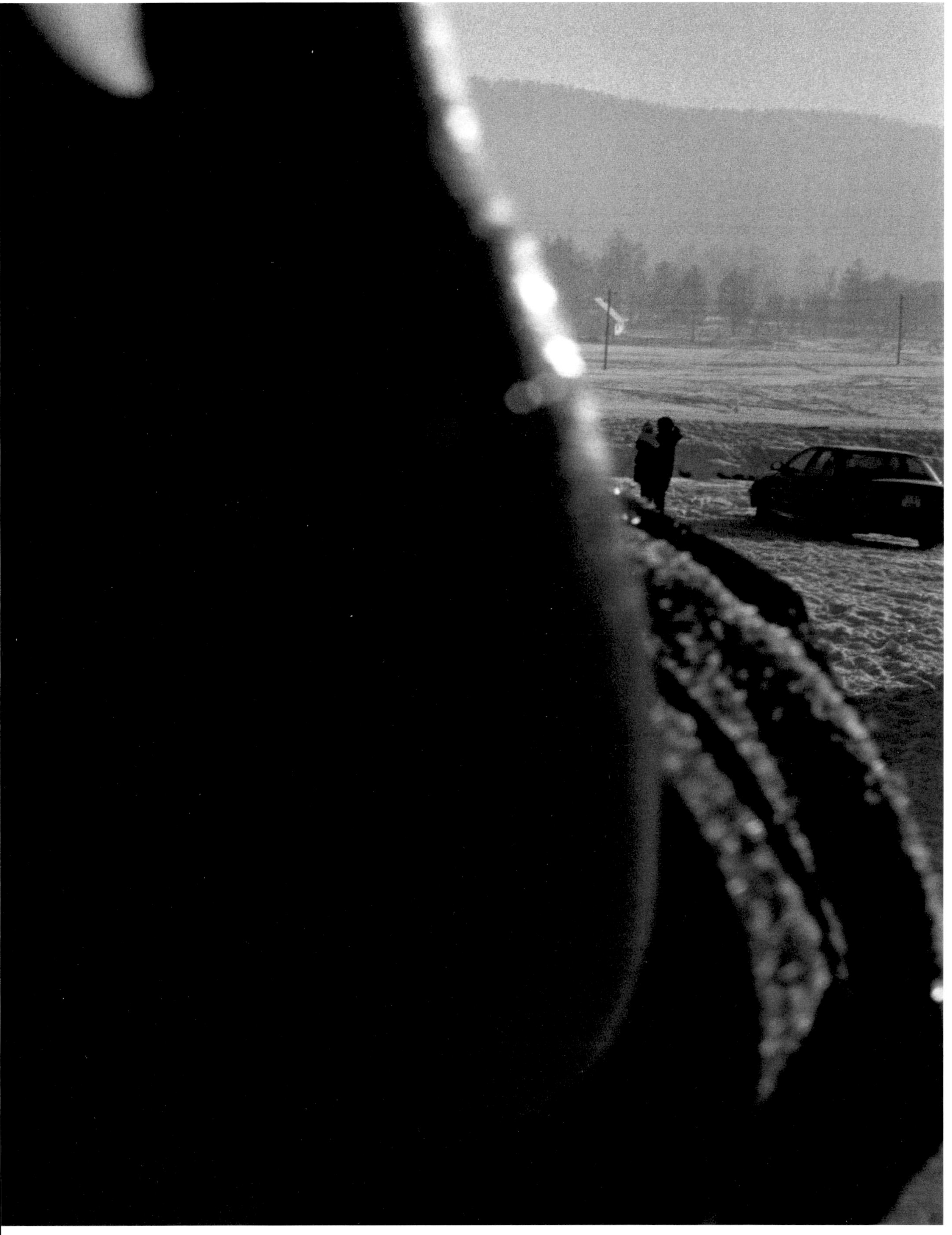

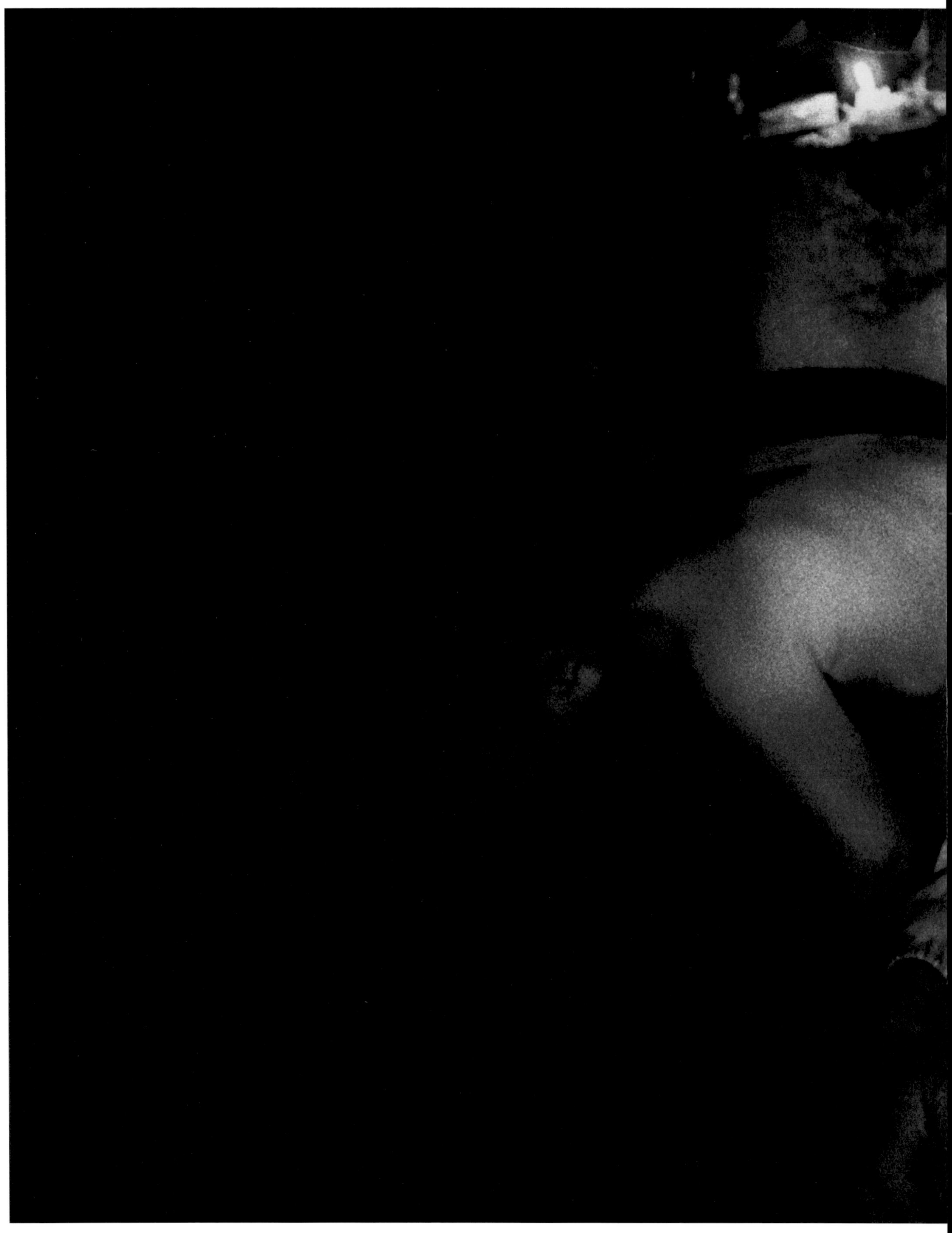

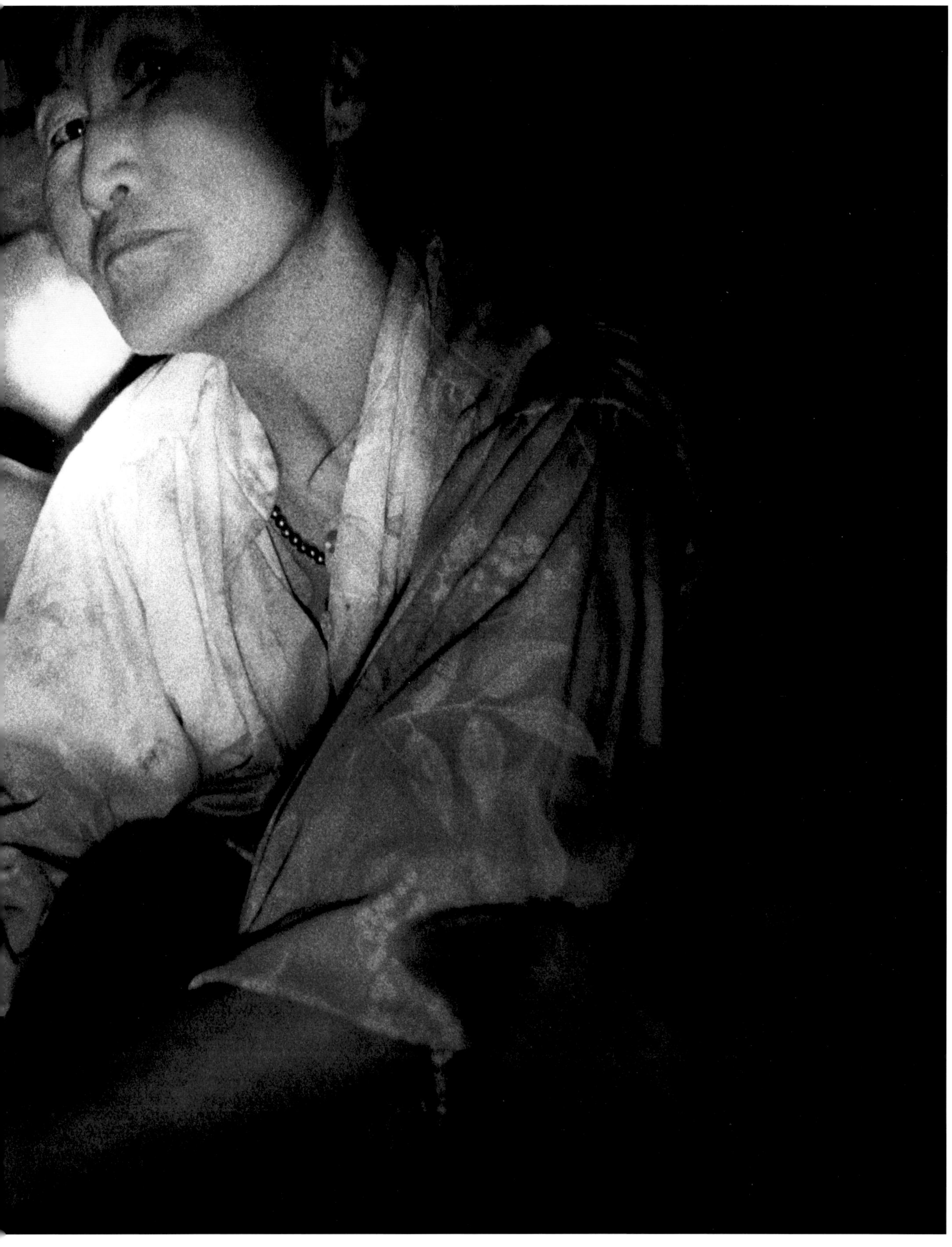

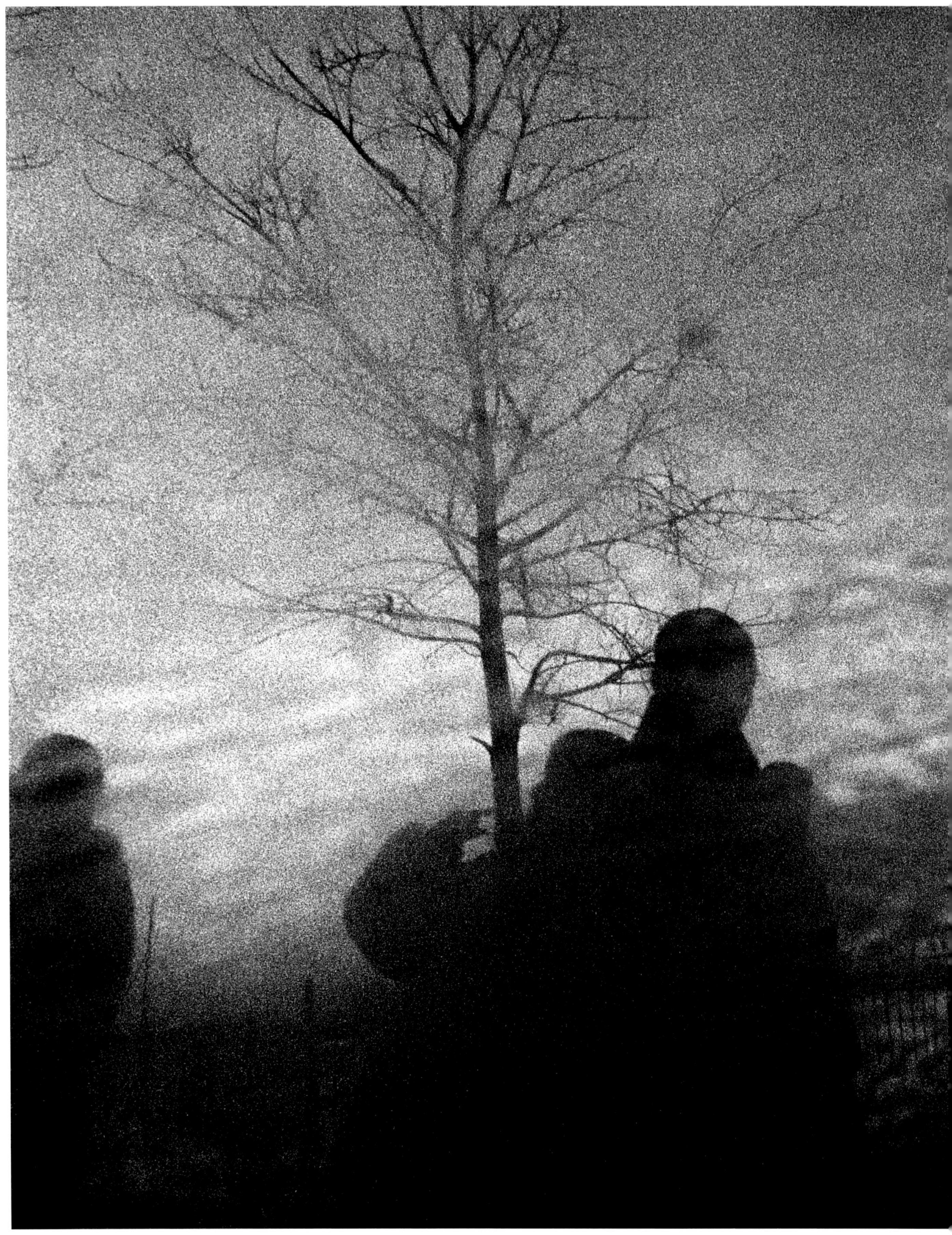

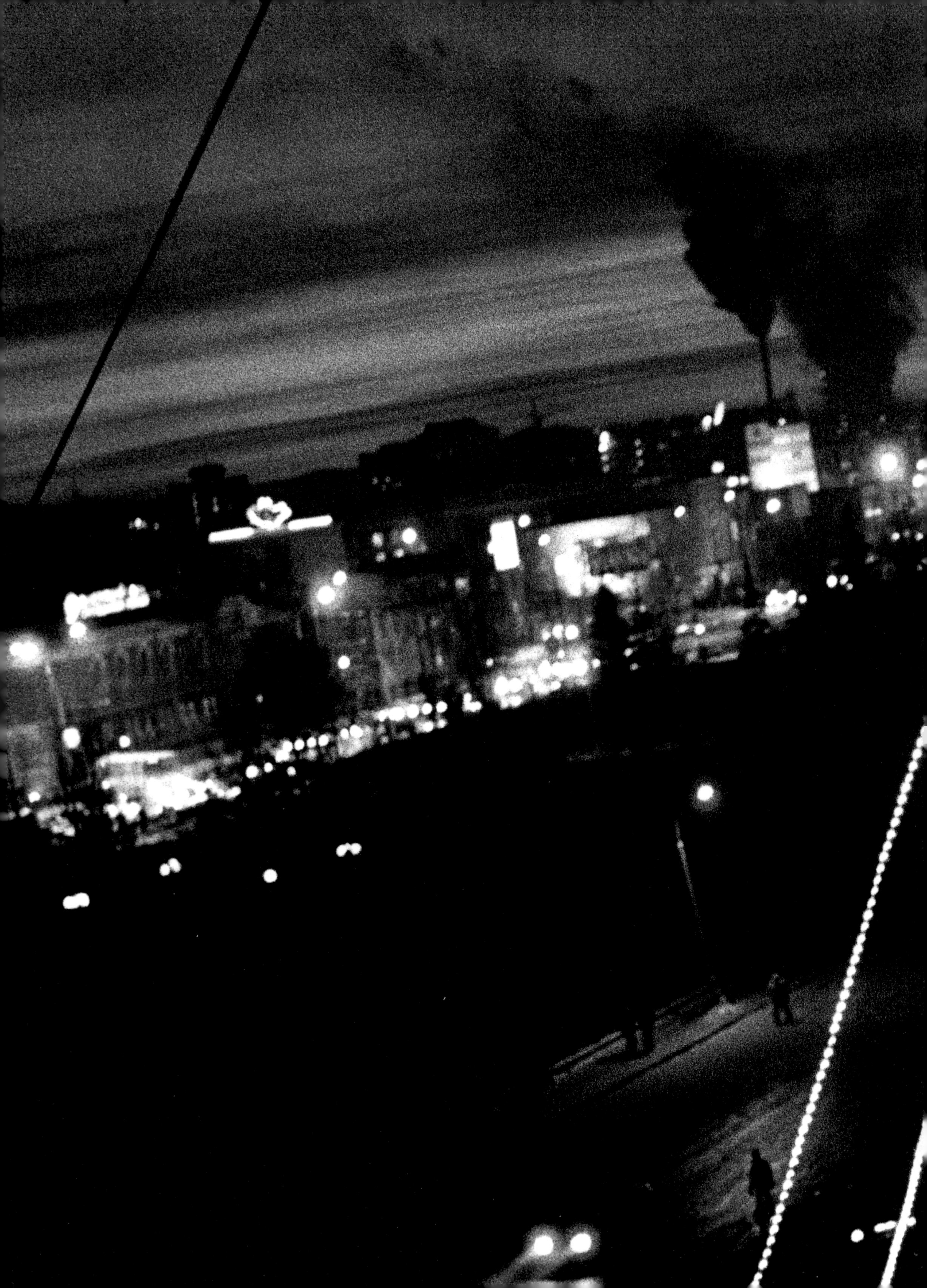

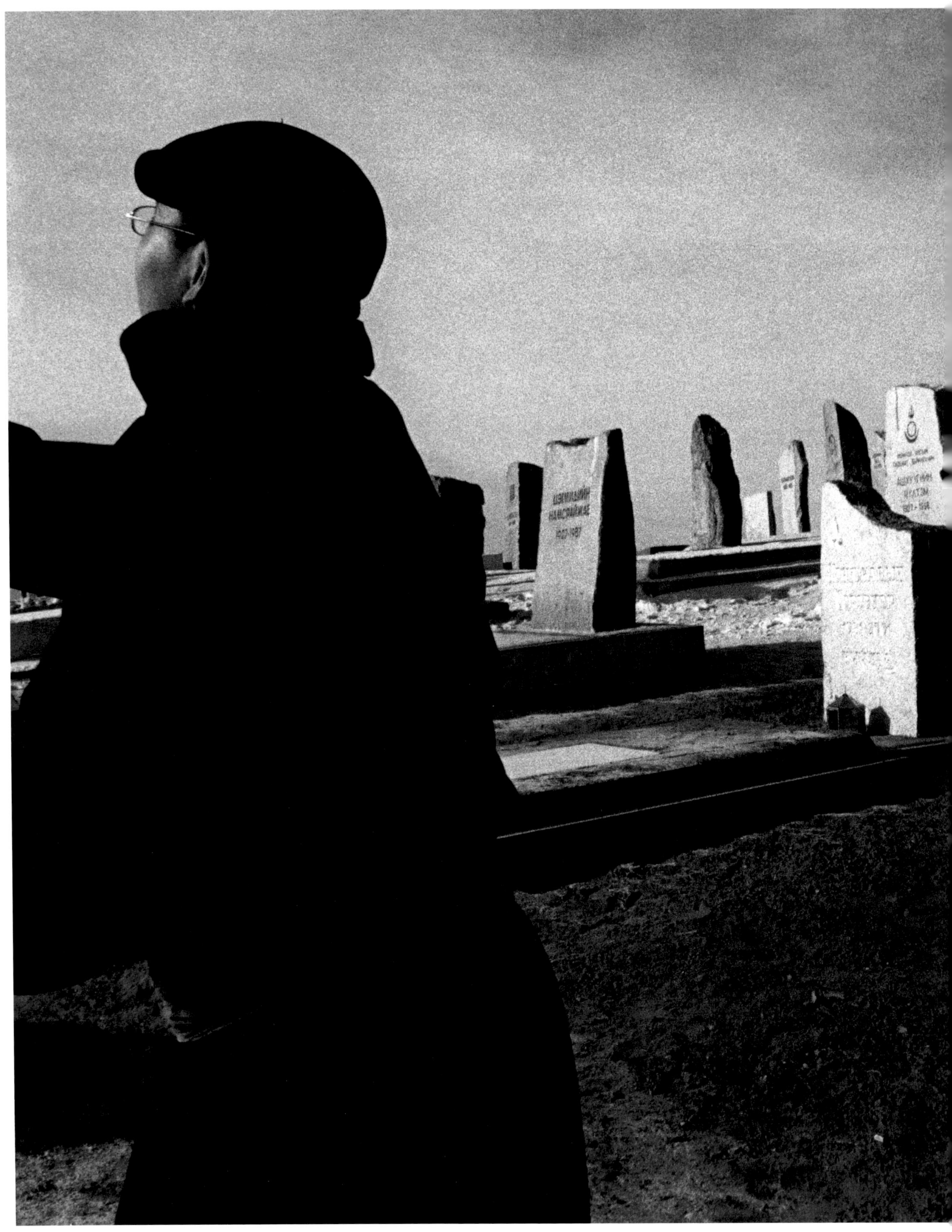

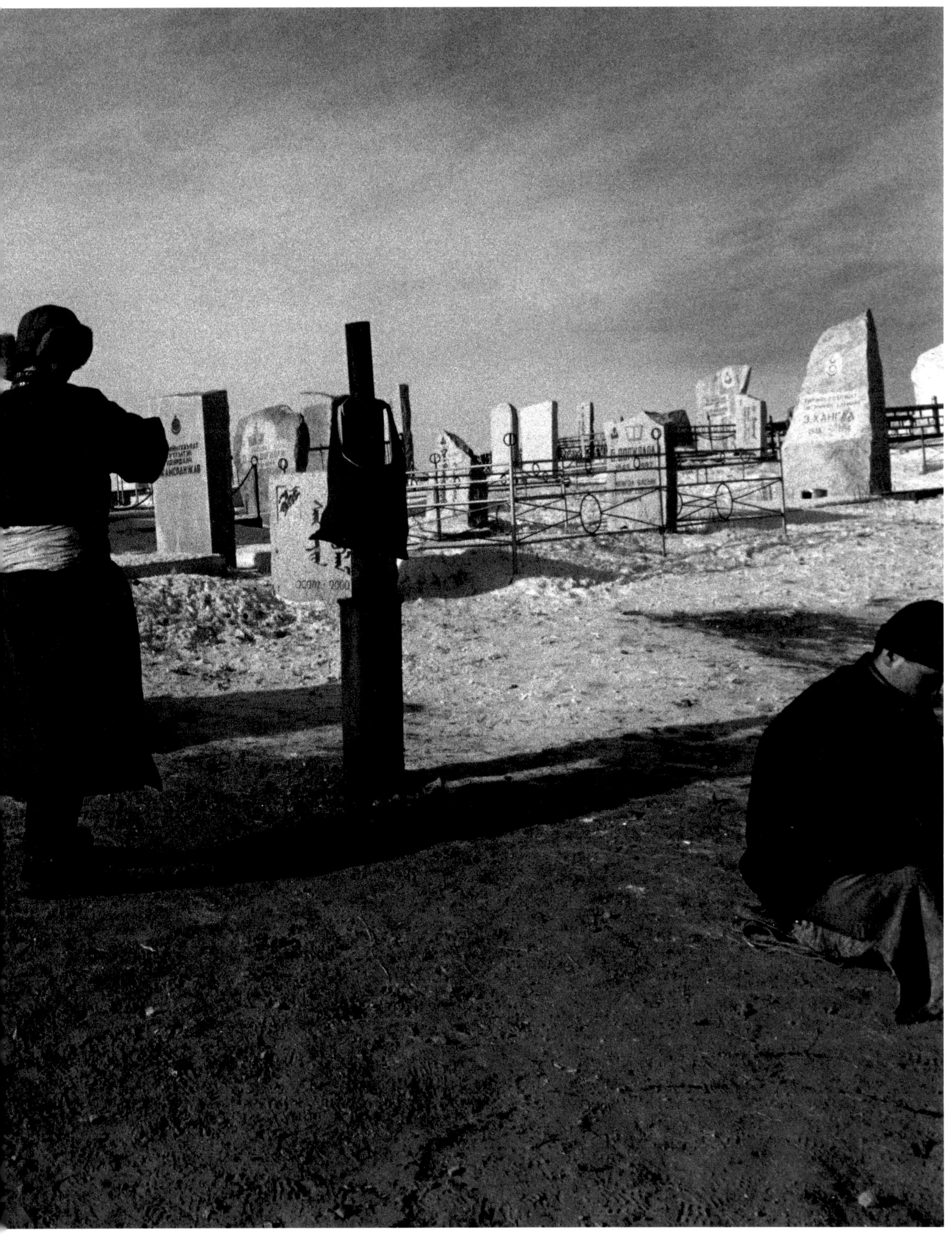

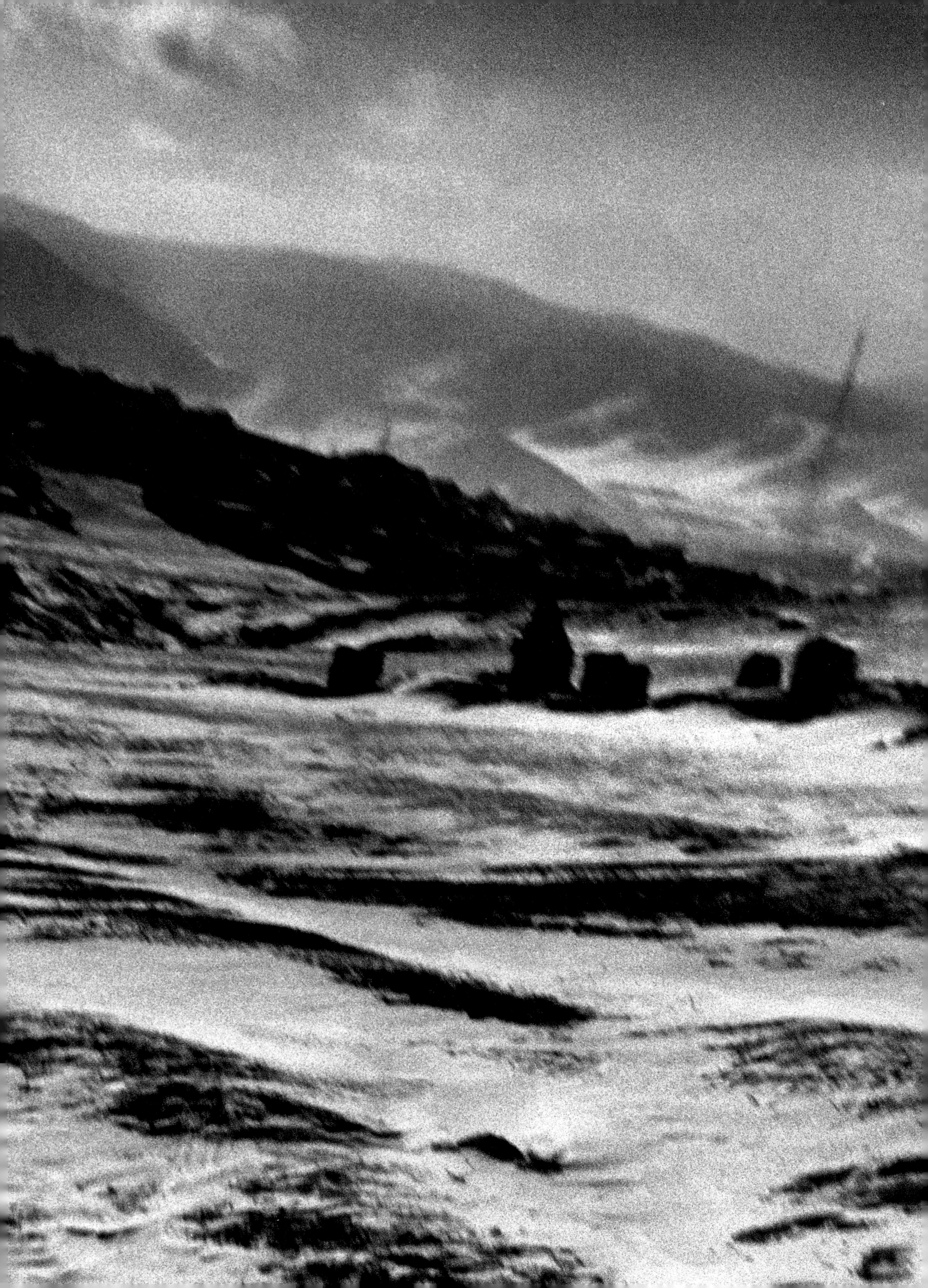

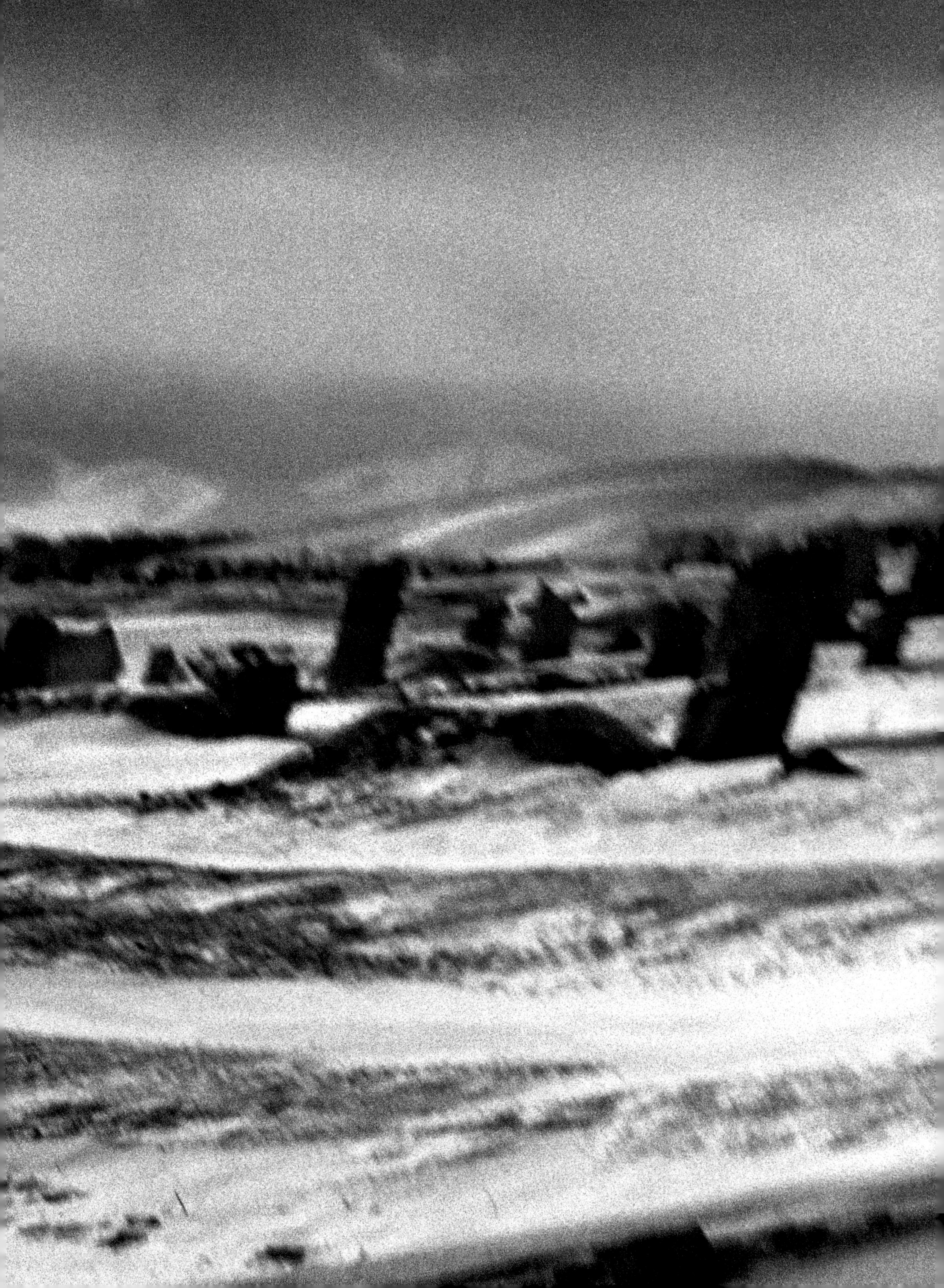

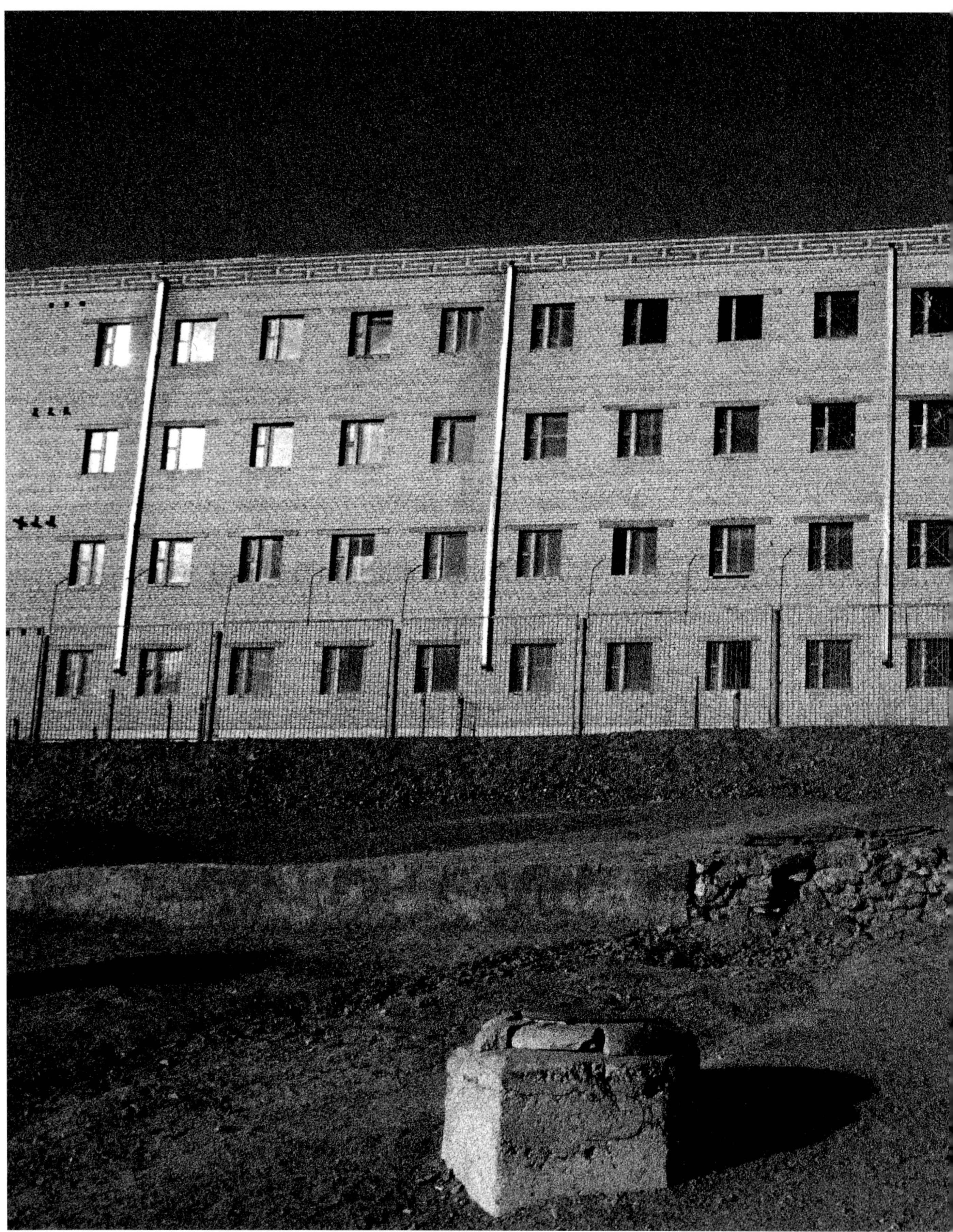

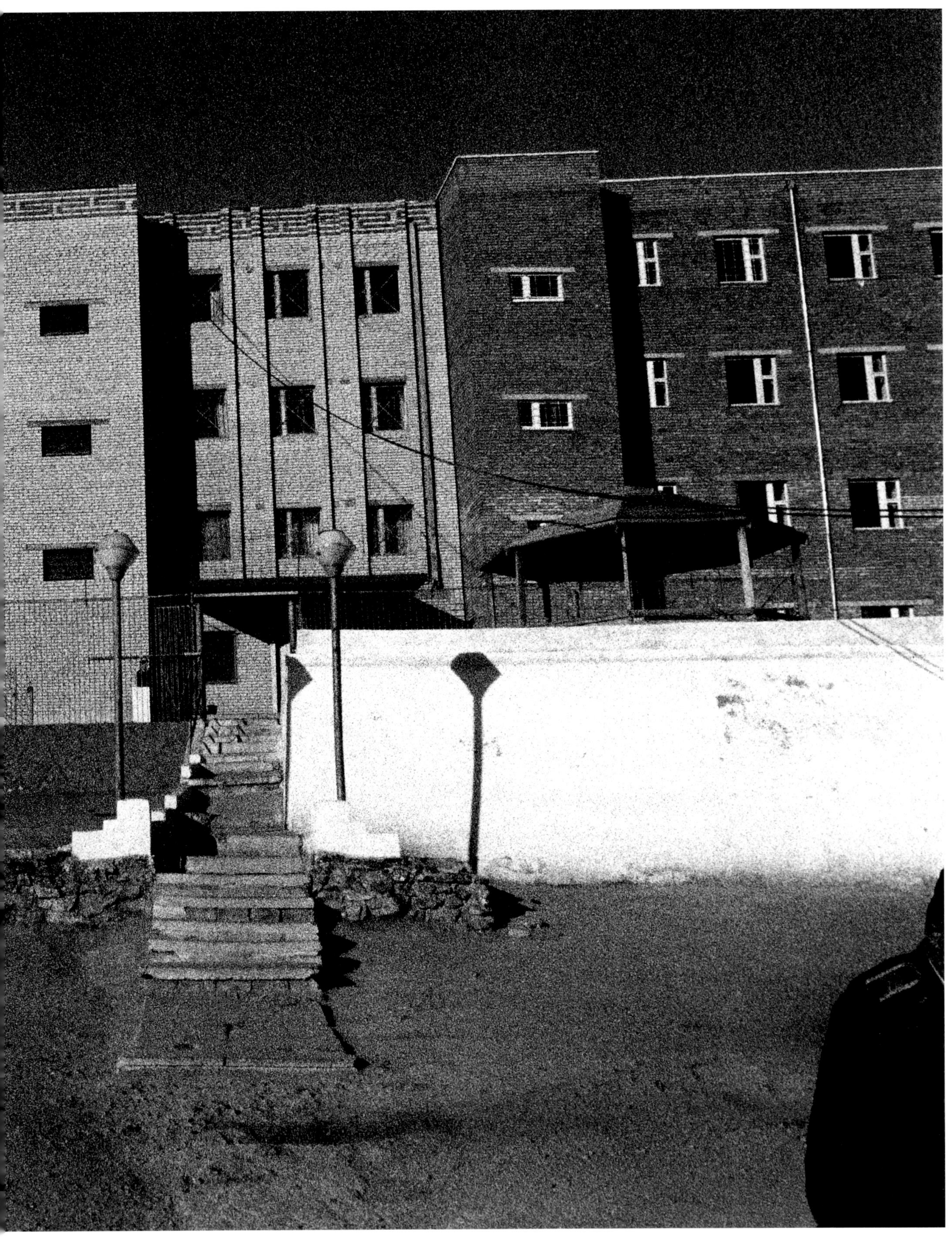

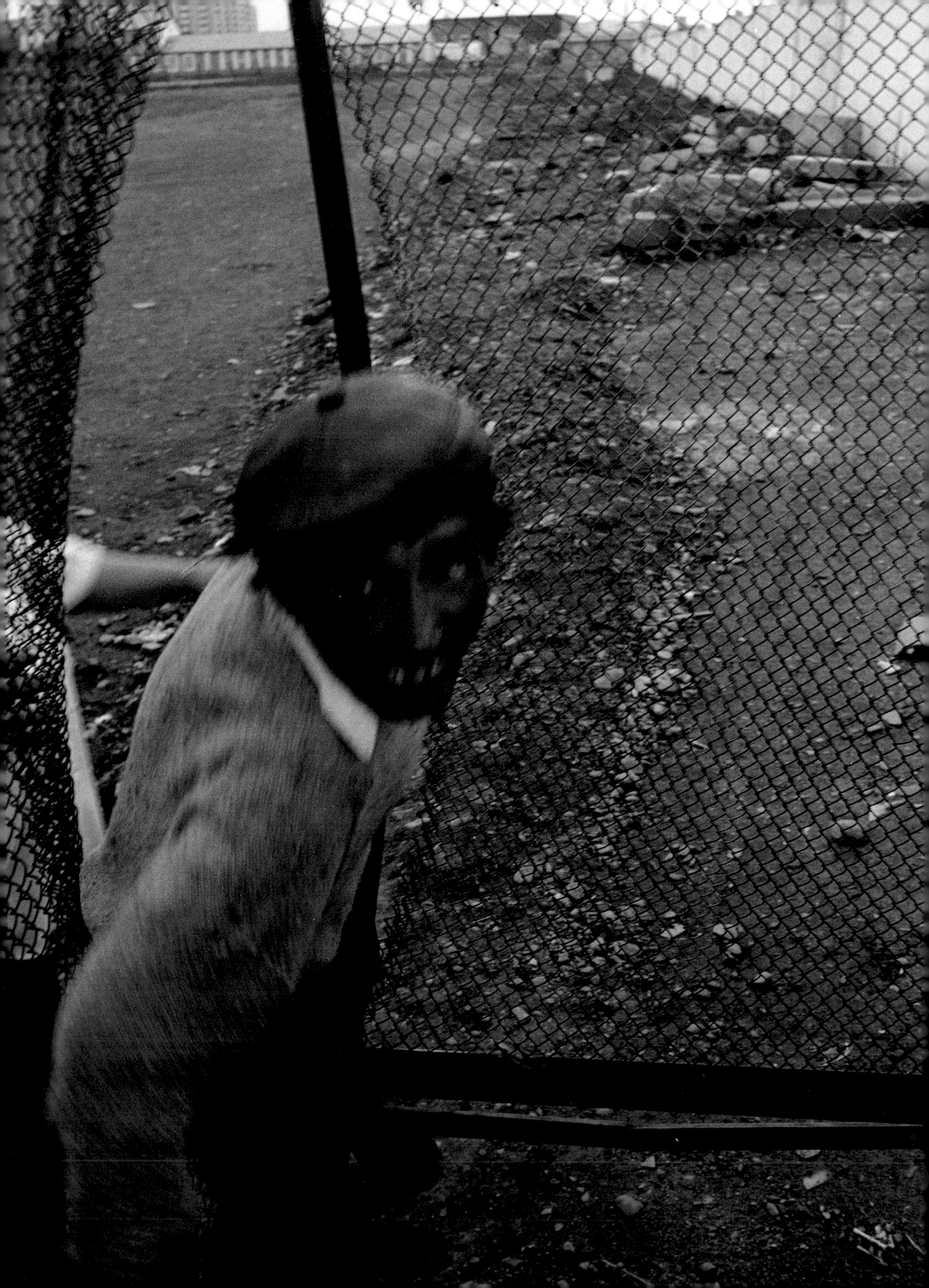

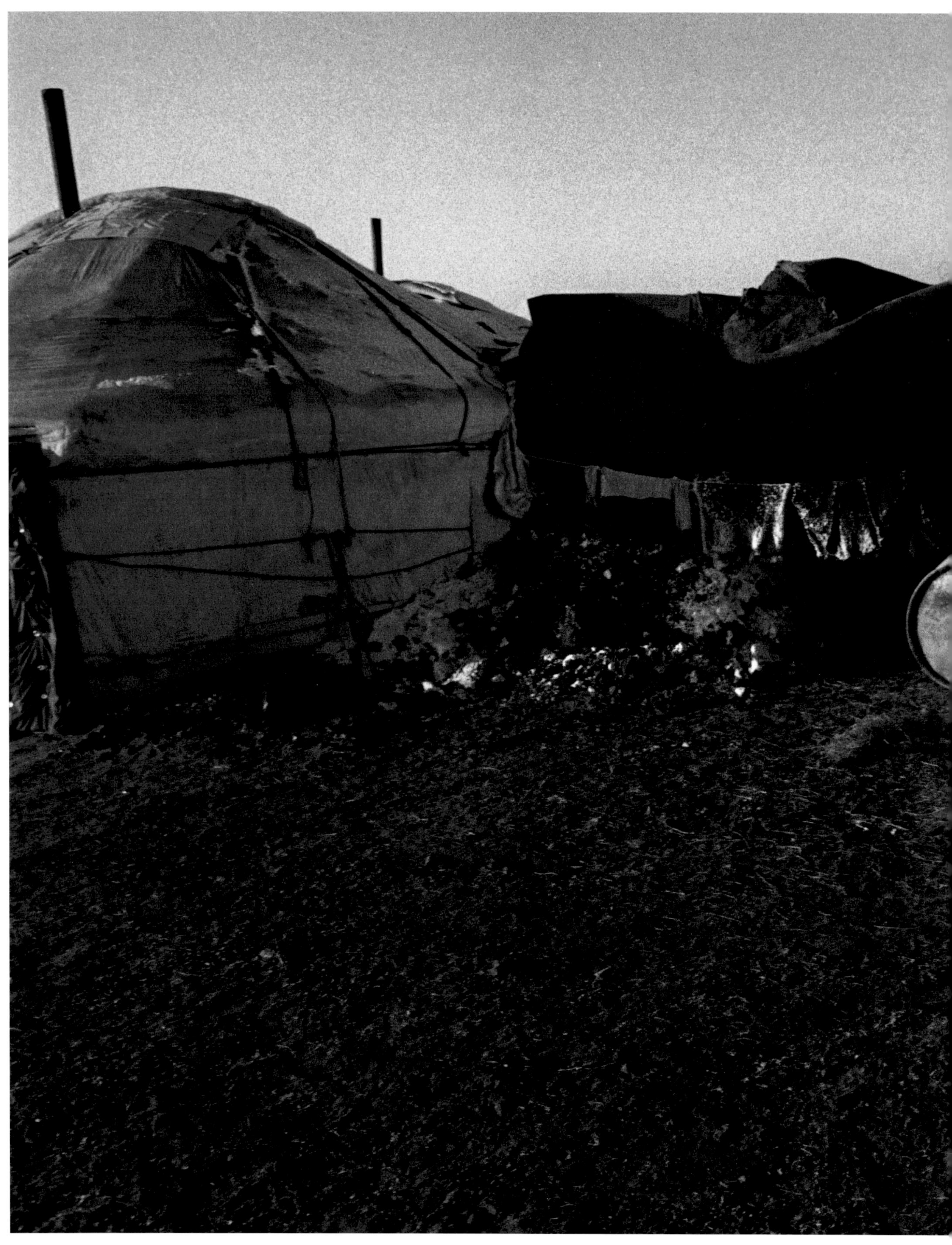

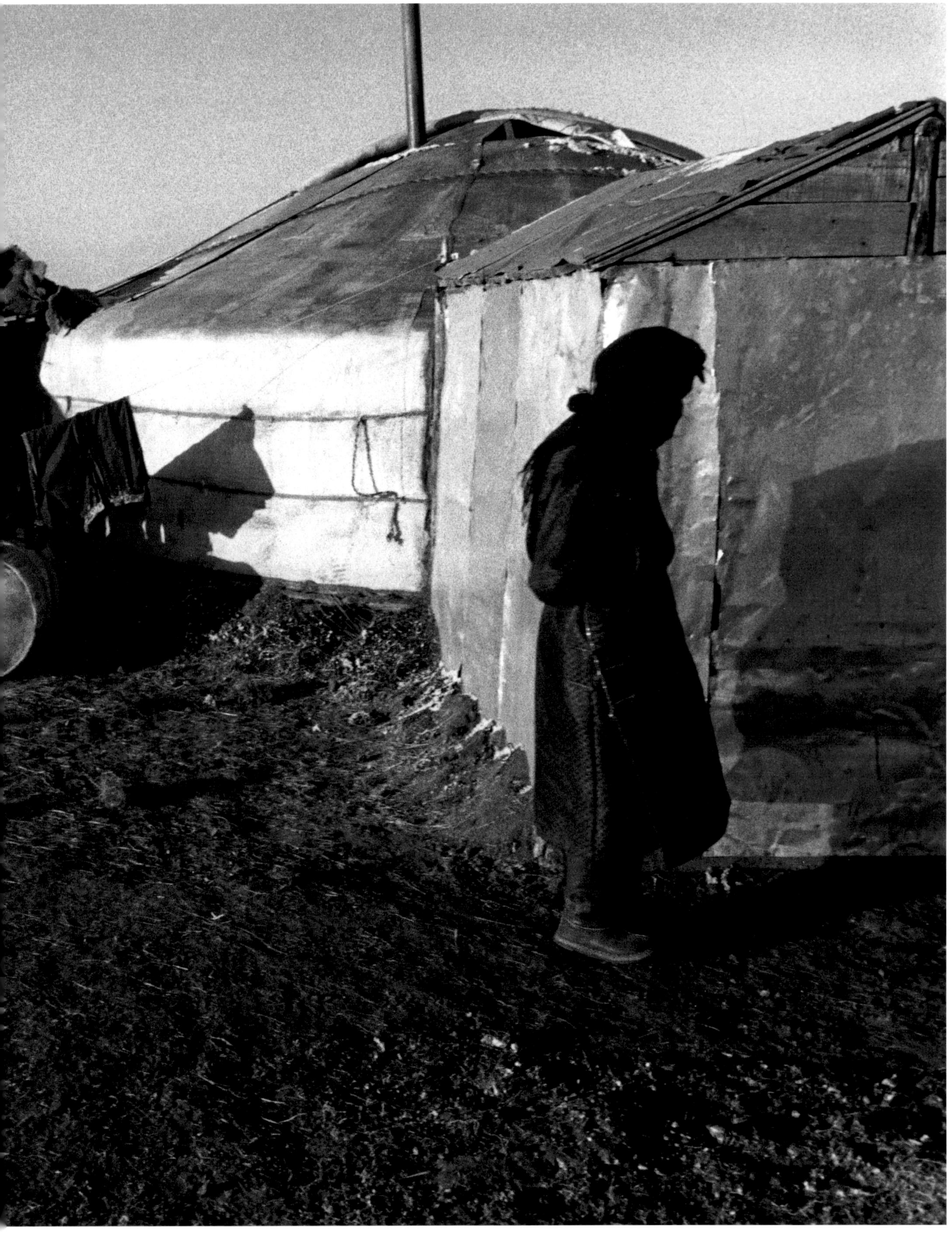

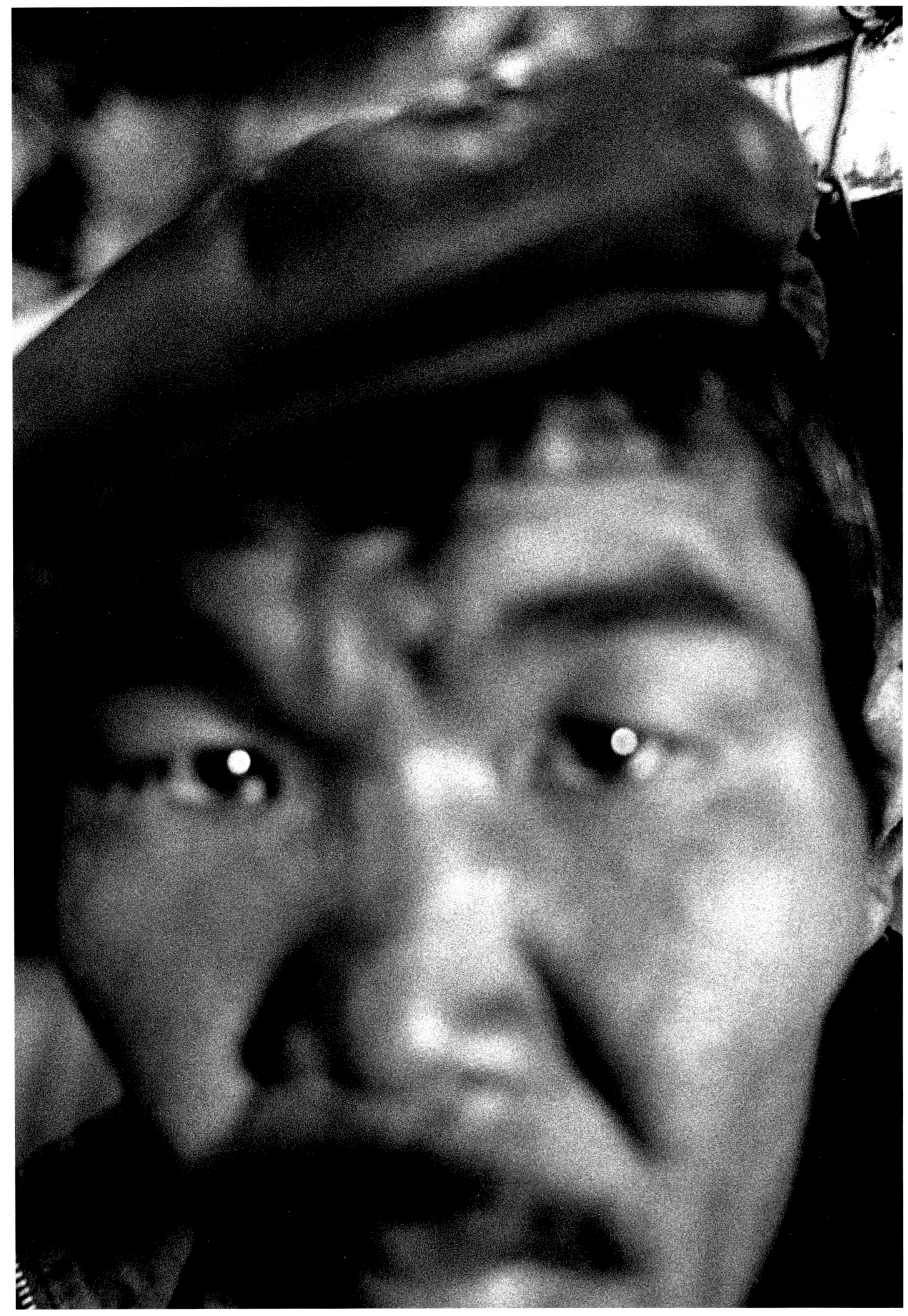

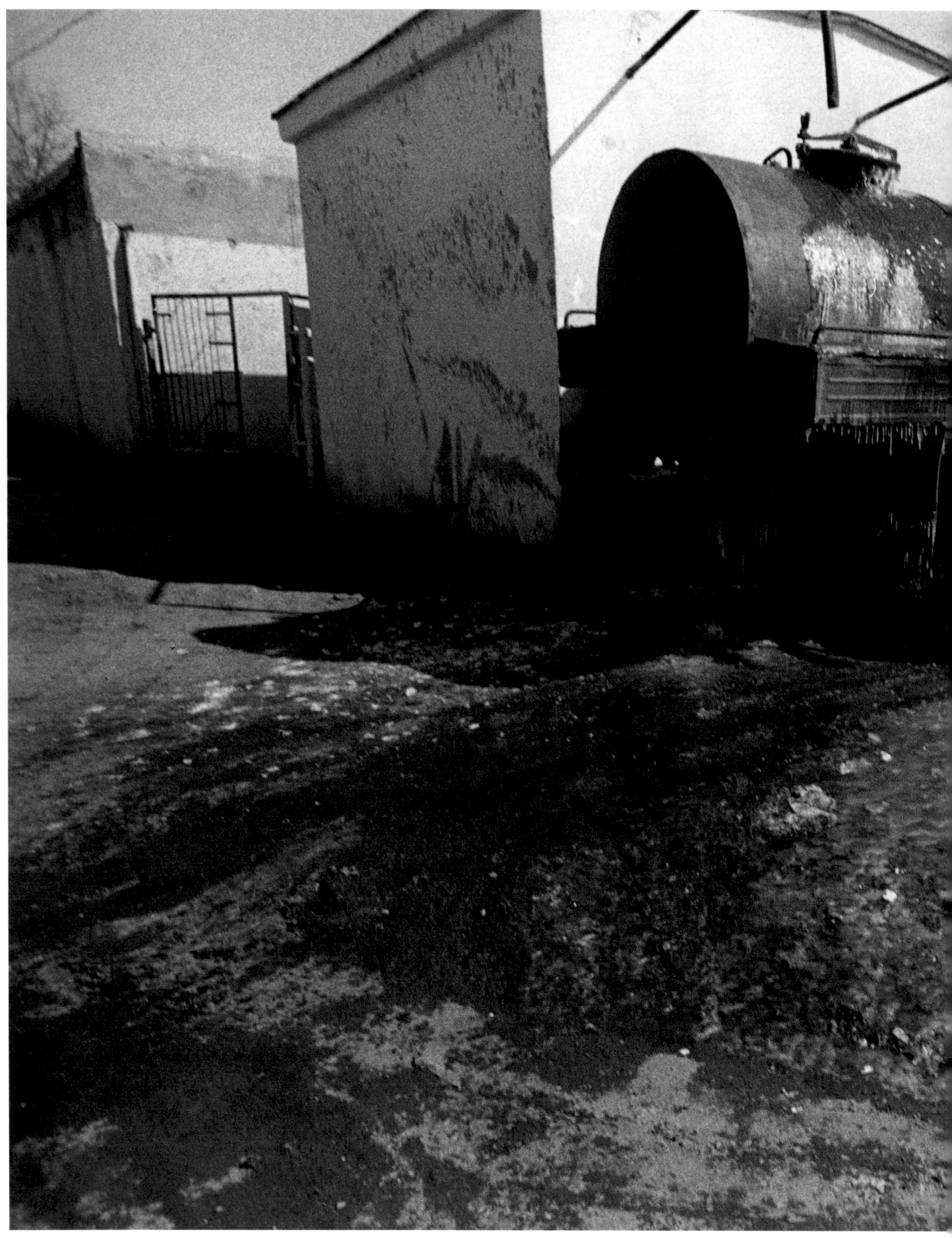

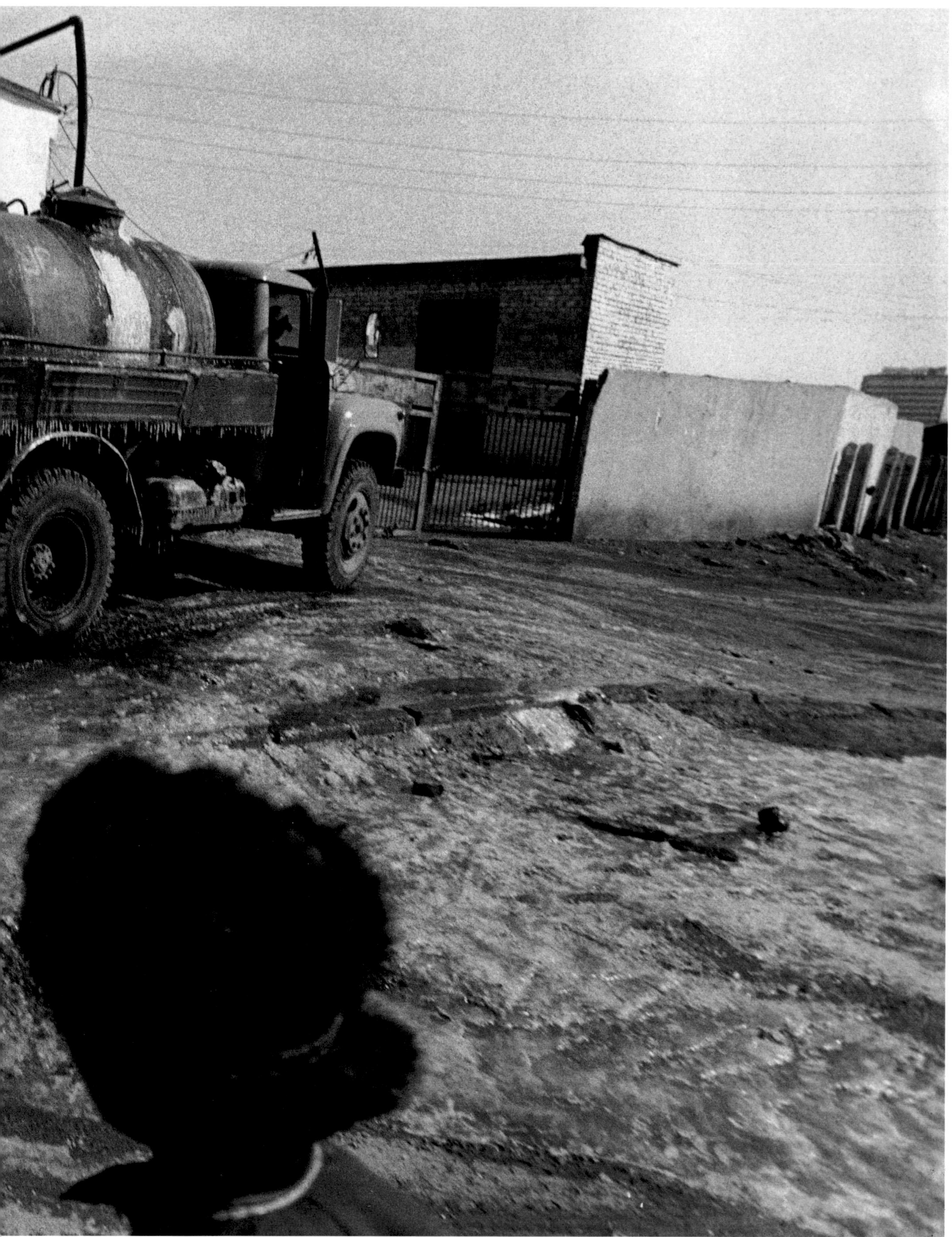

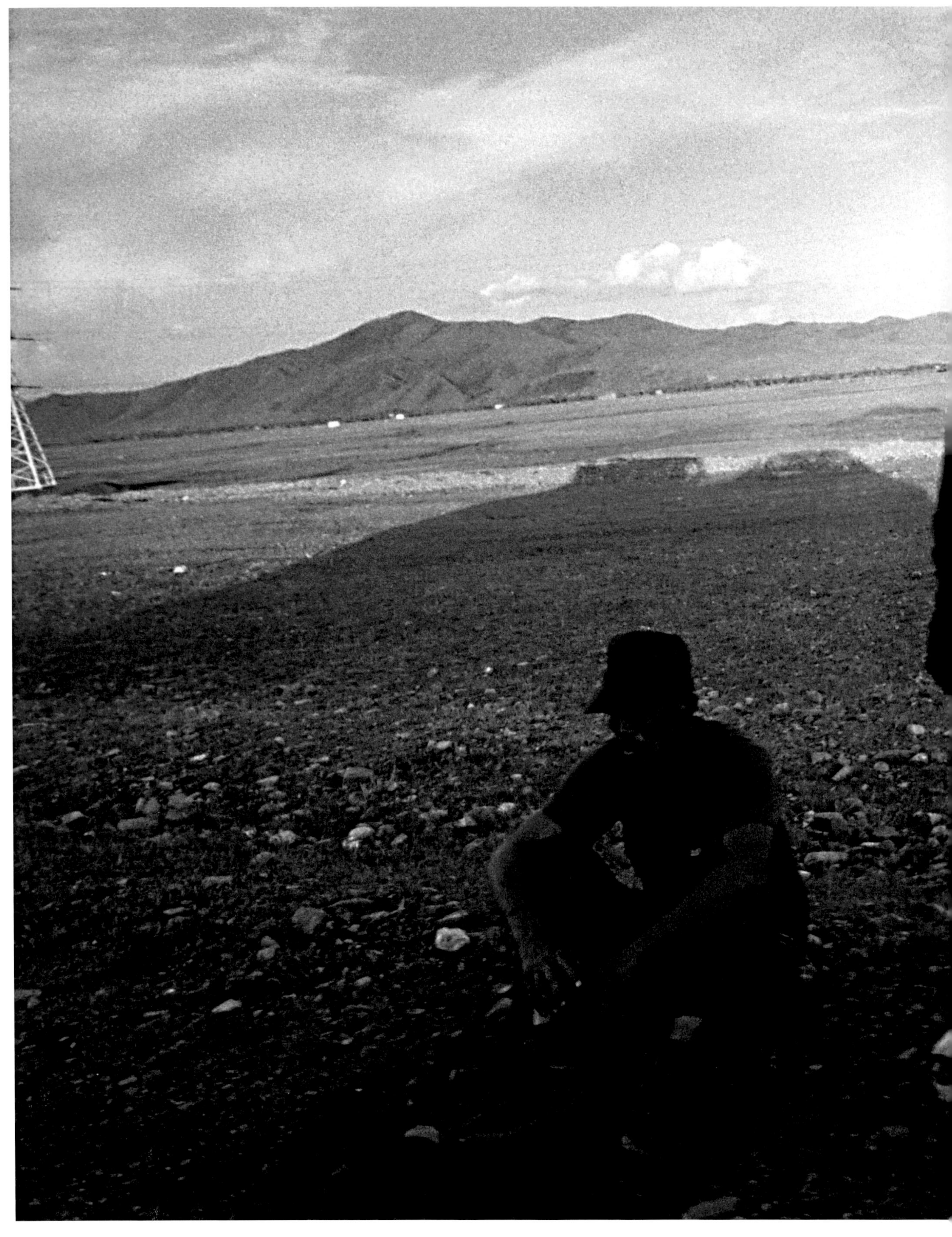

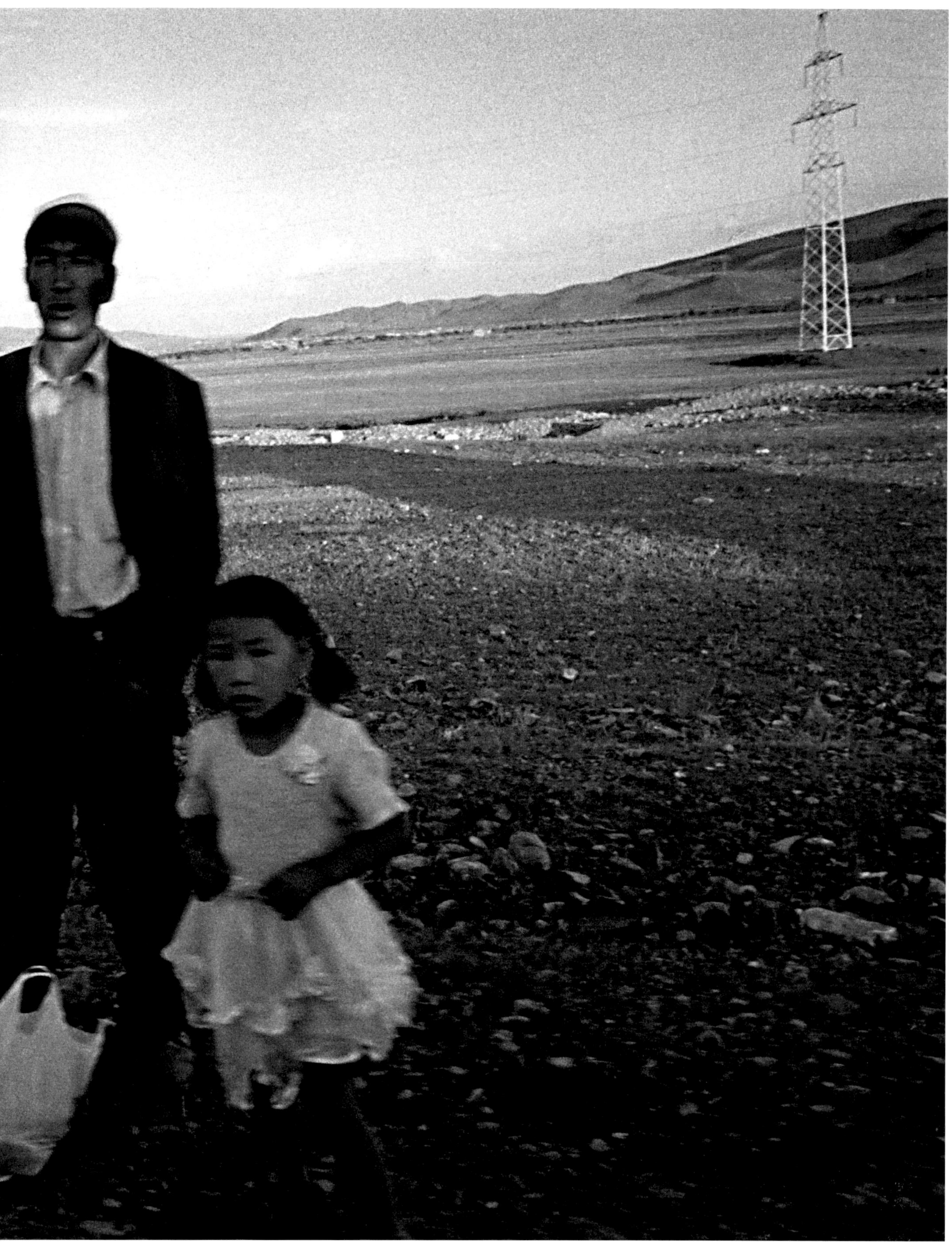

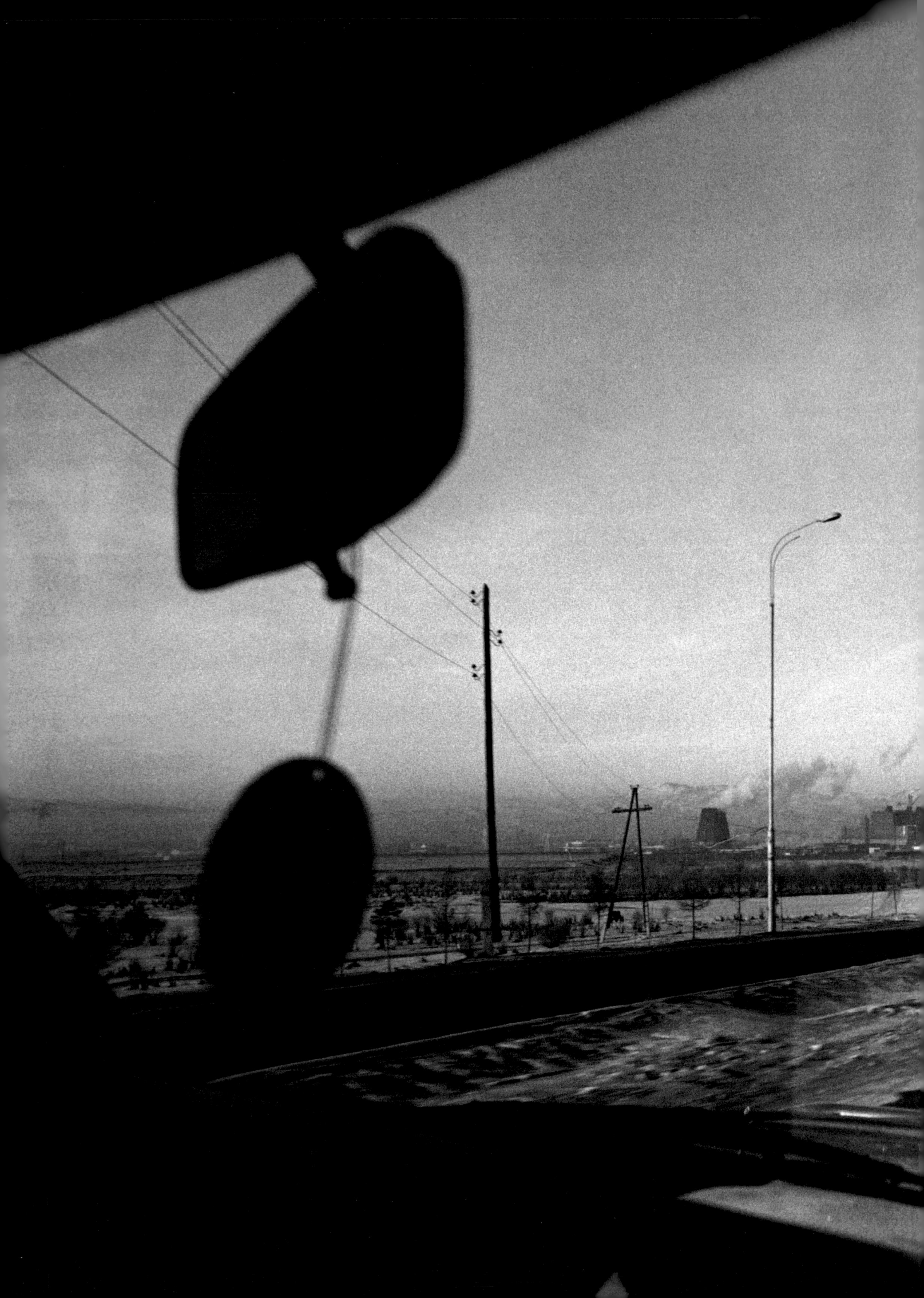

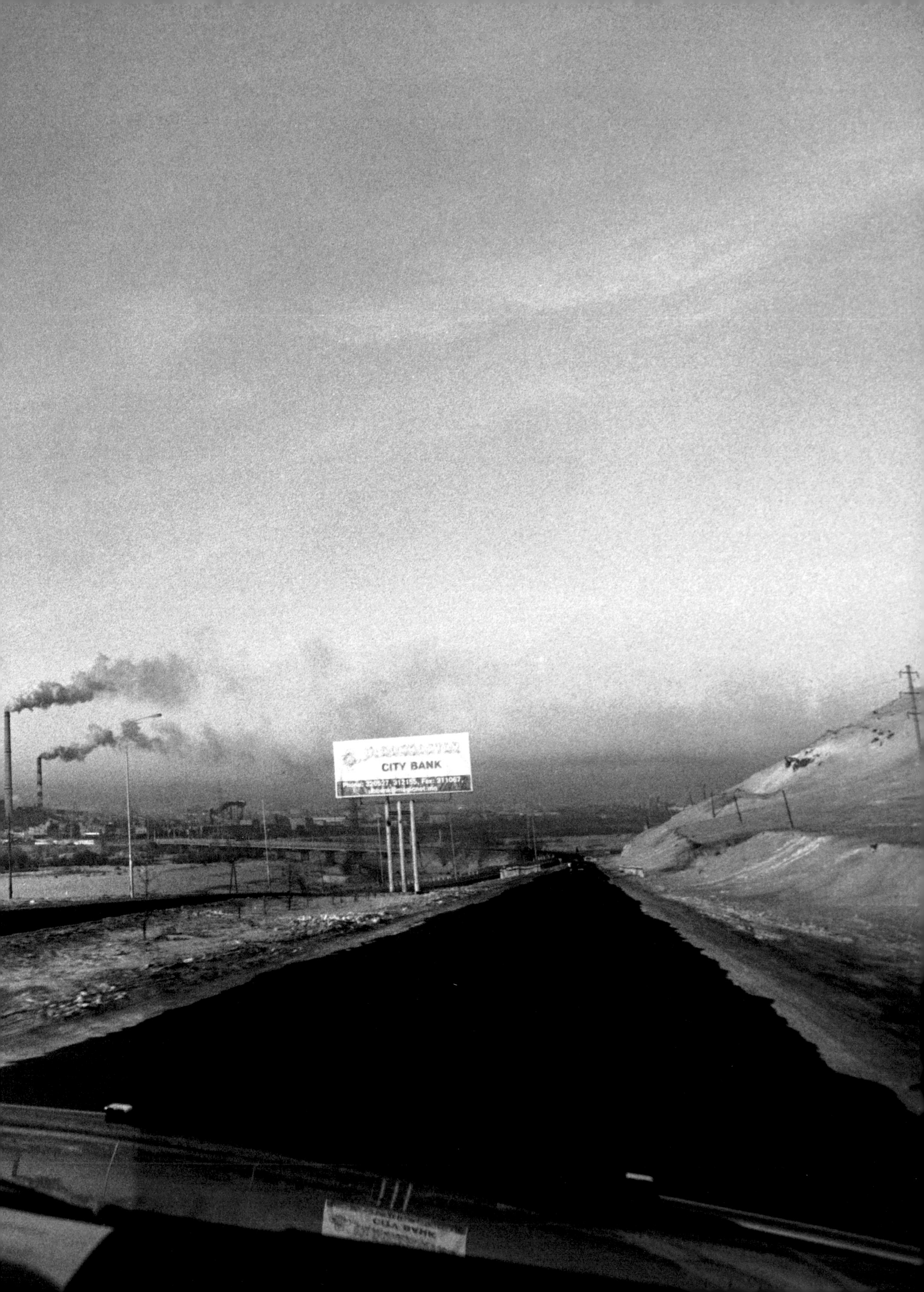
CITY BANK

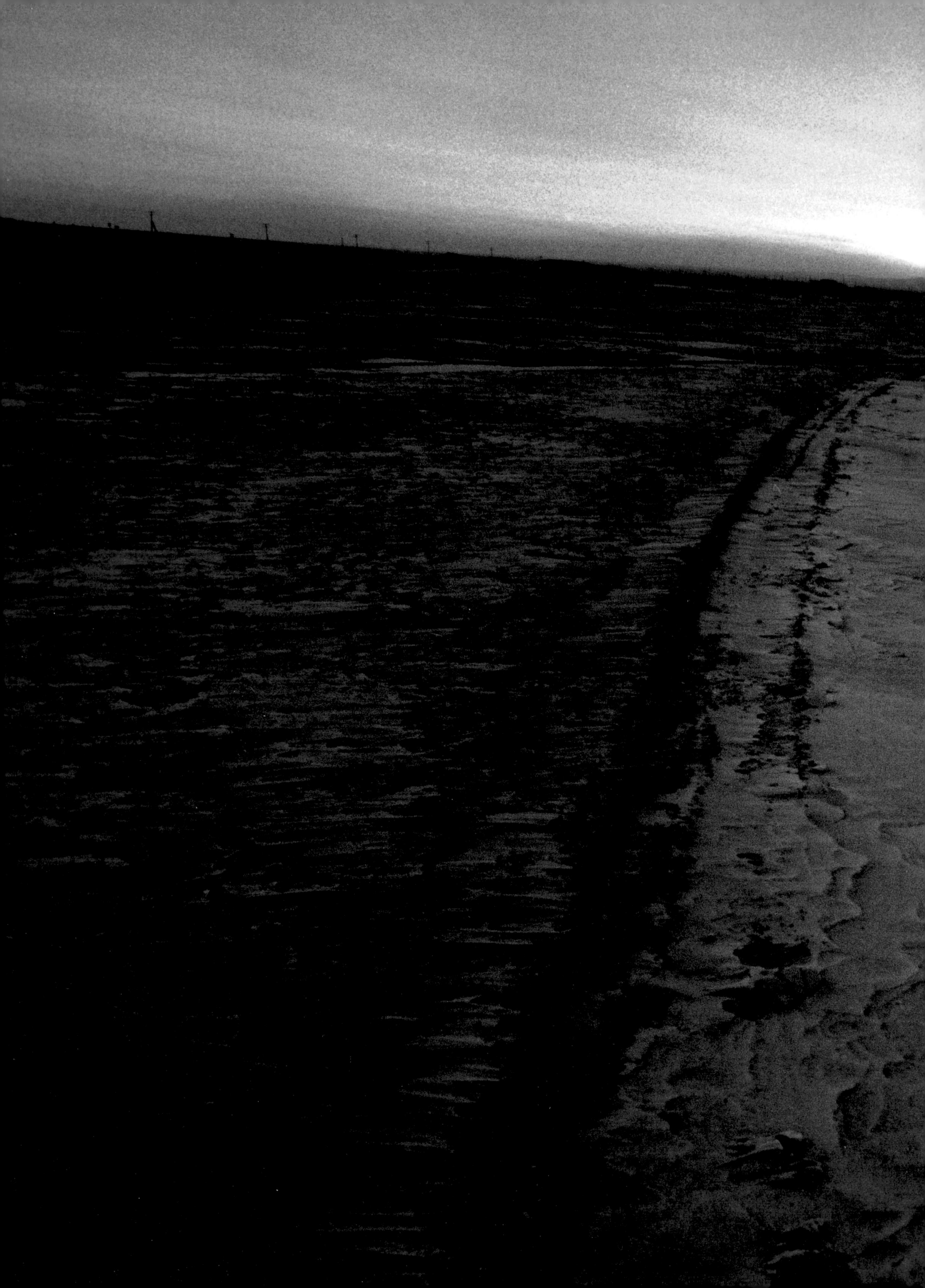

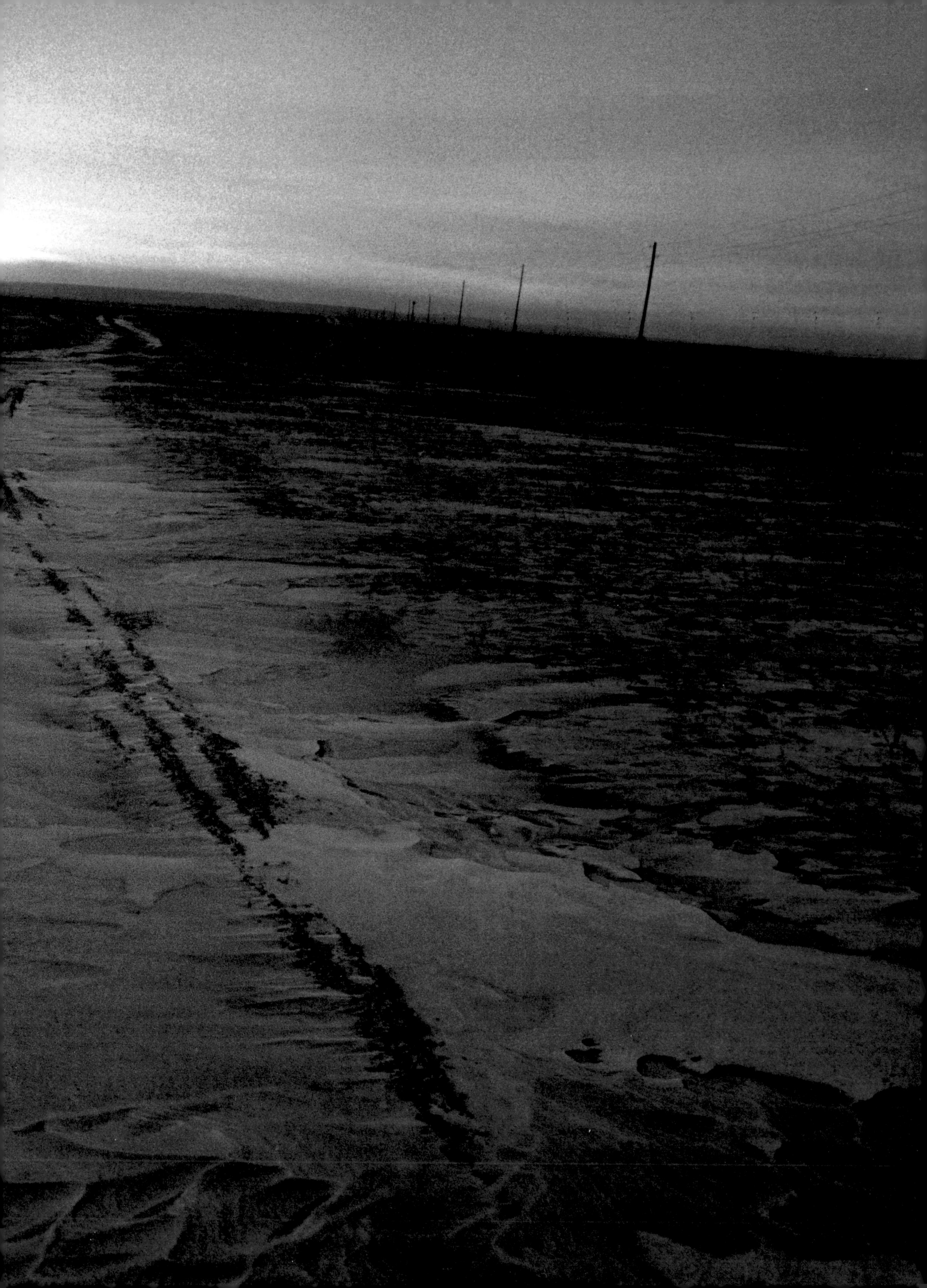

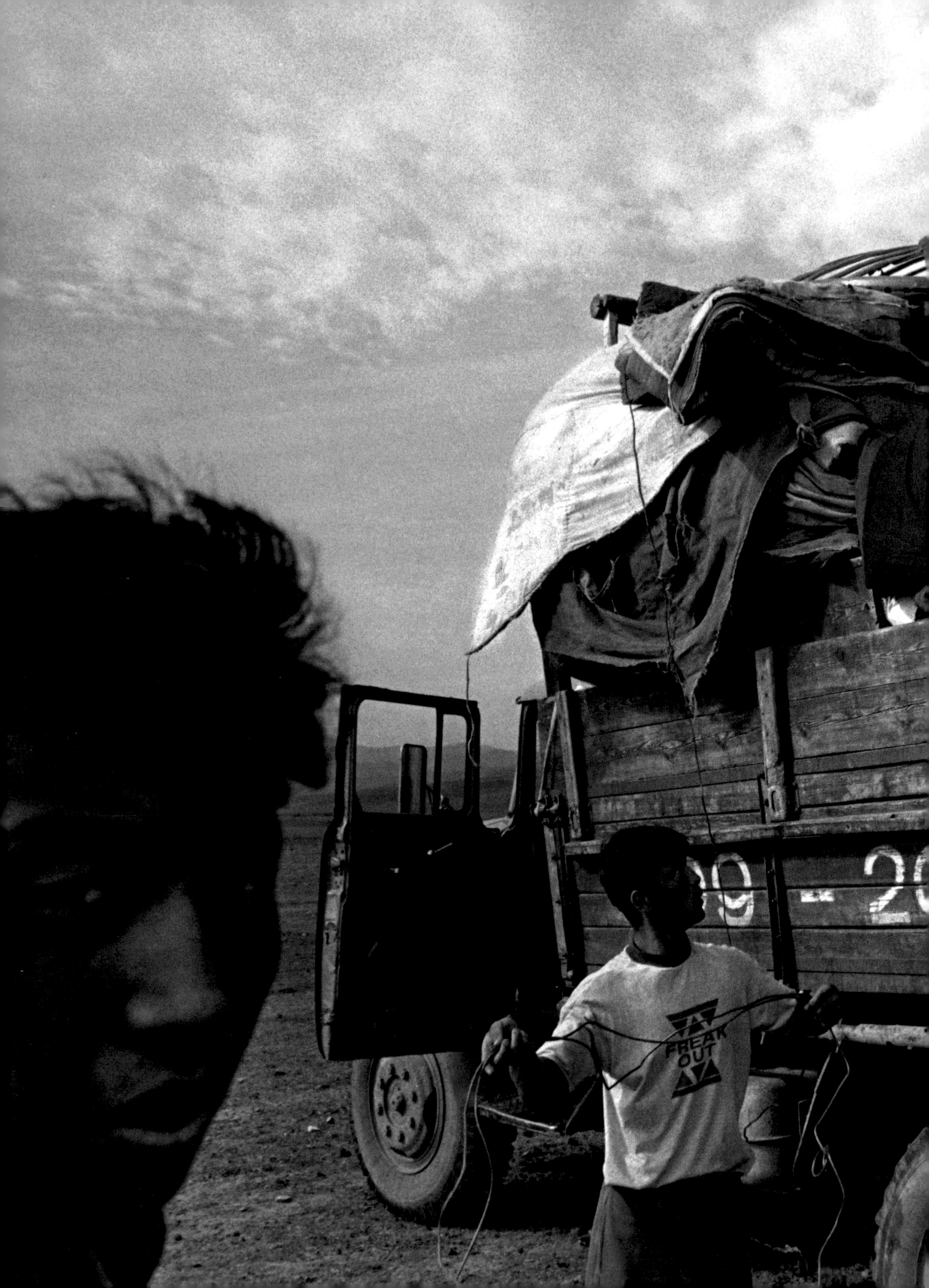
FREAK
OUT

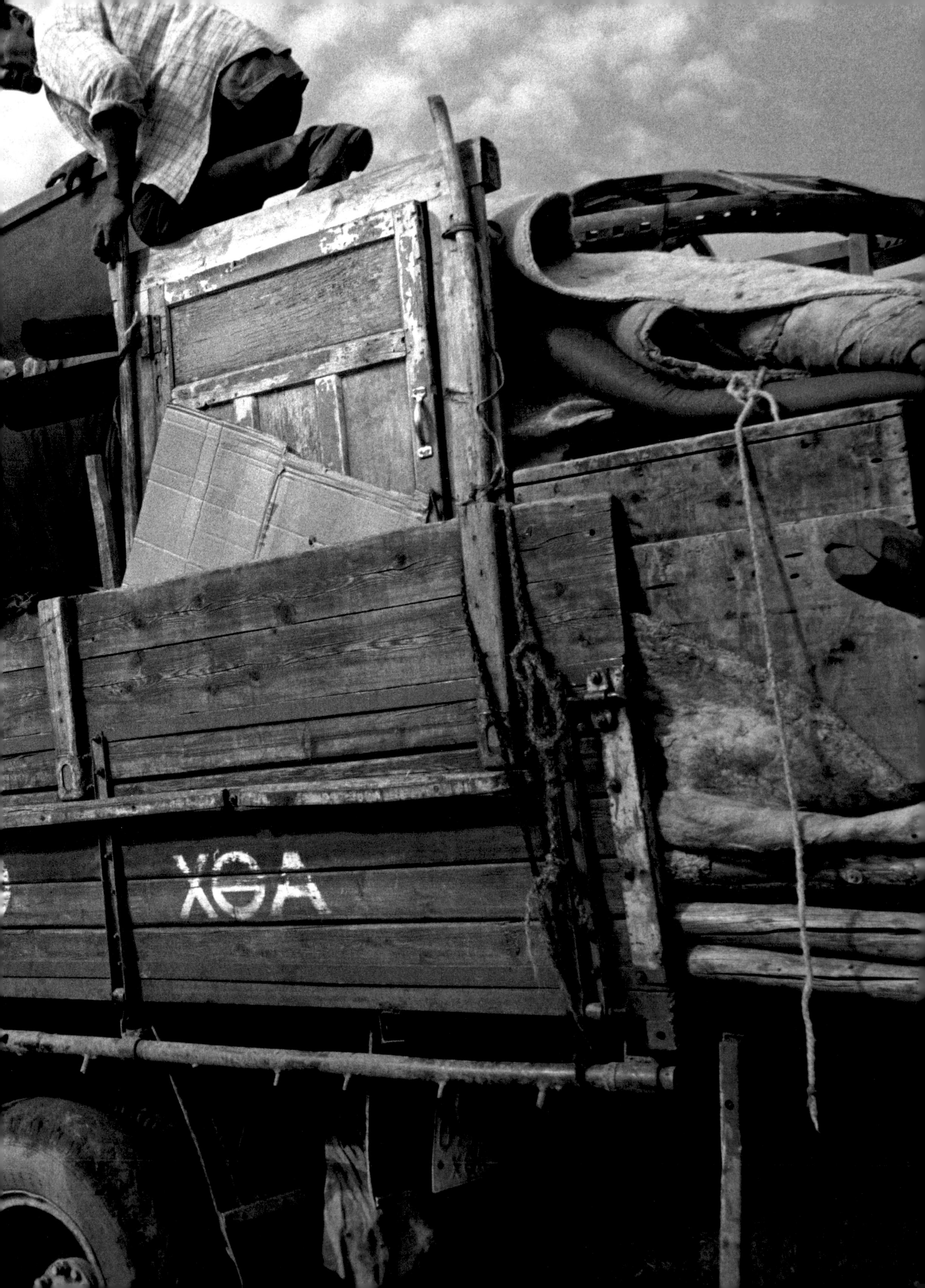
XΘA

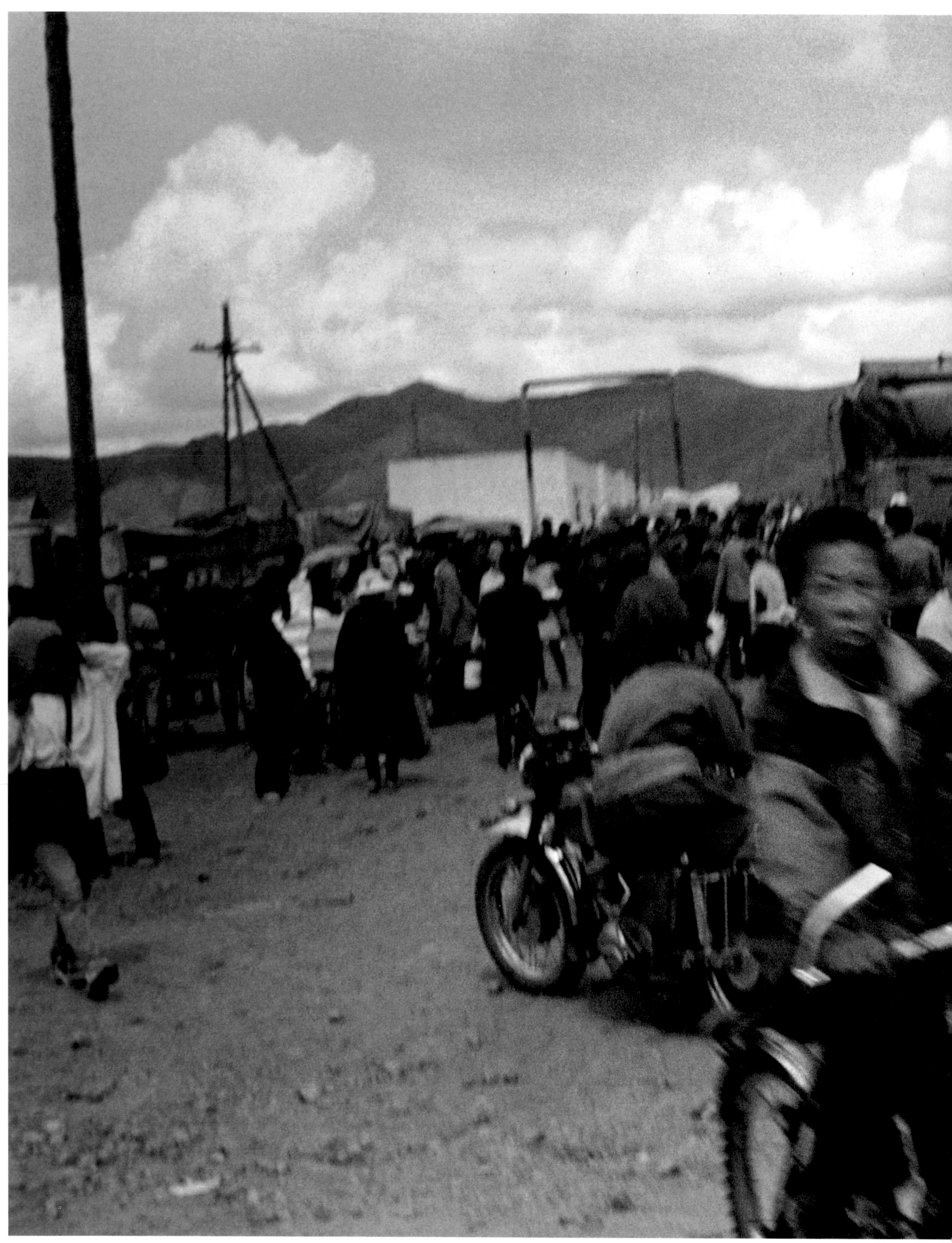

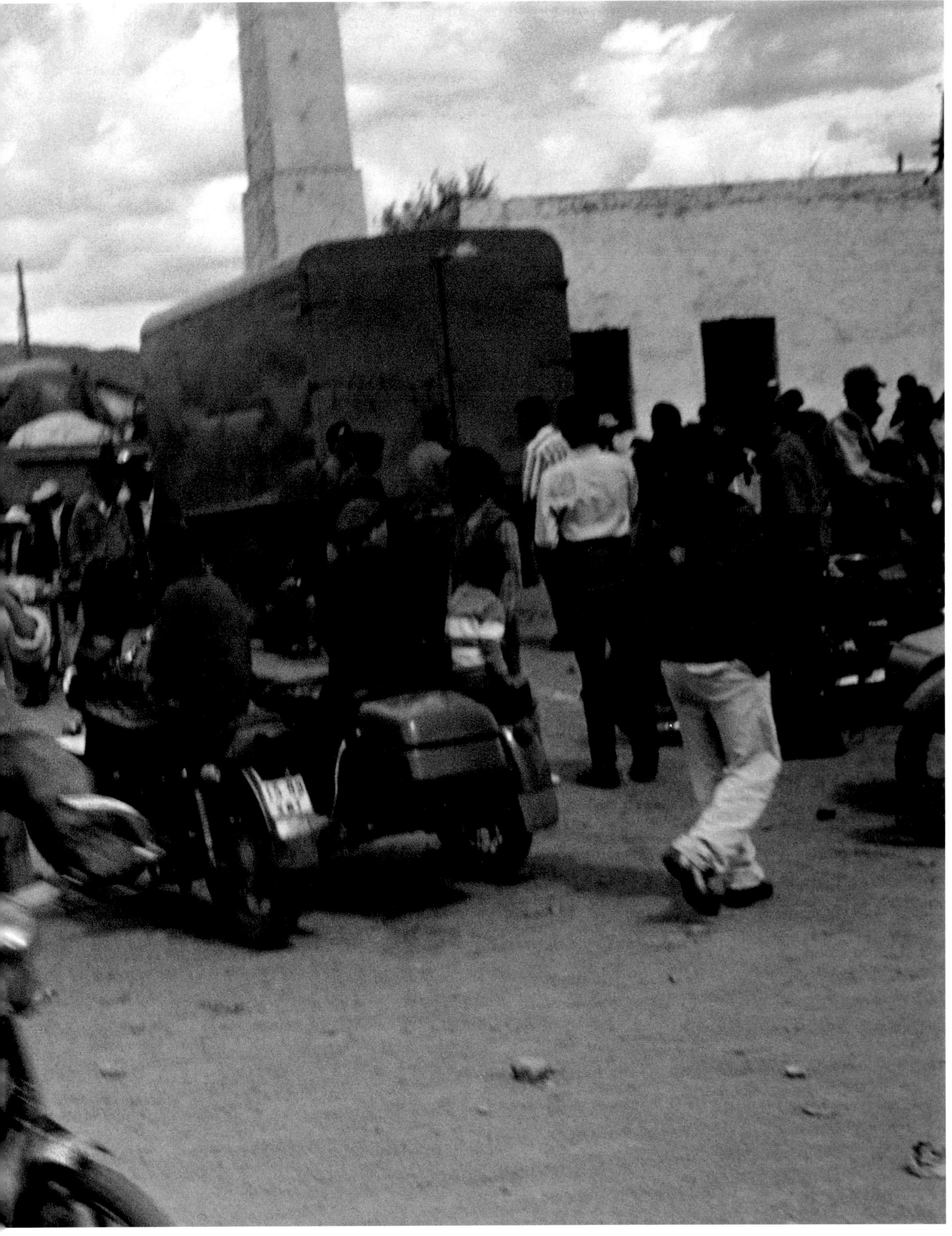

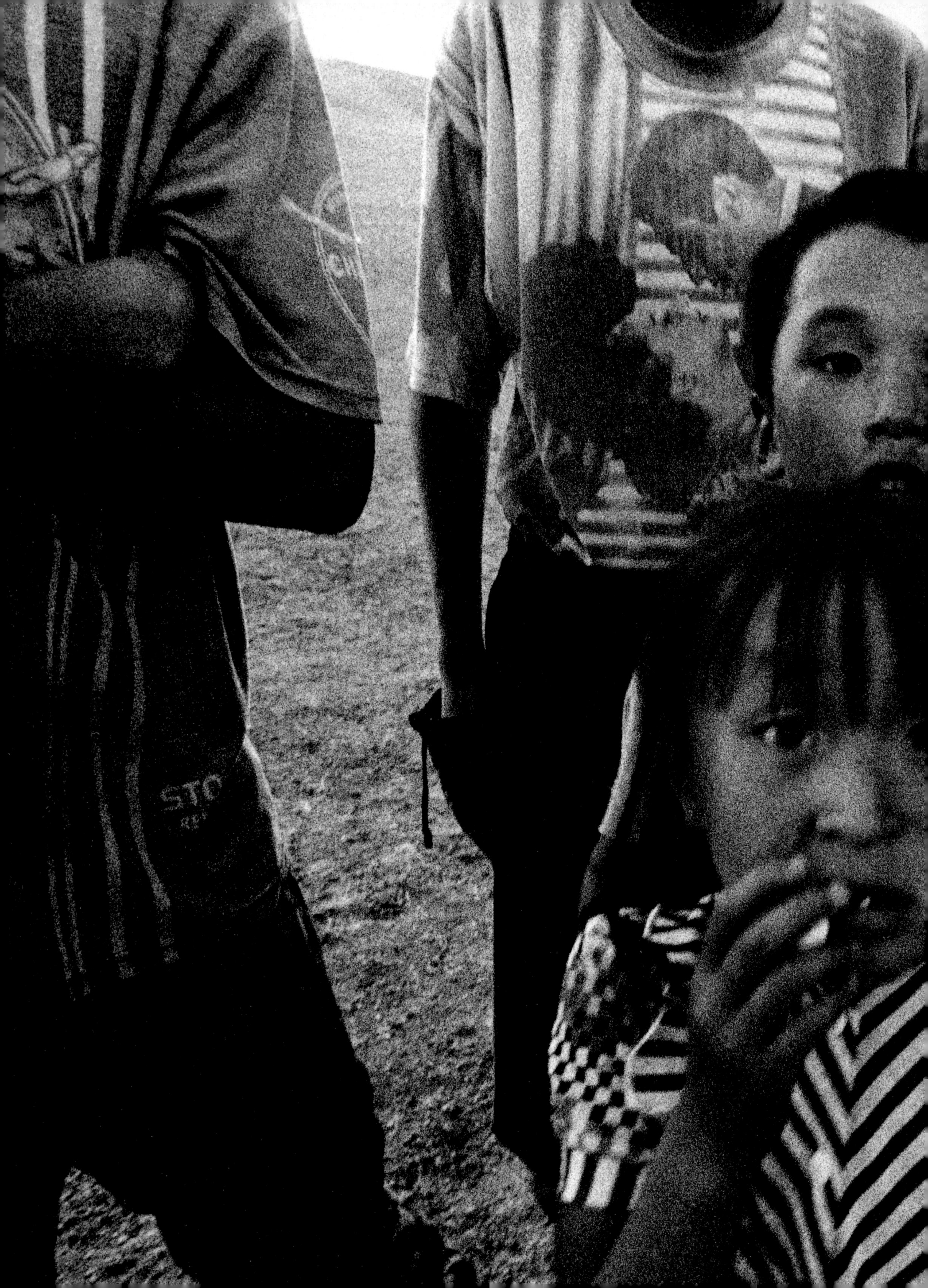

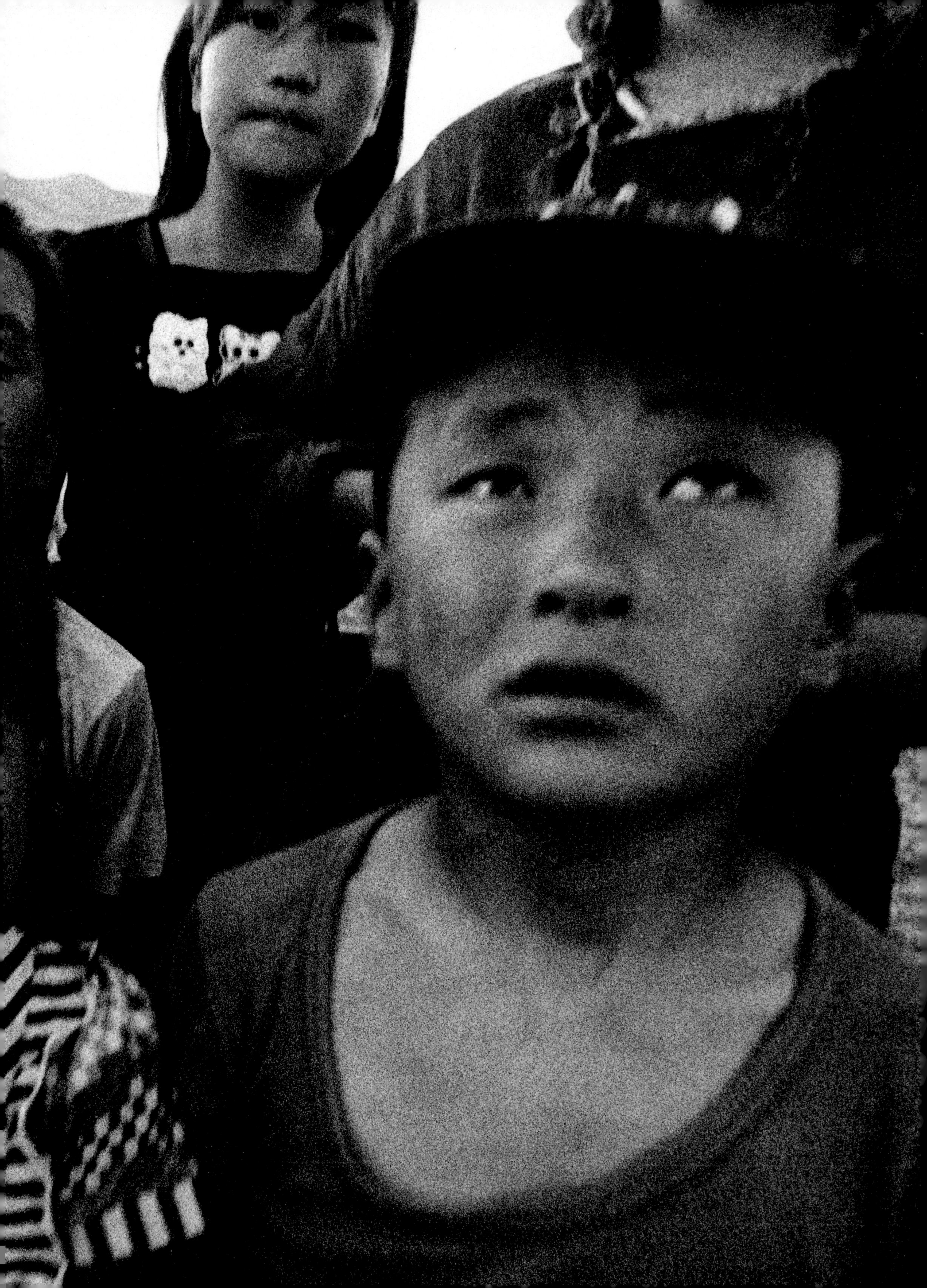

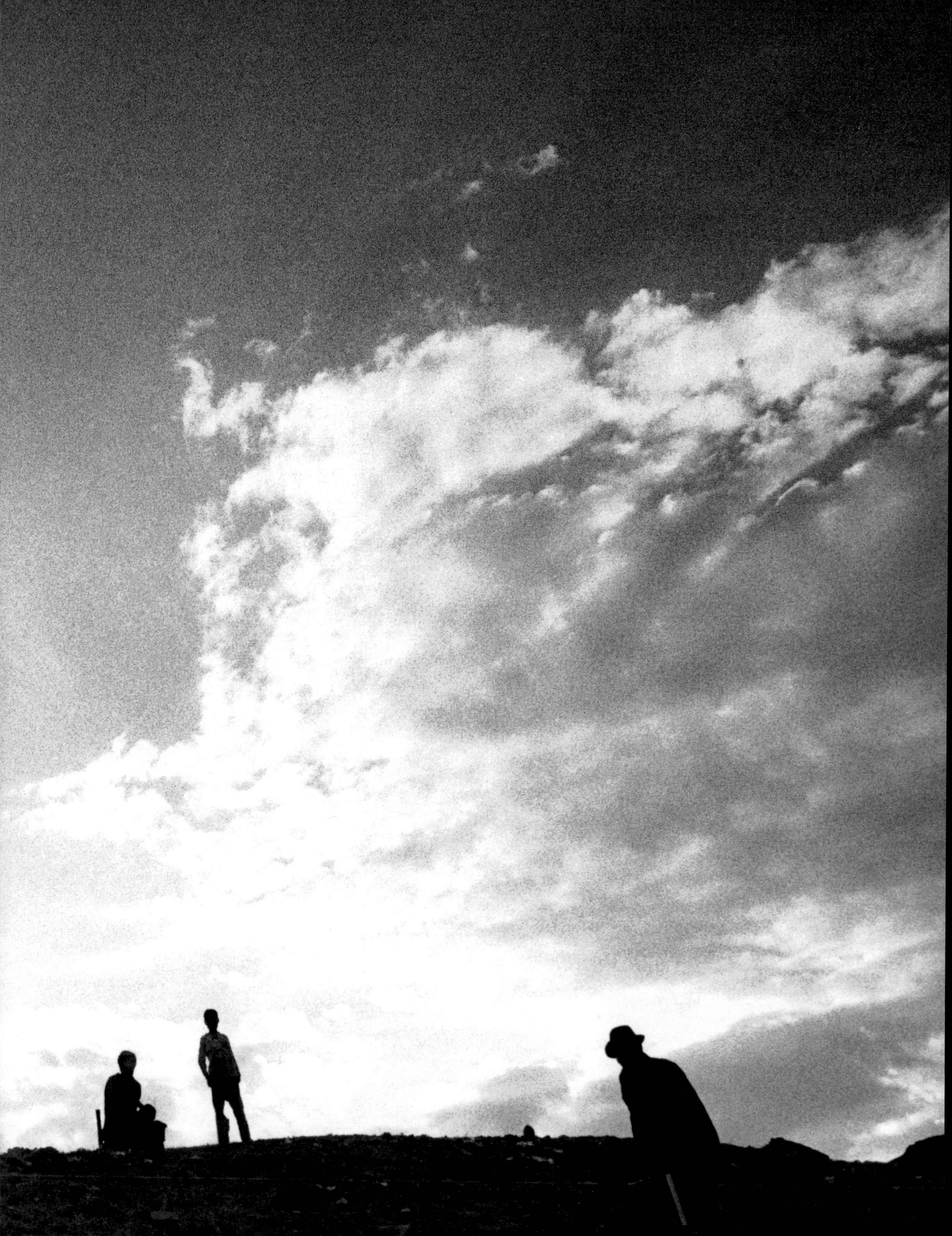

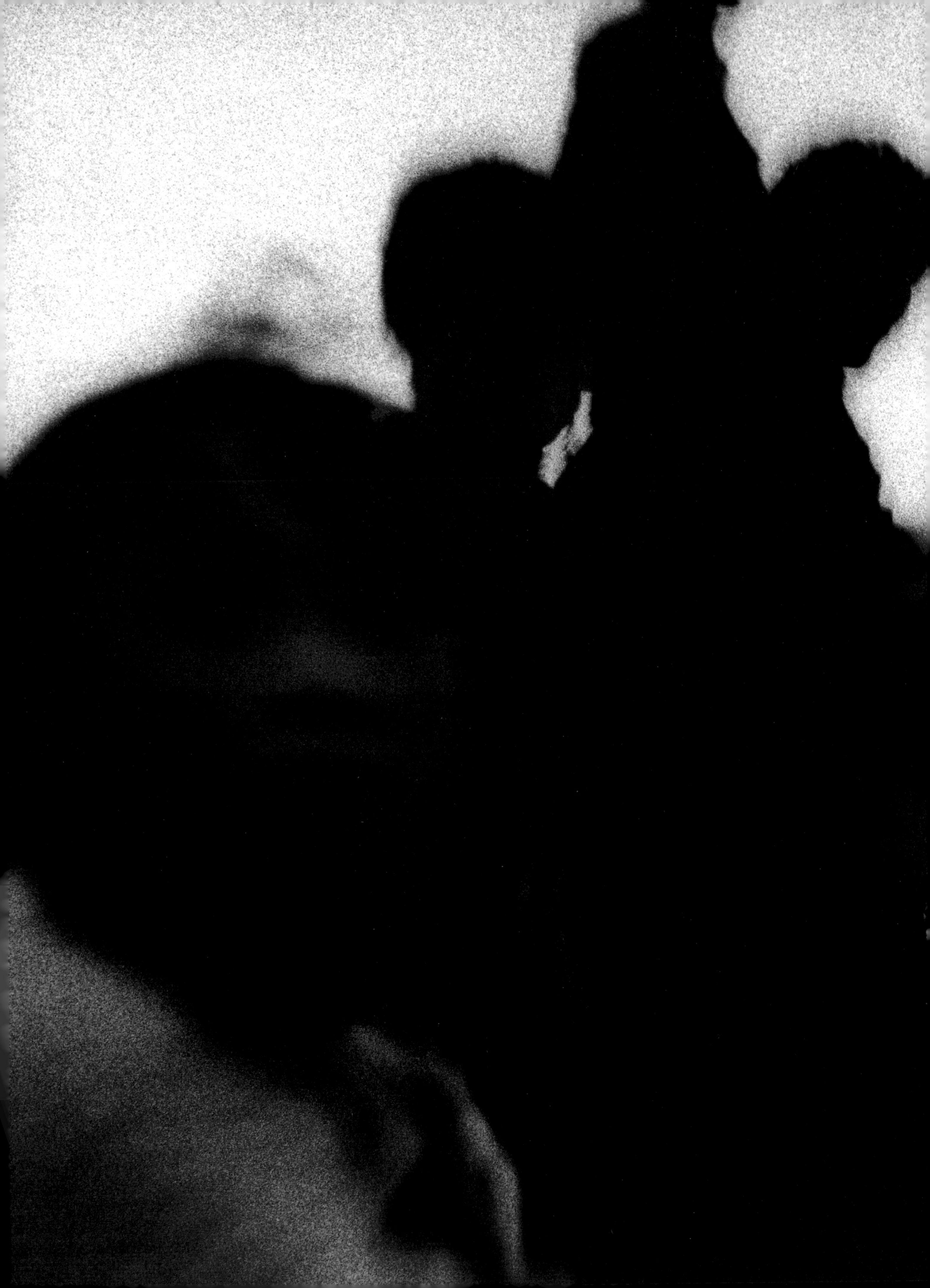

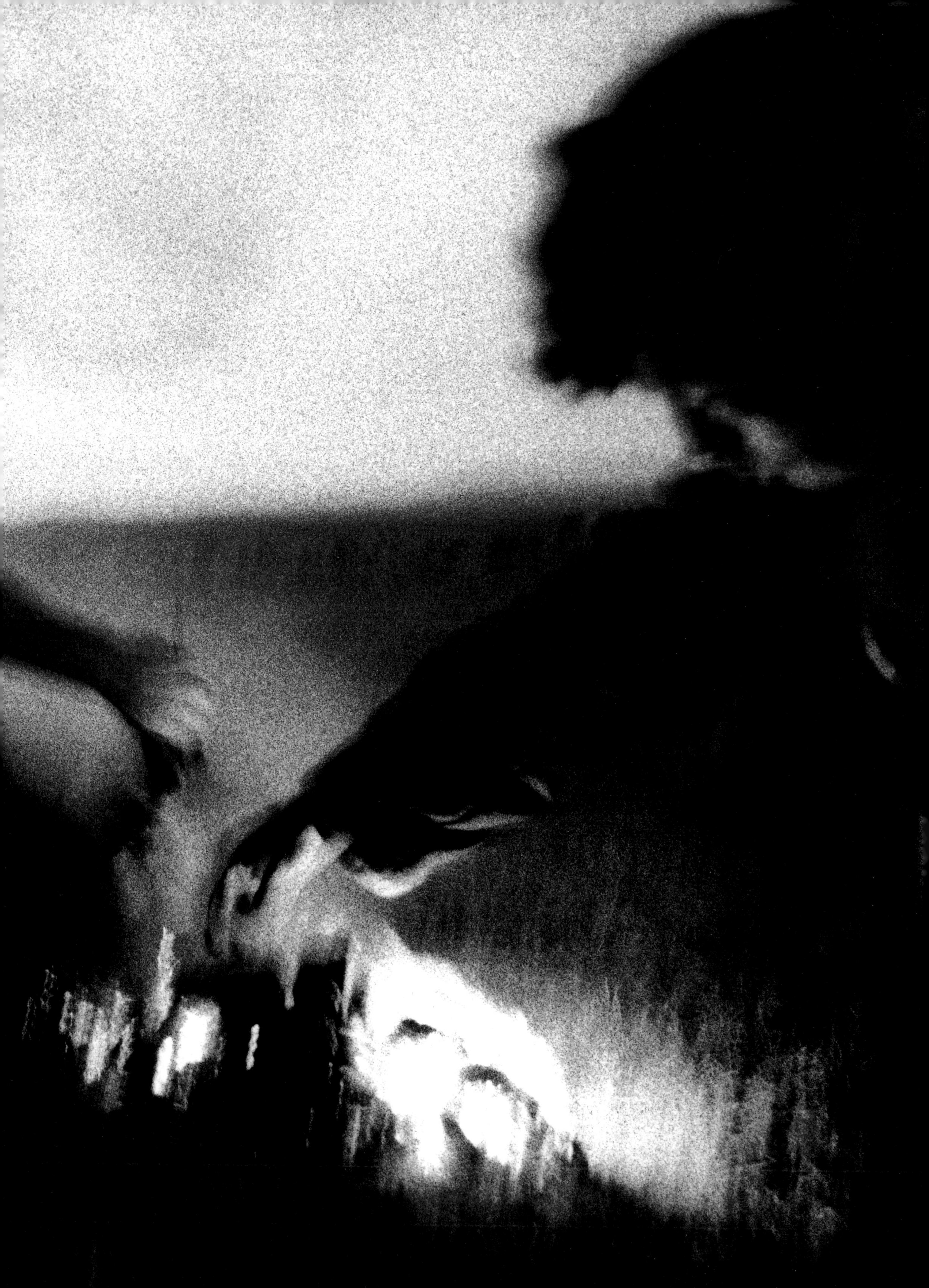

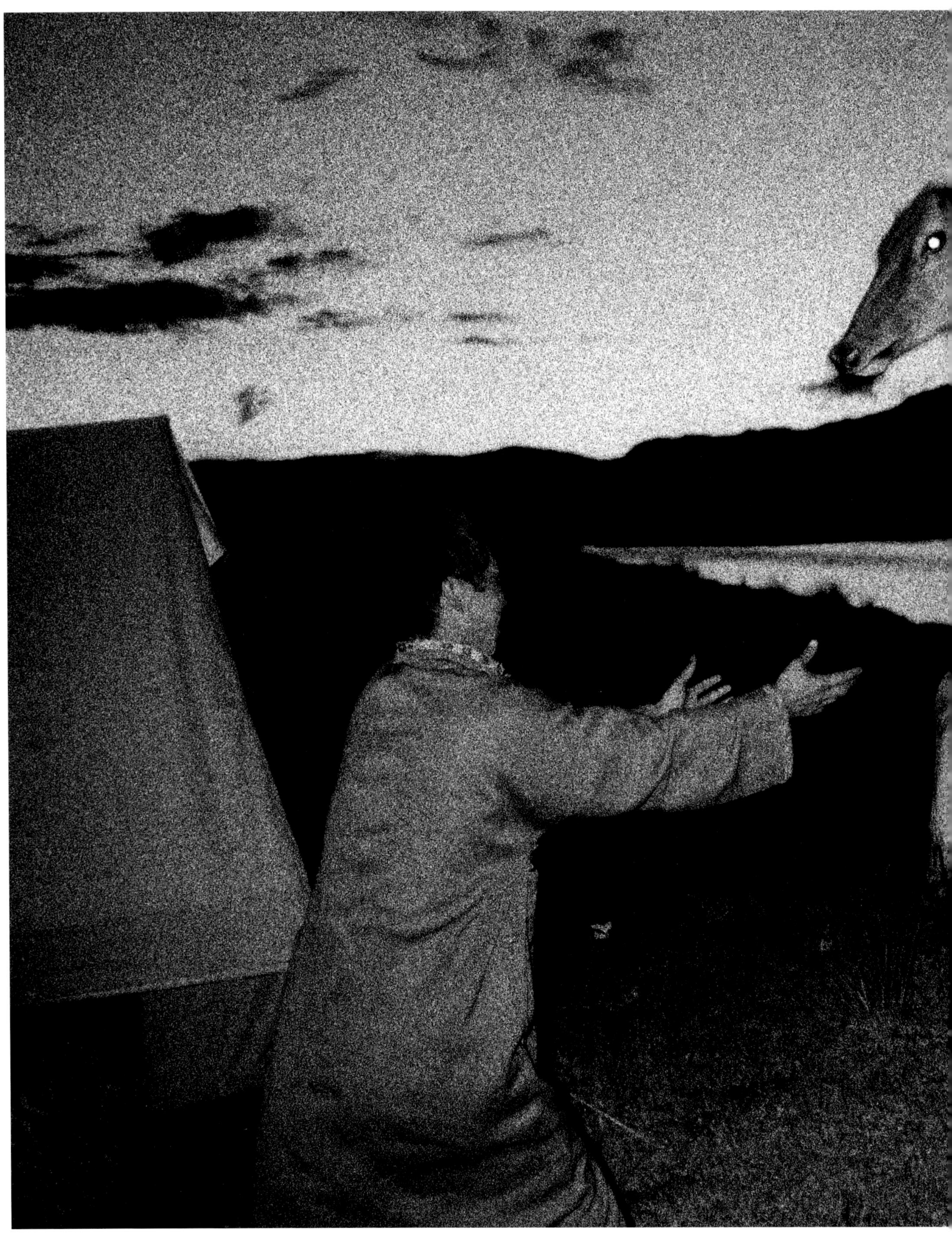

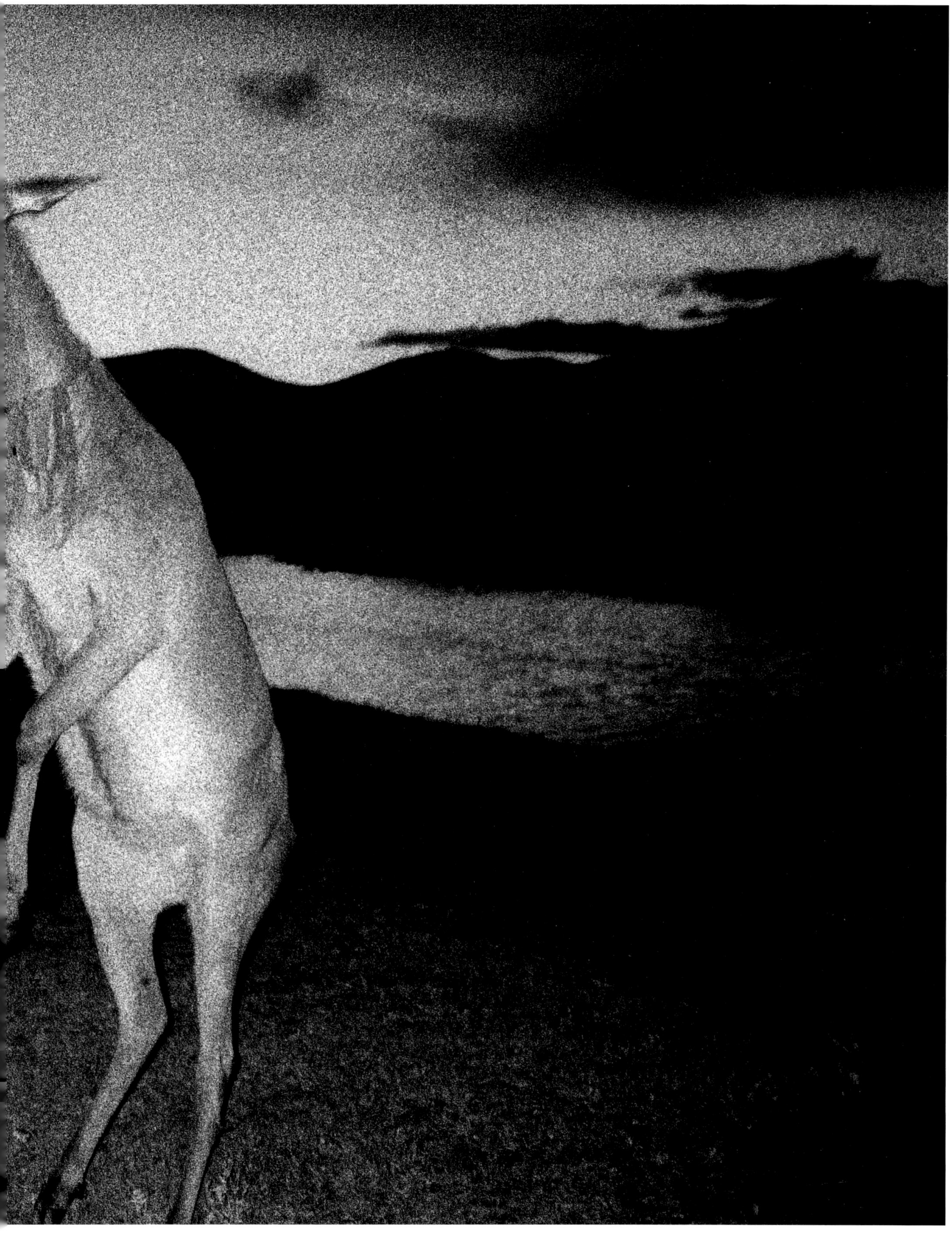

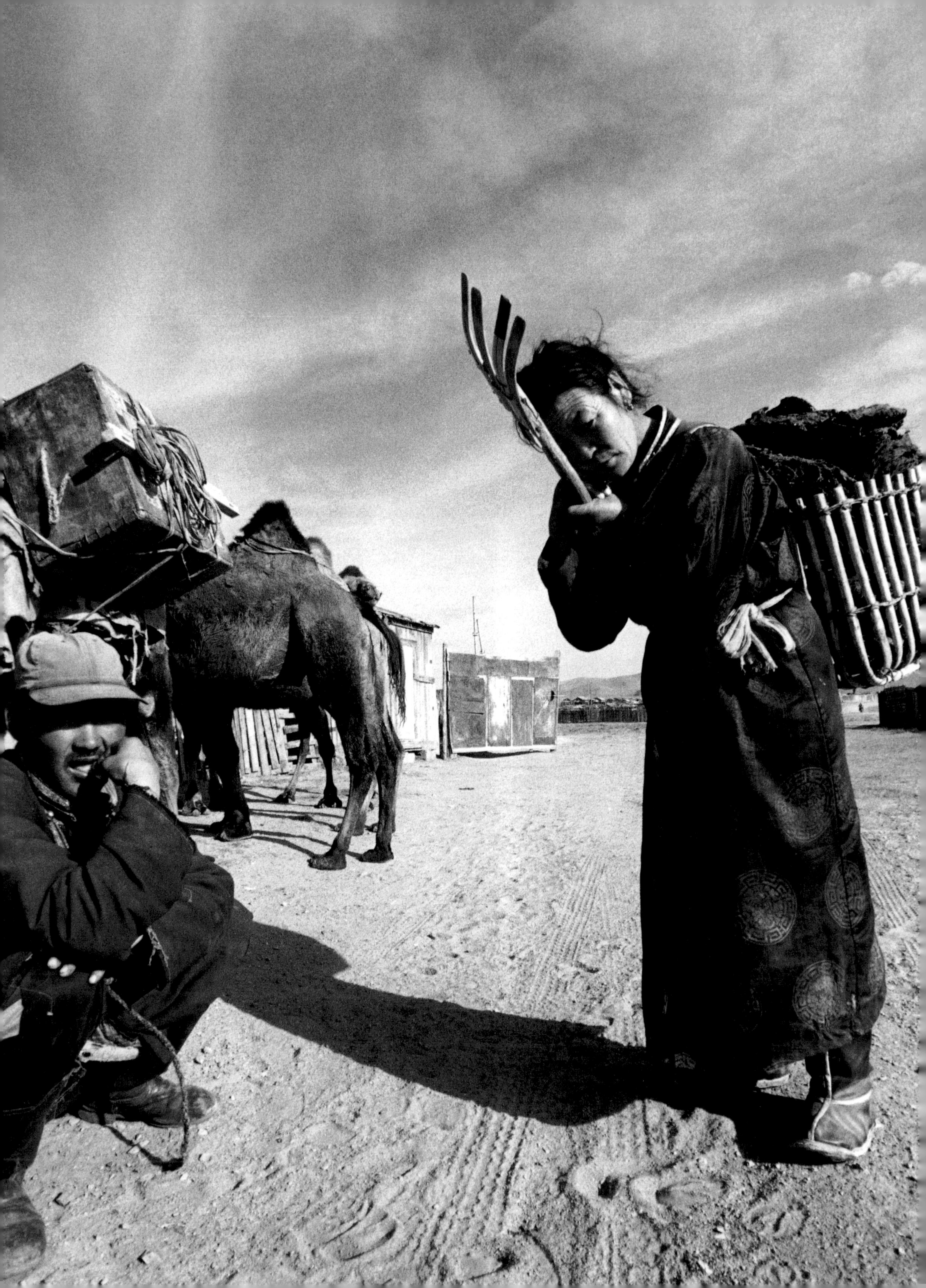

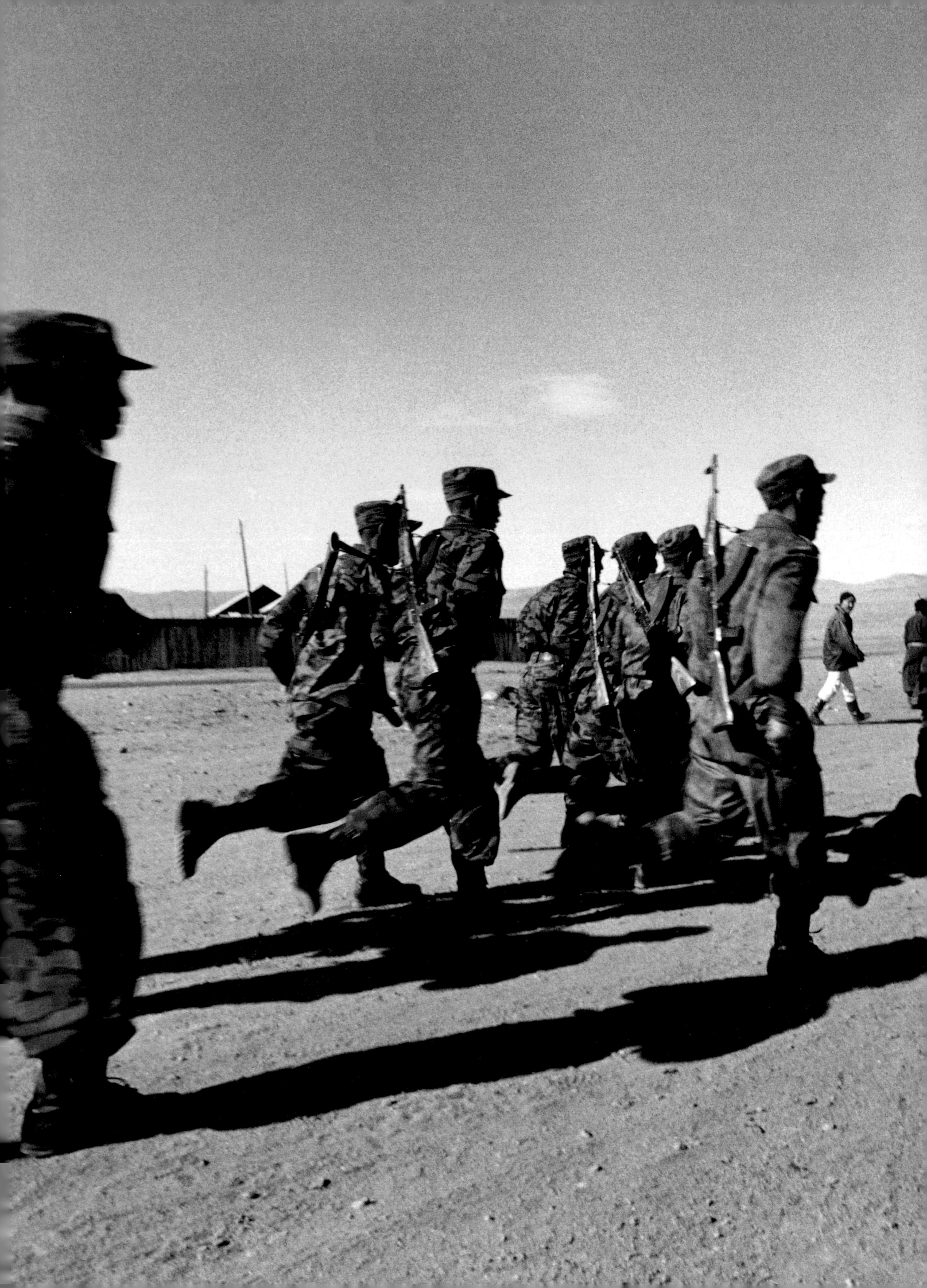

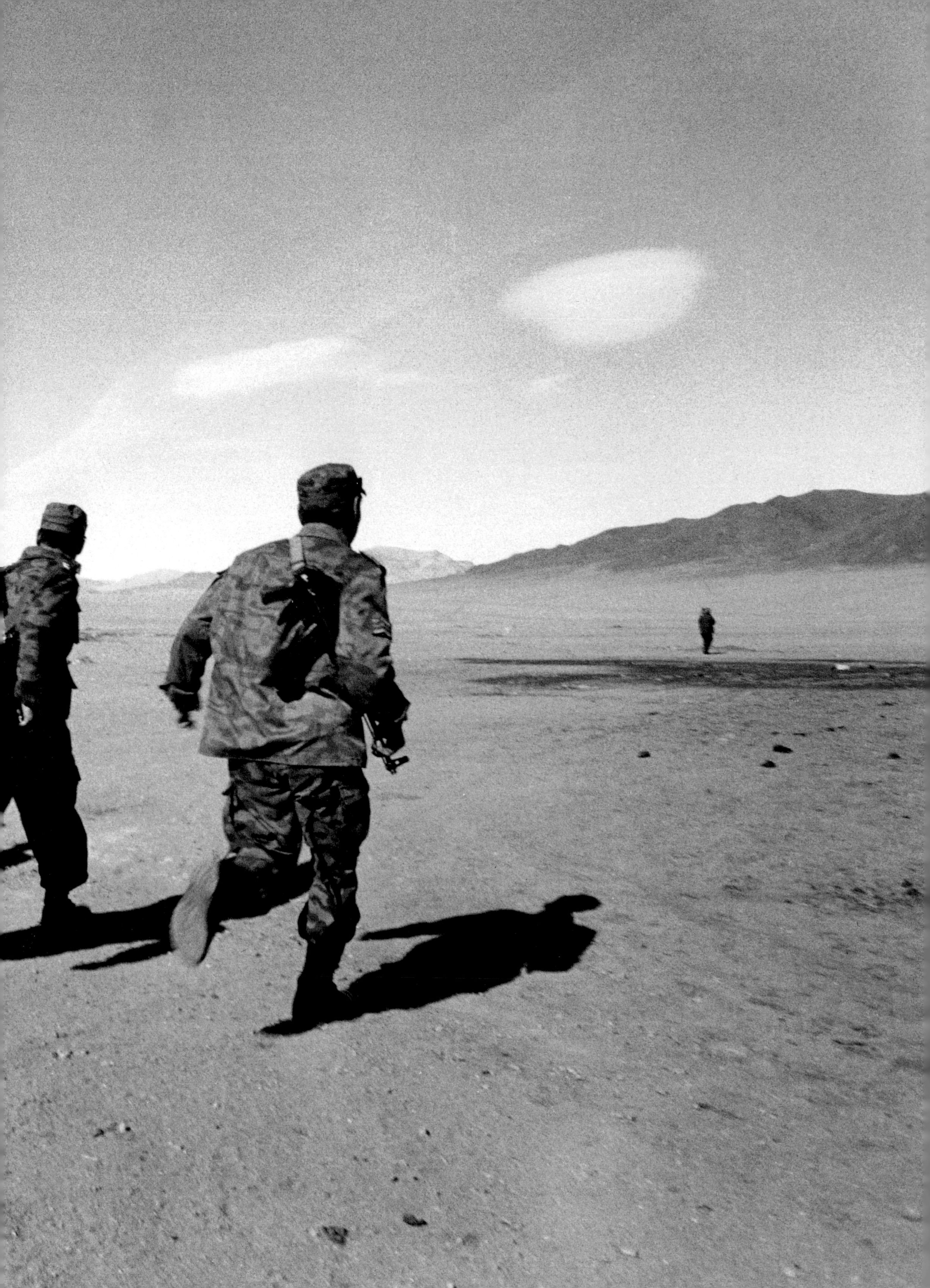

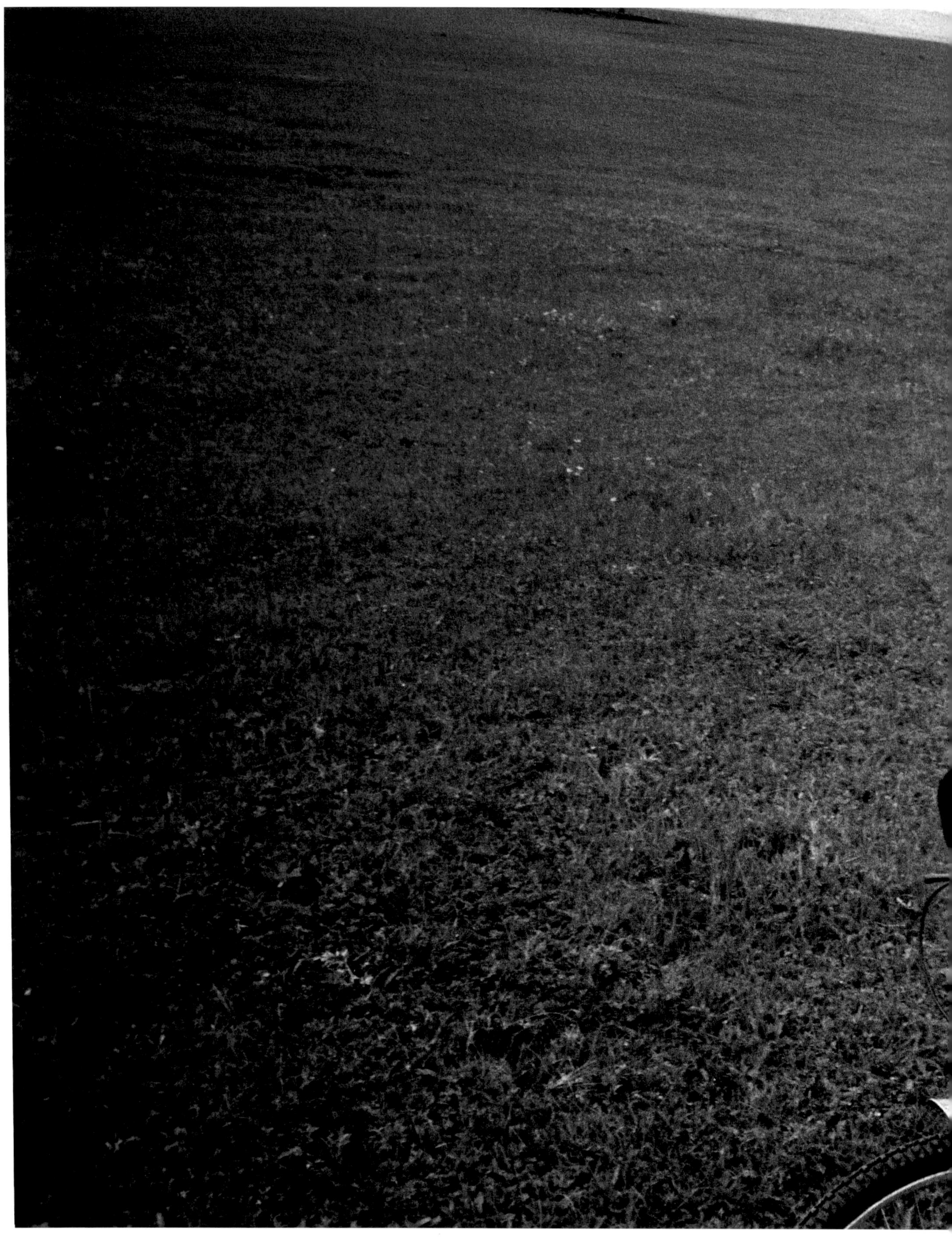

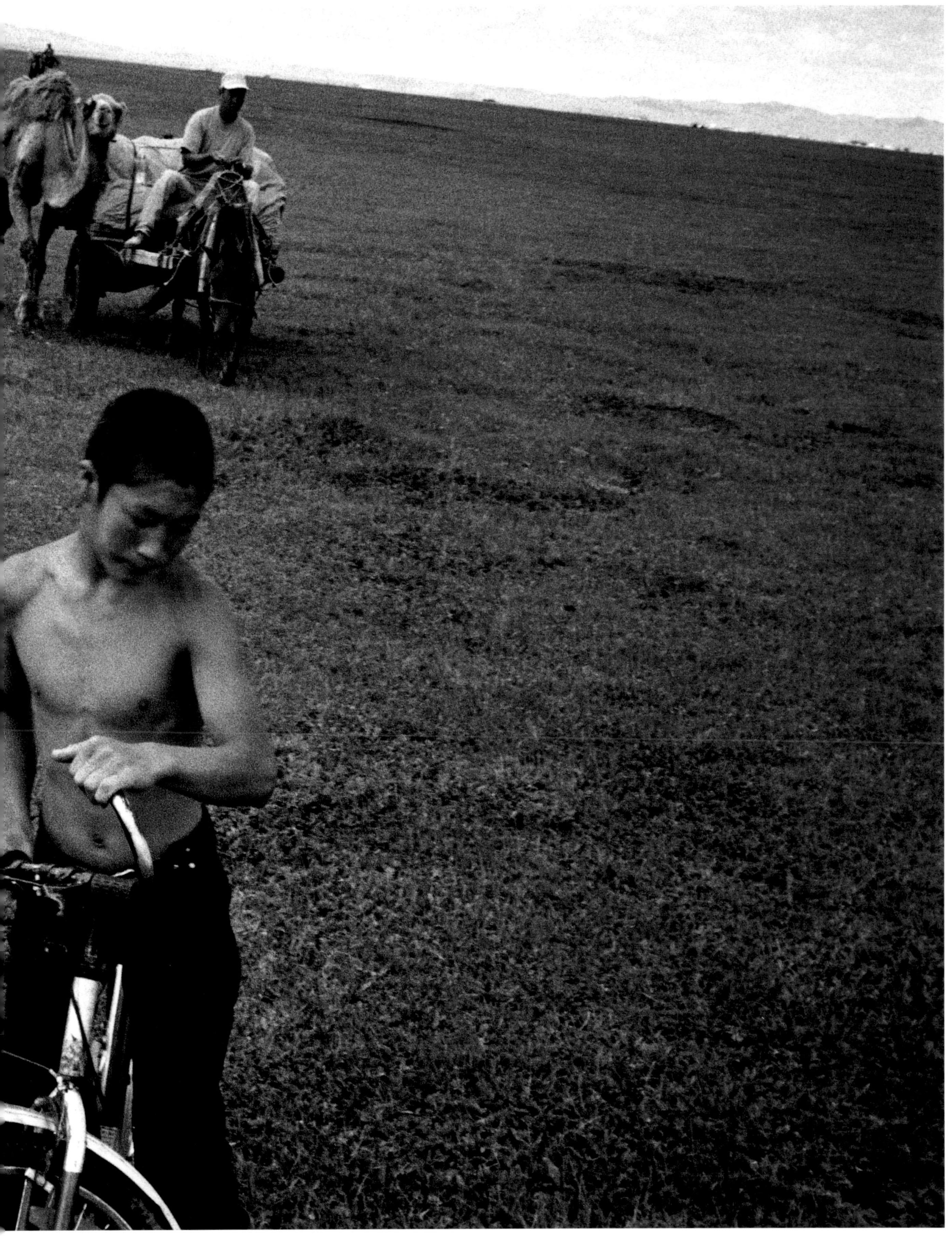

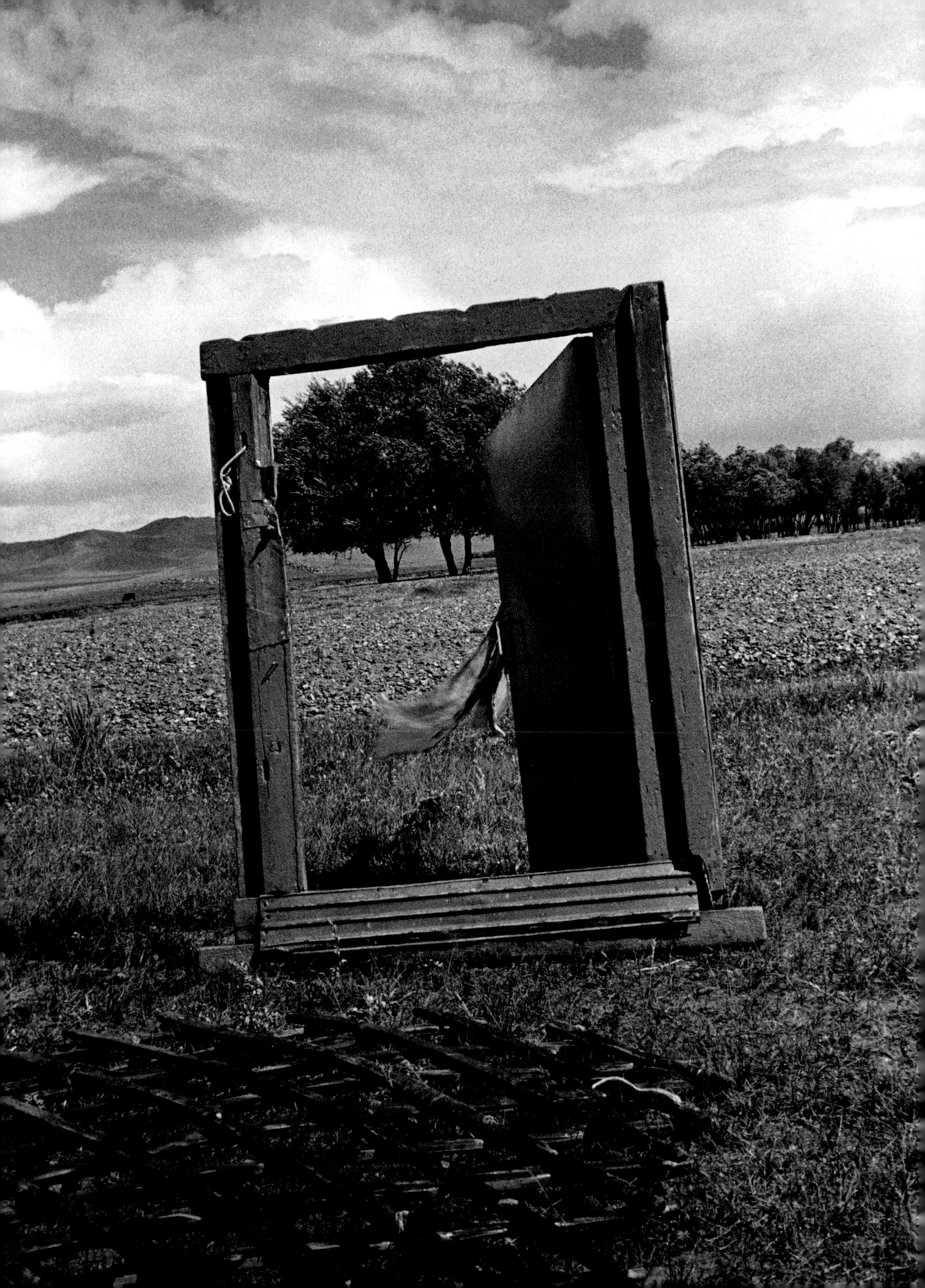

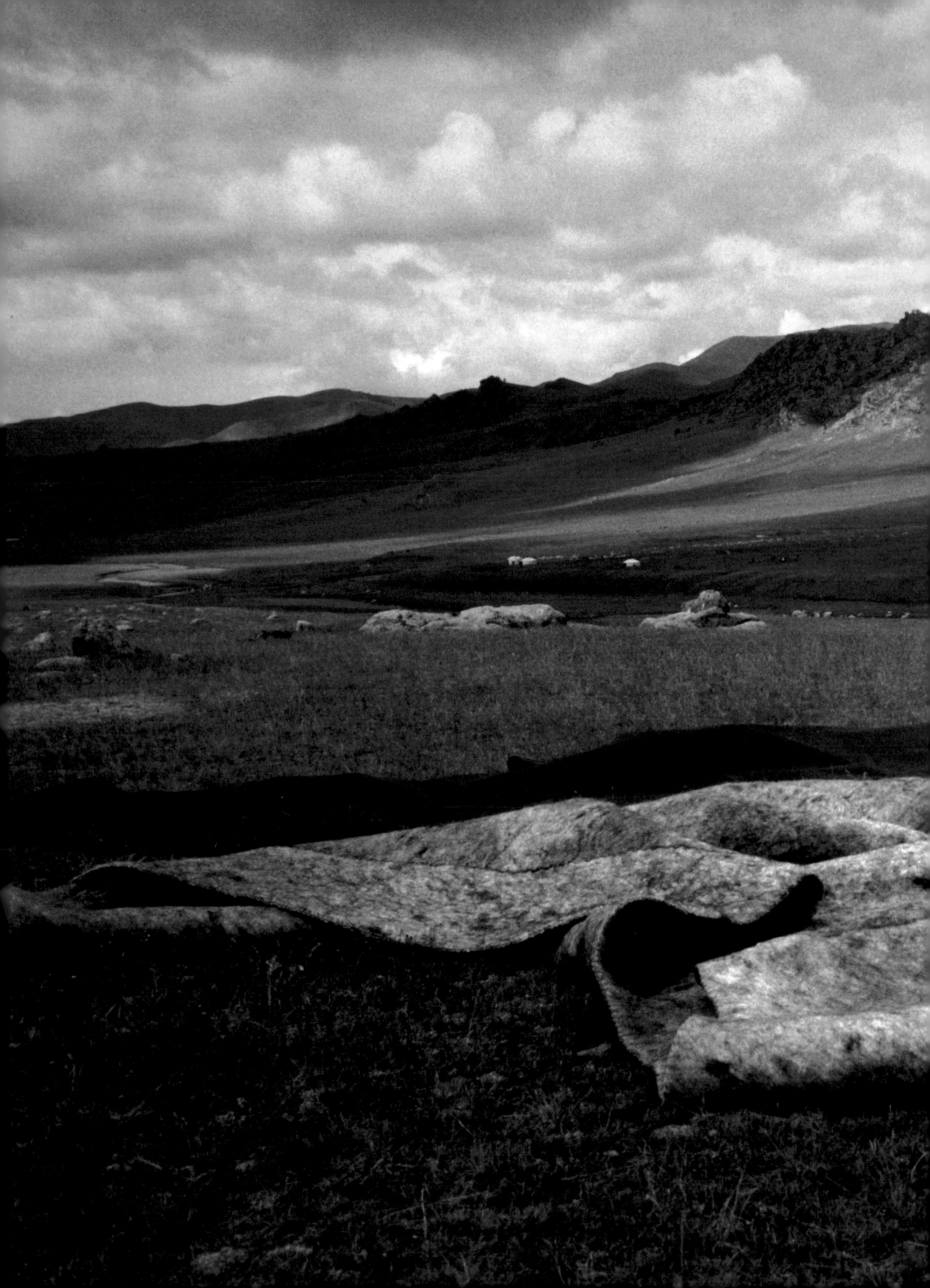

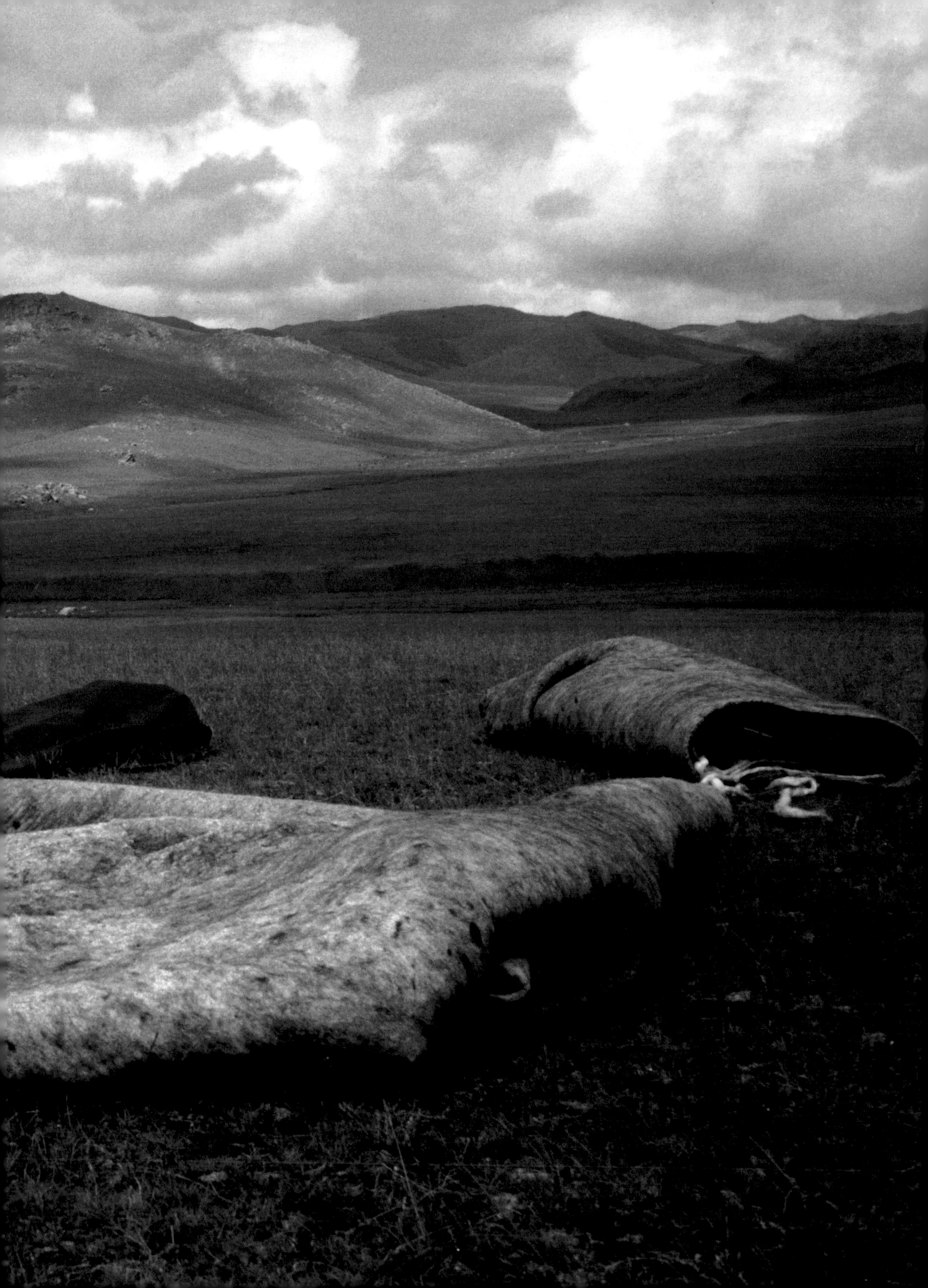

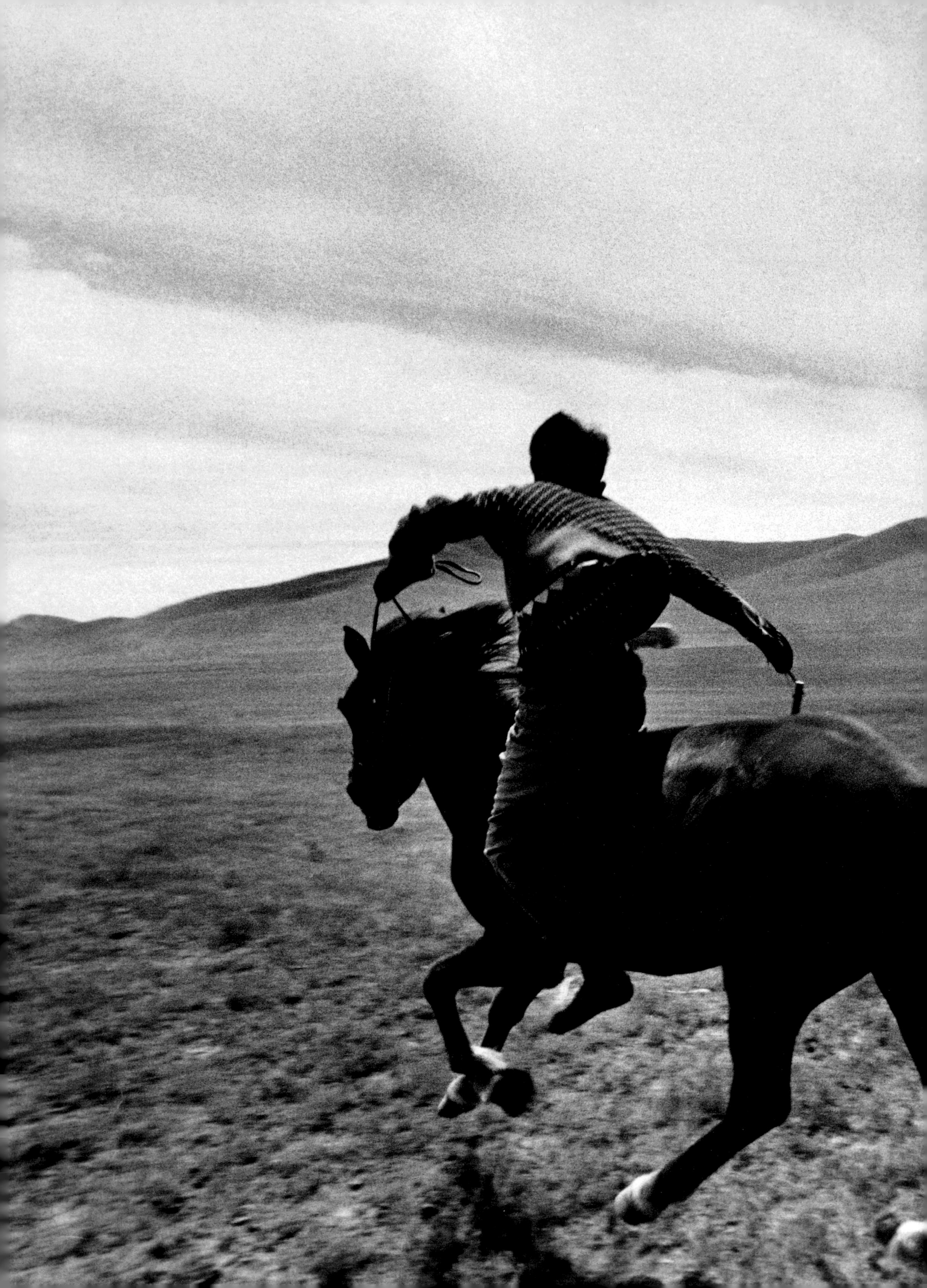

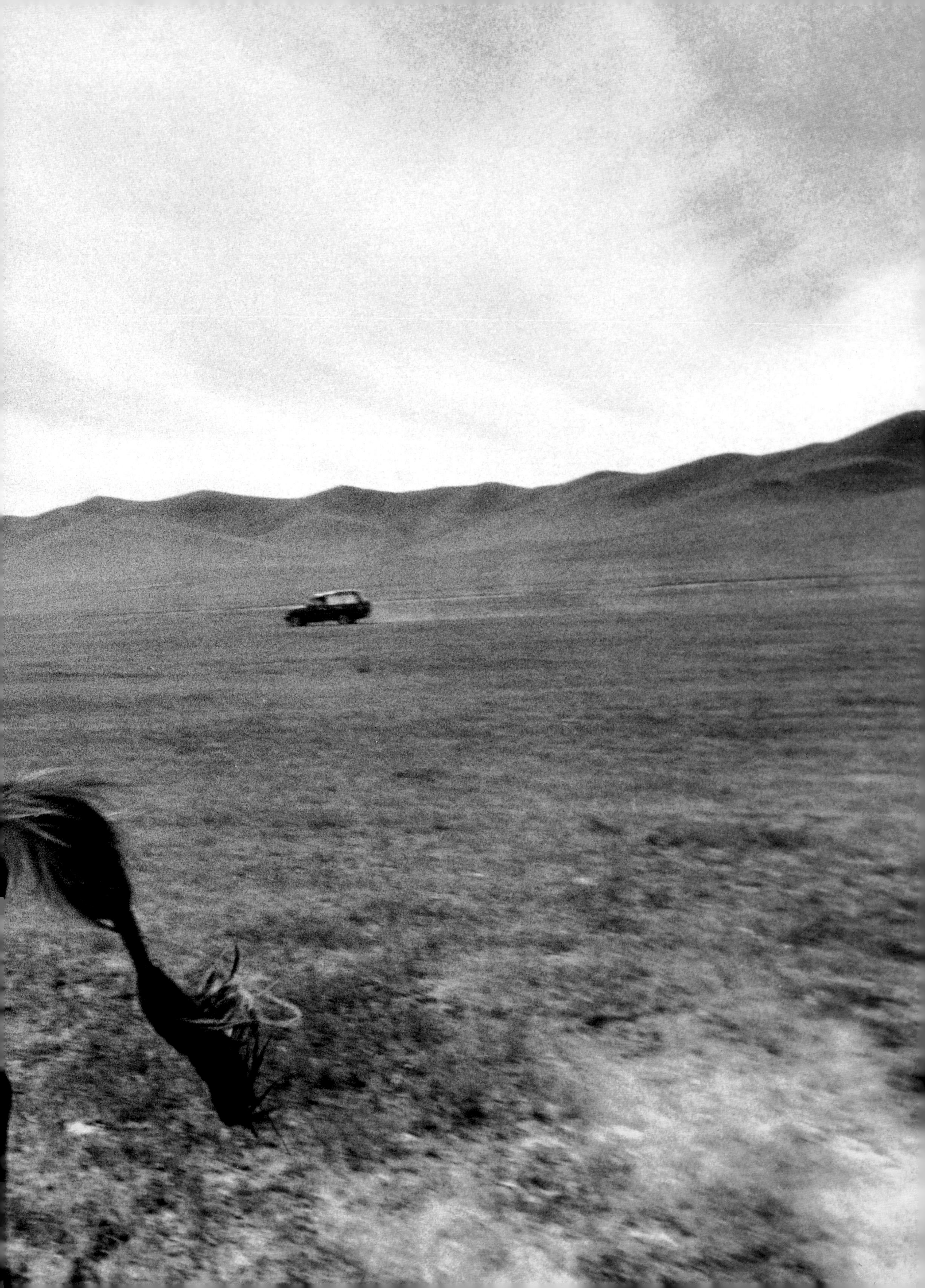

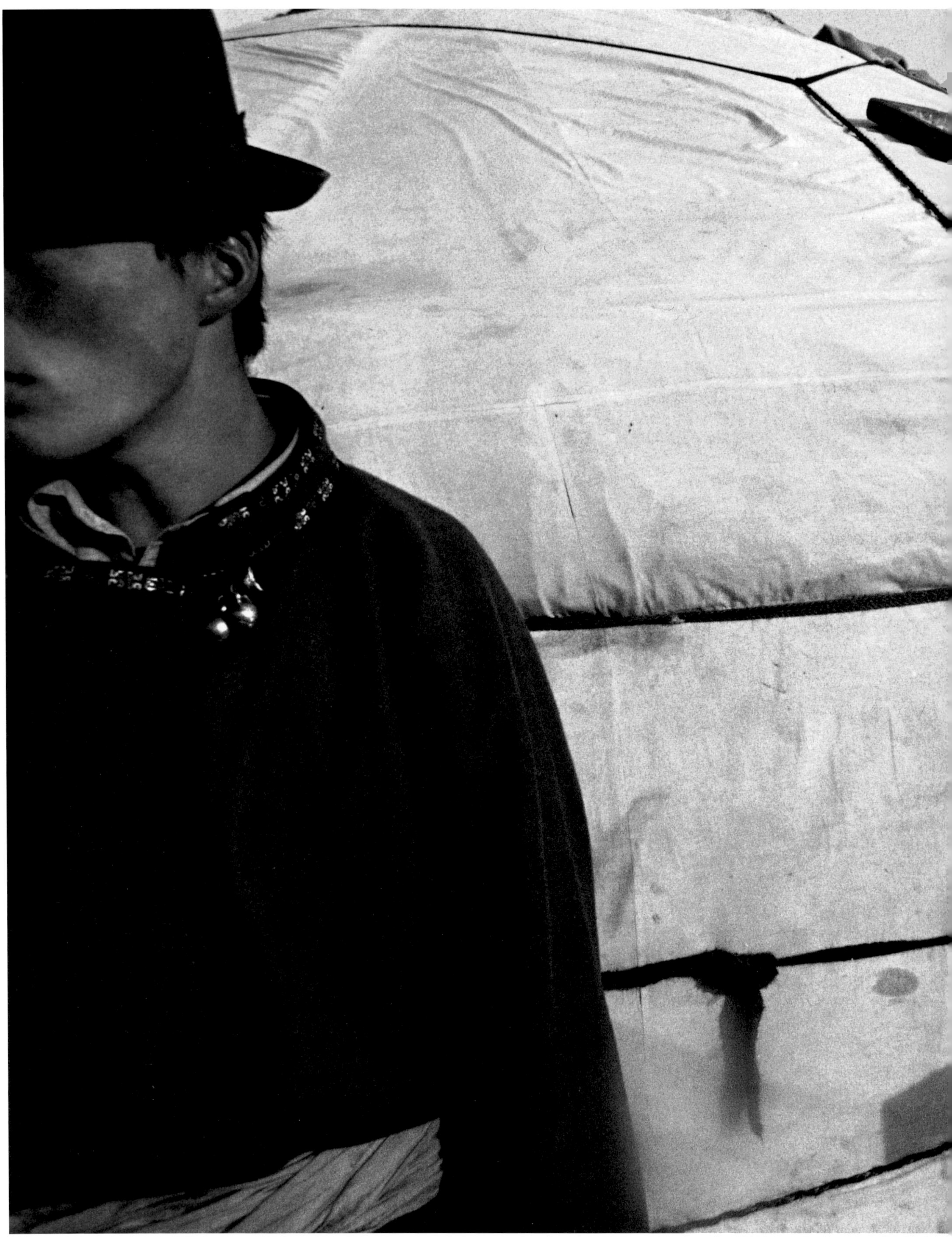

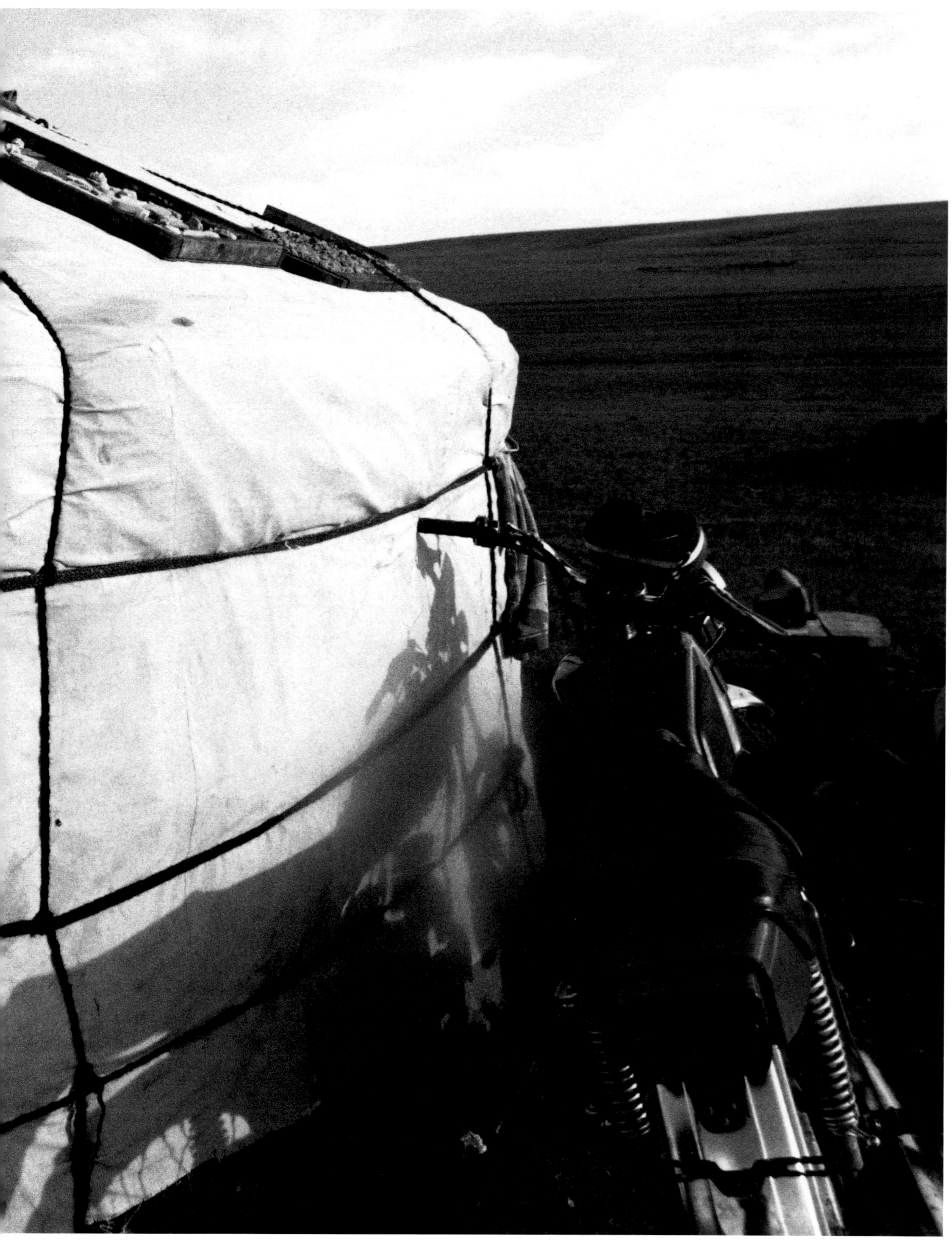

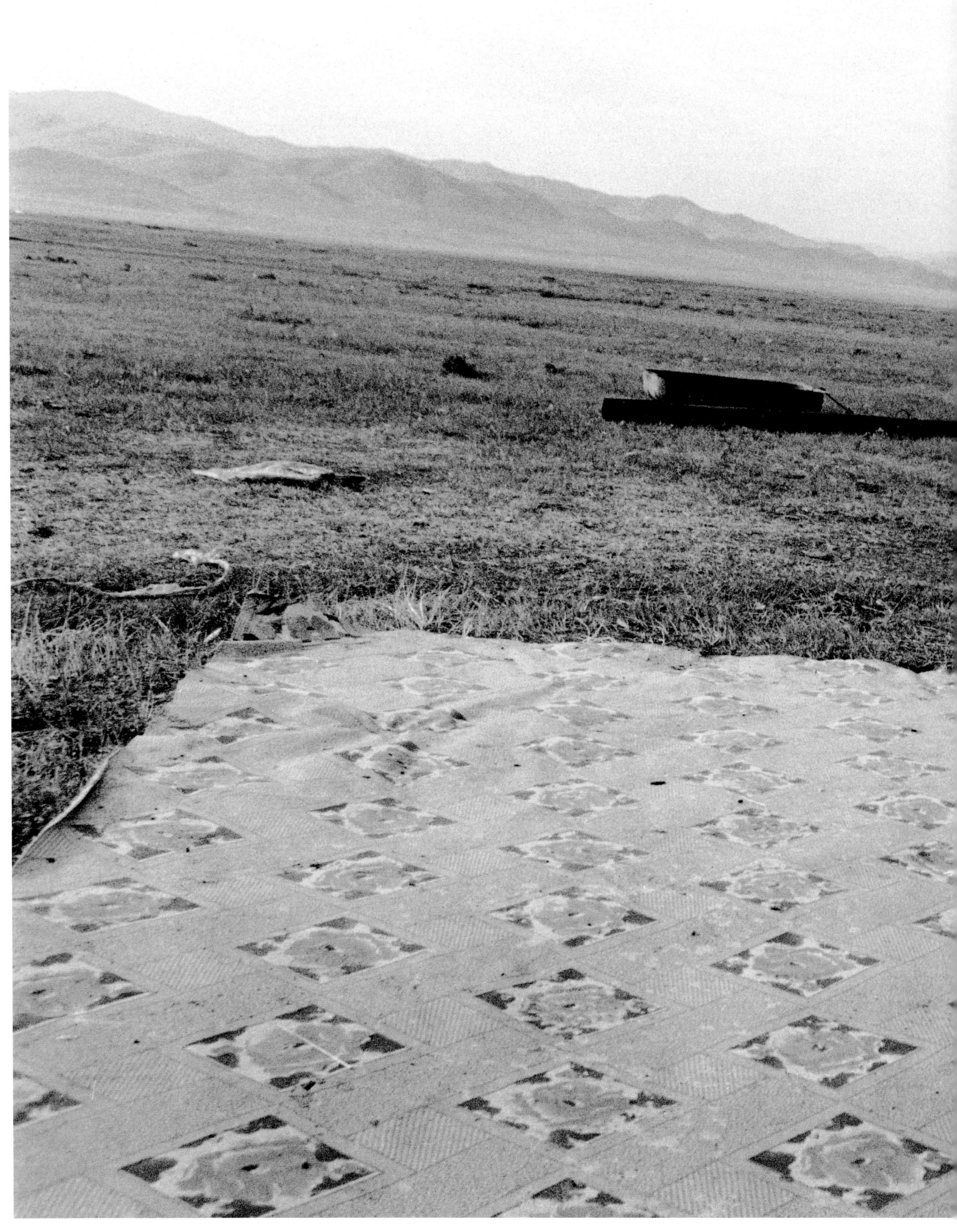

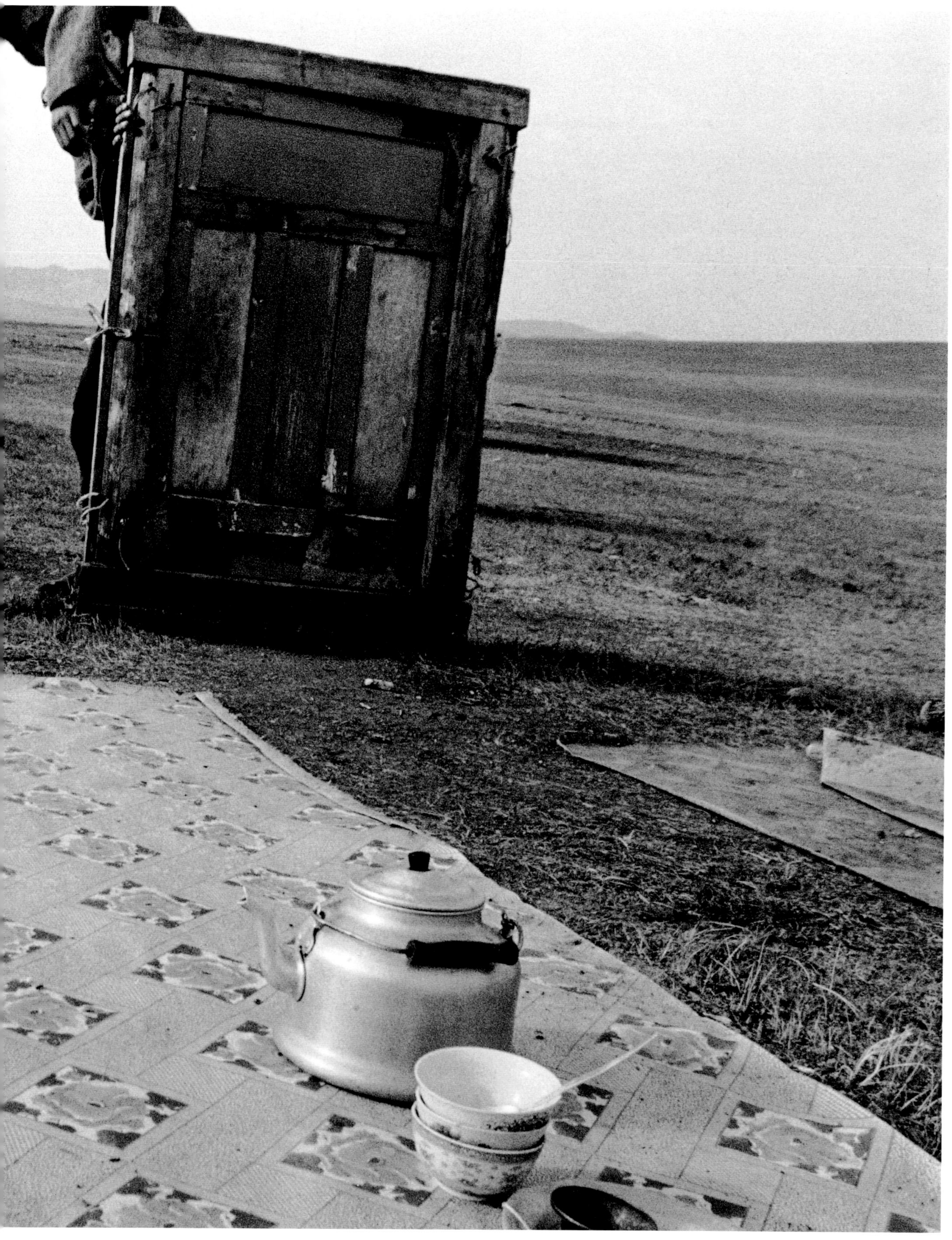

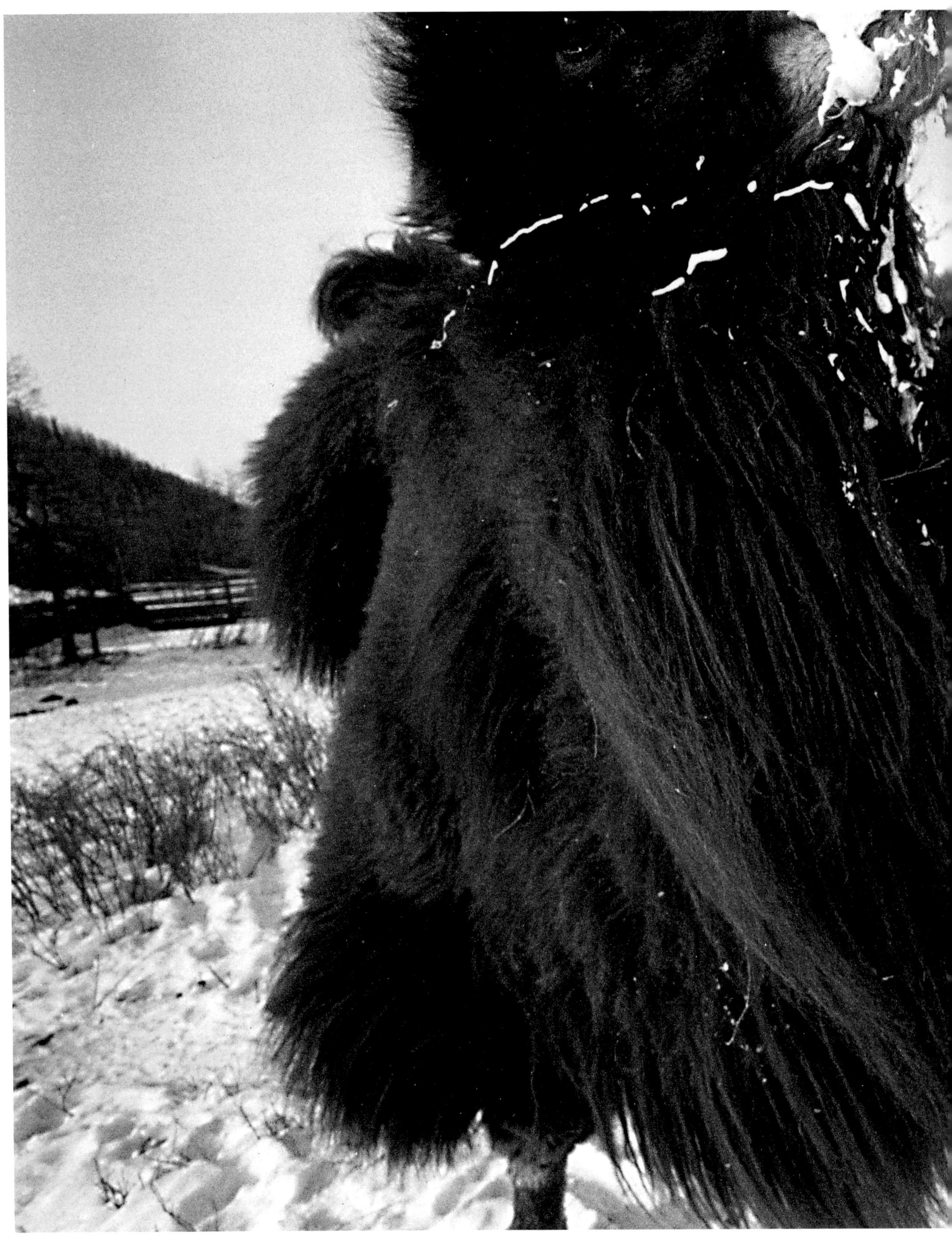

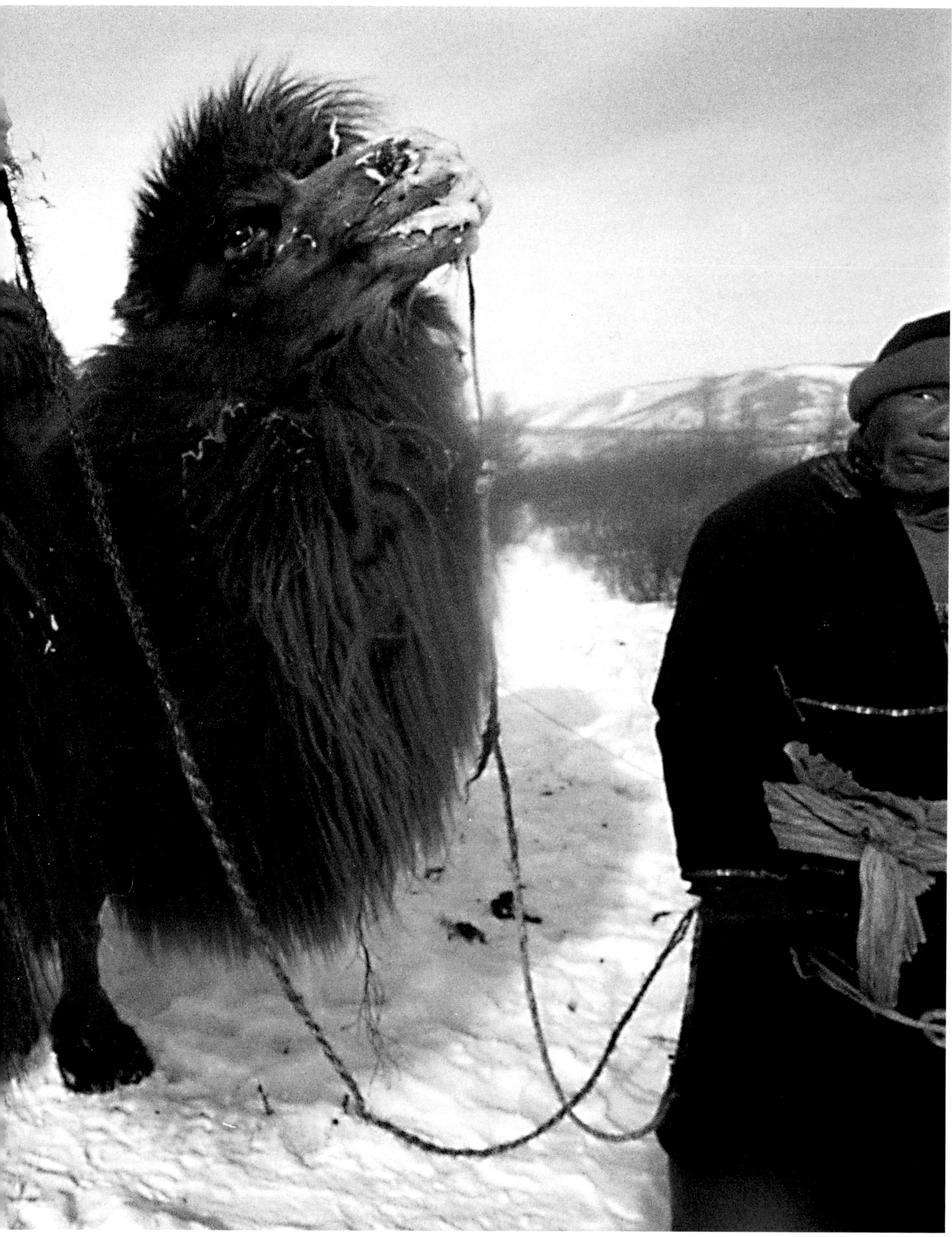

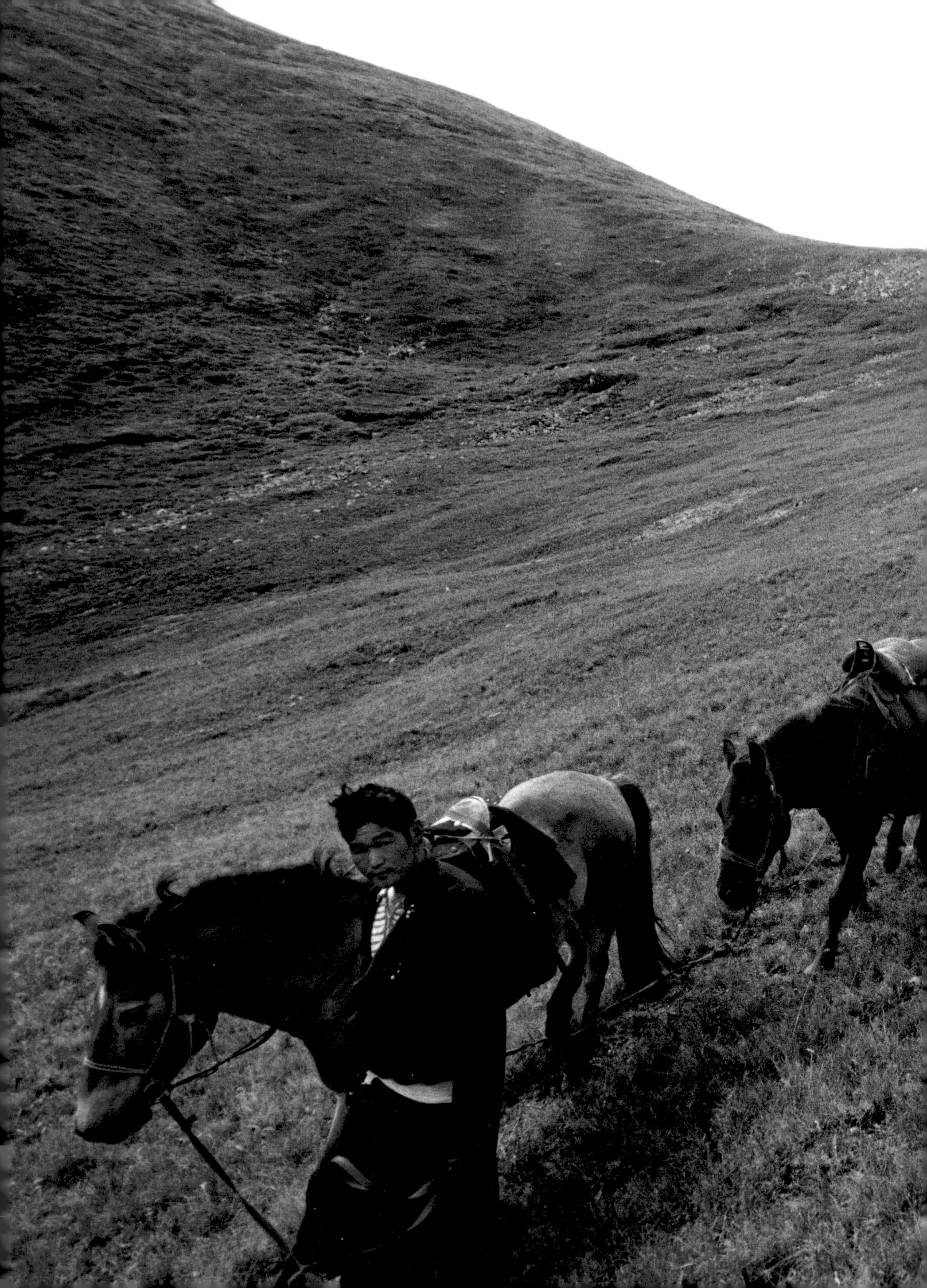

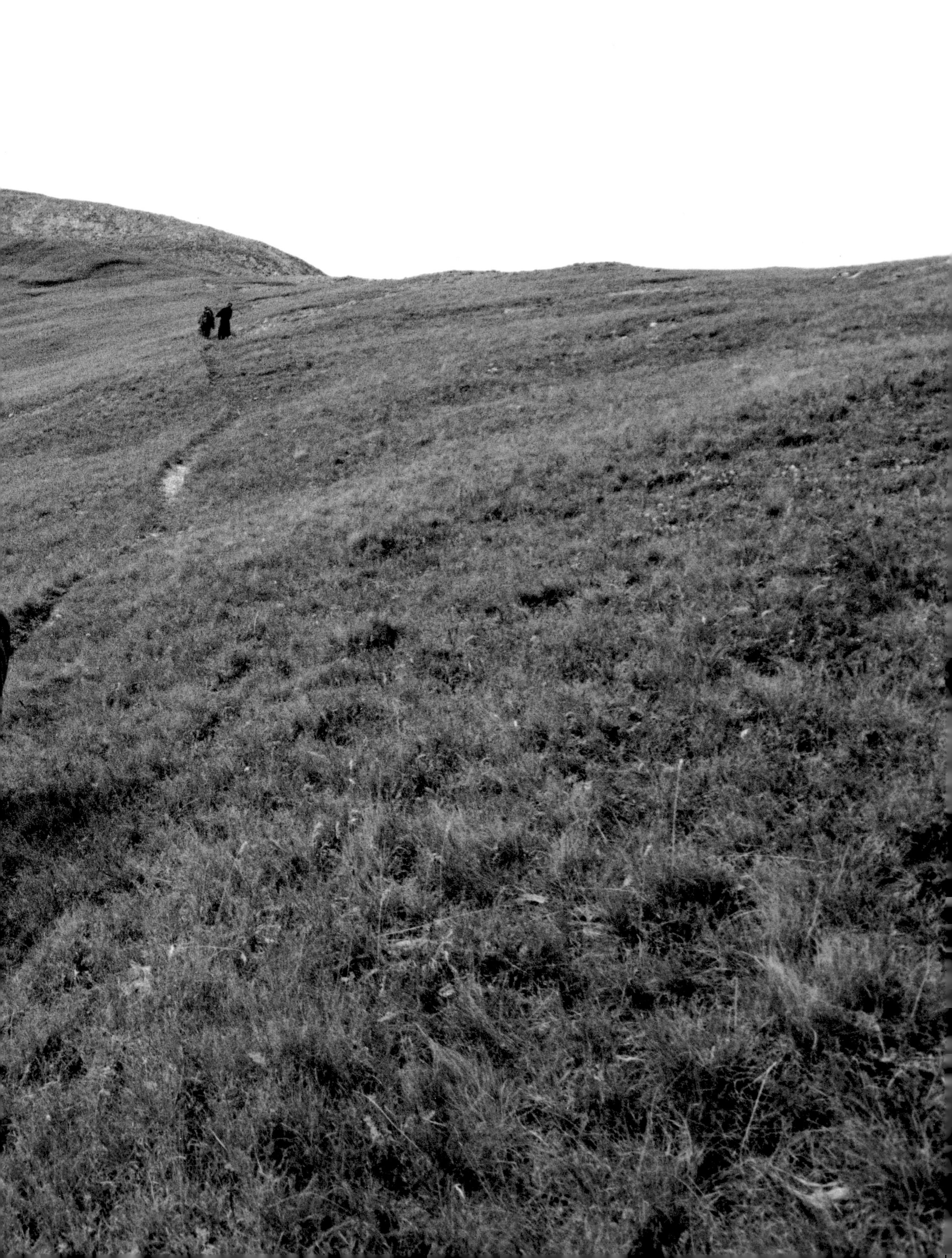

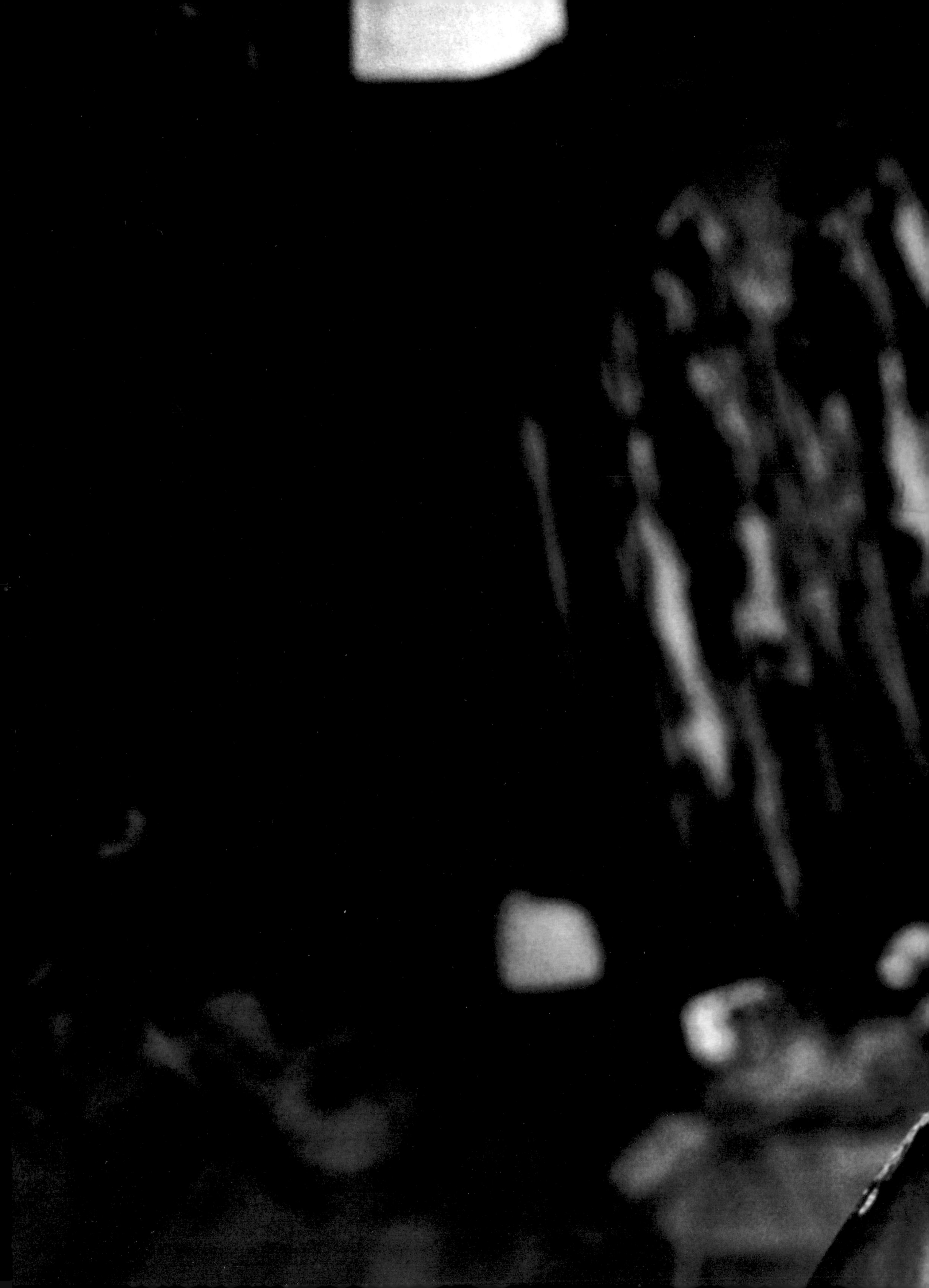

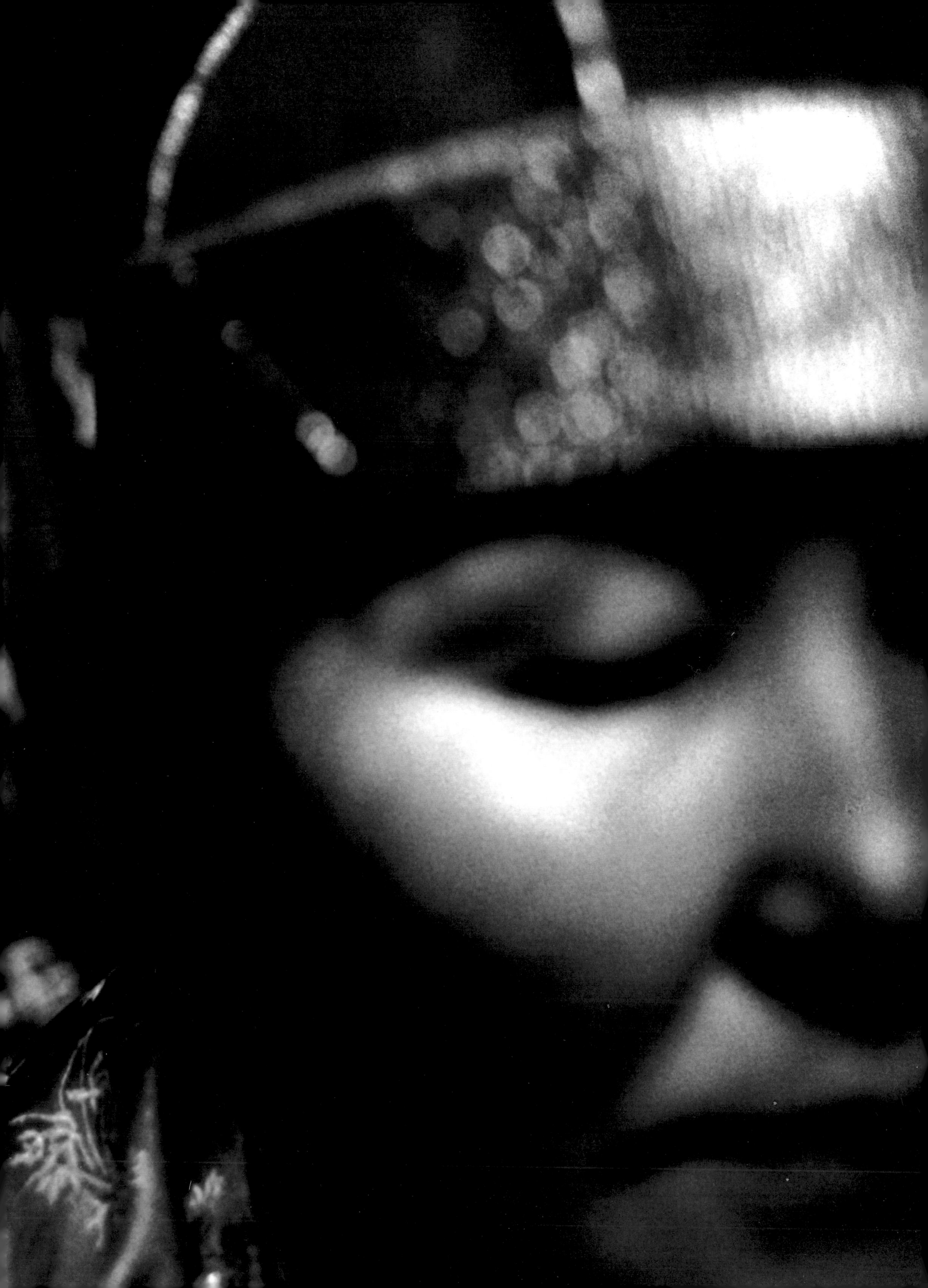

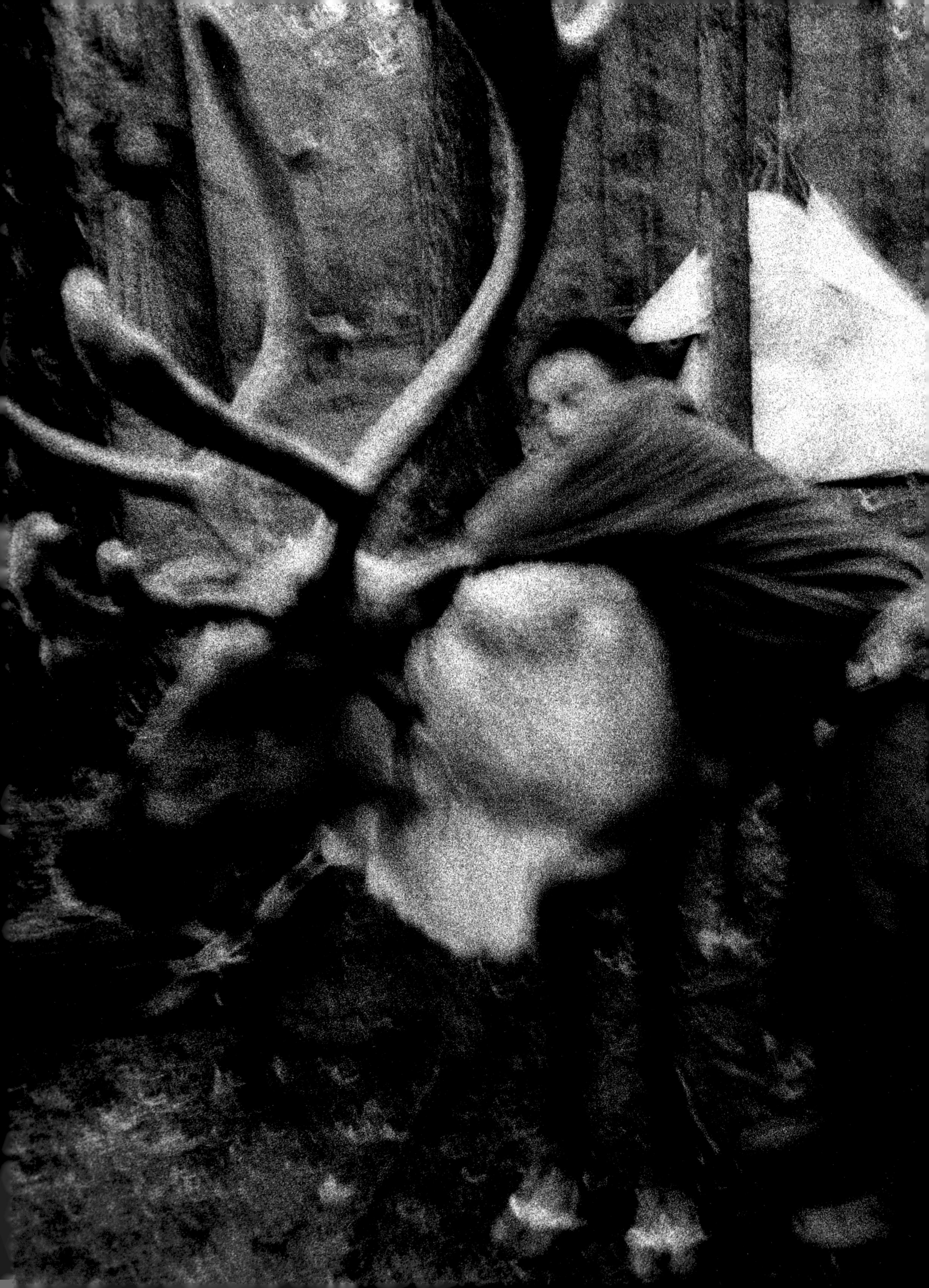

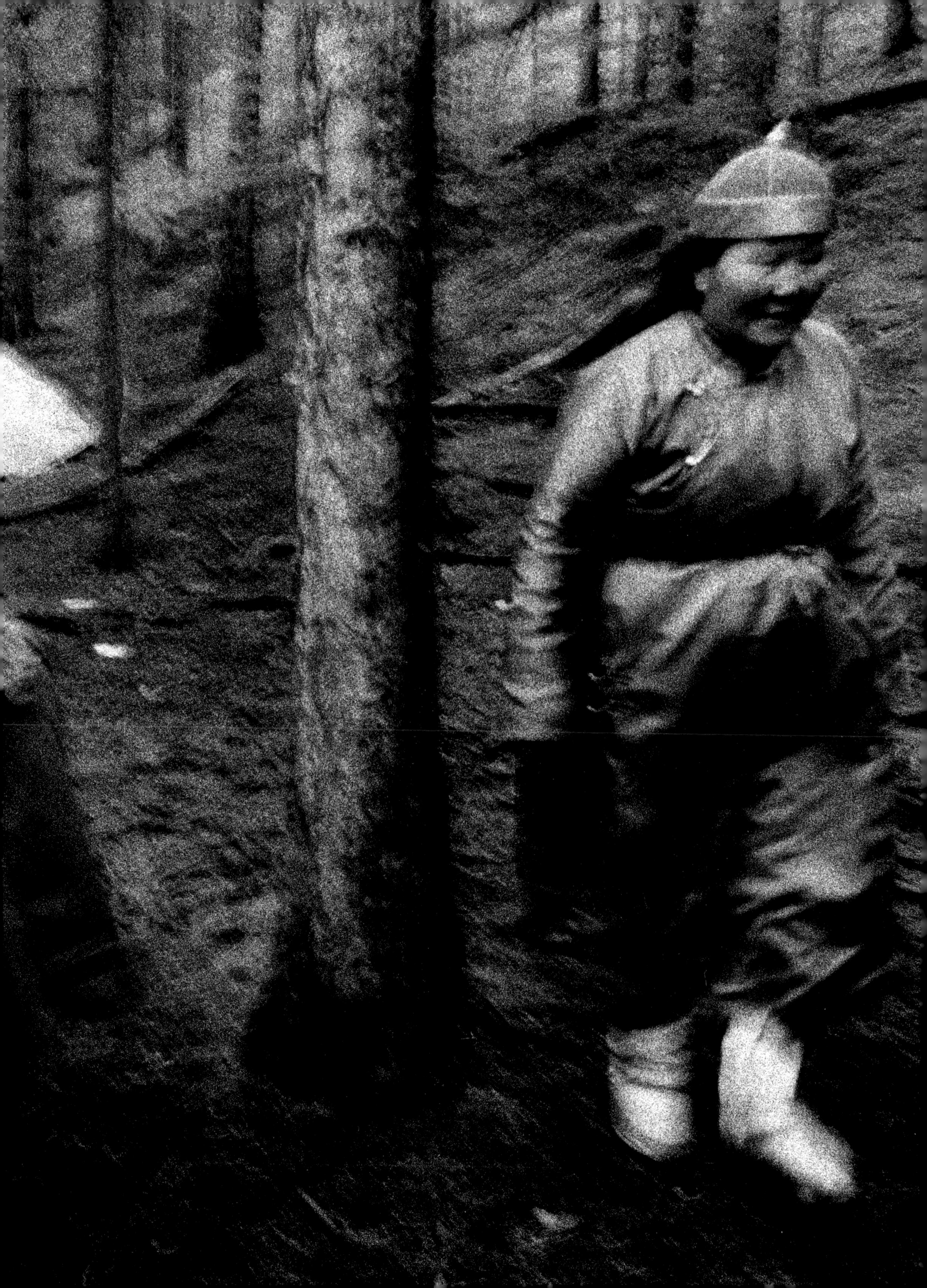

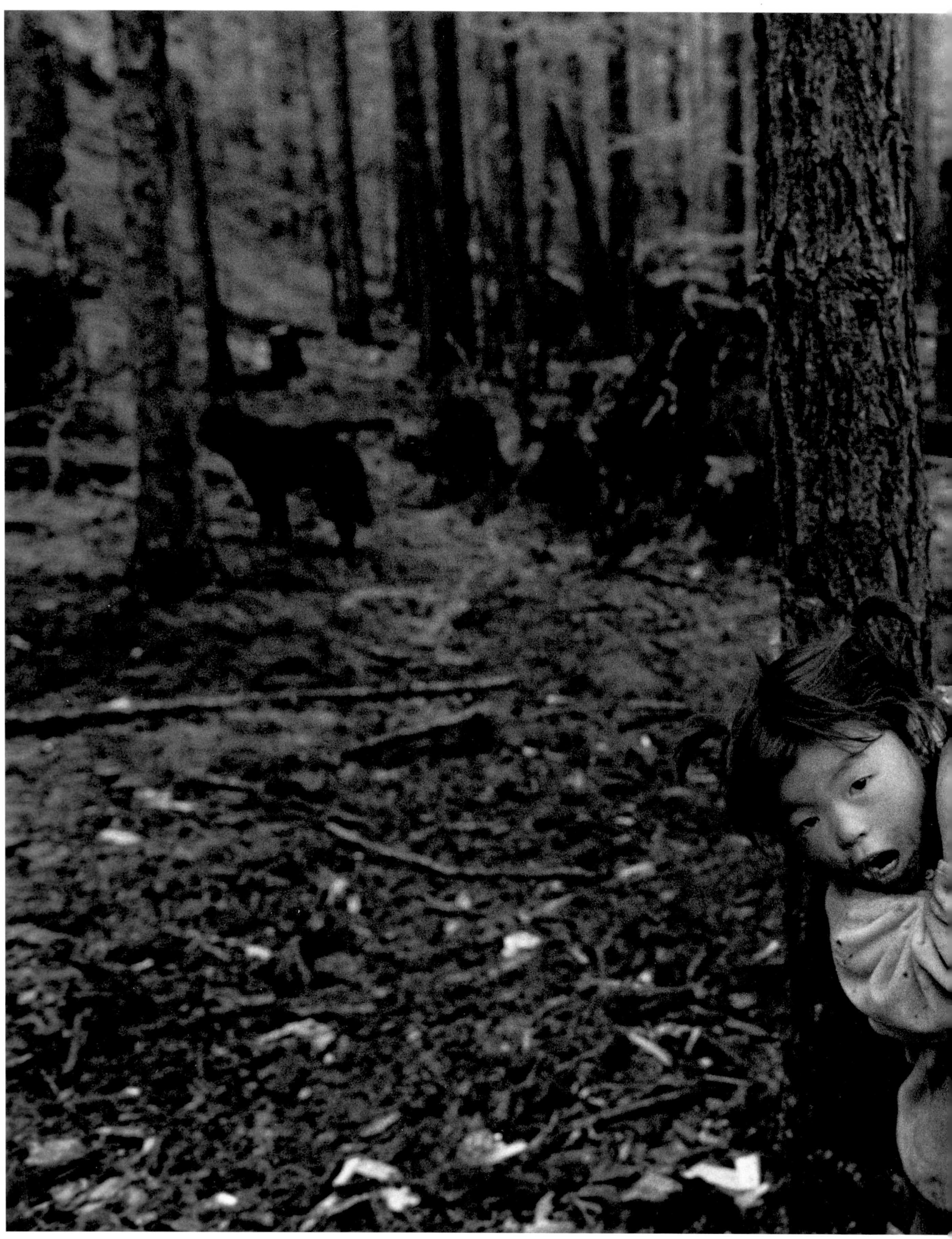

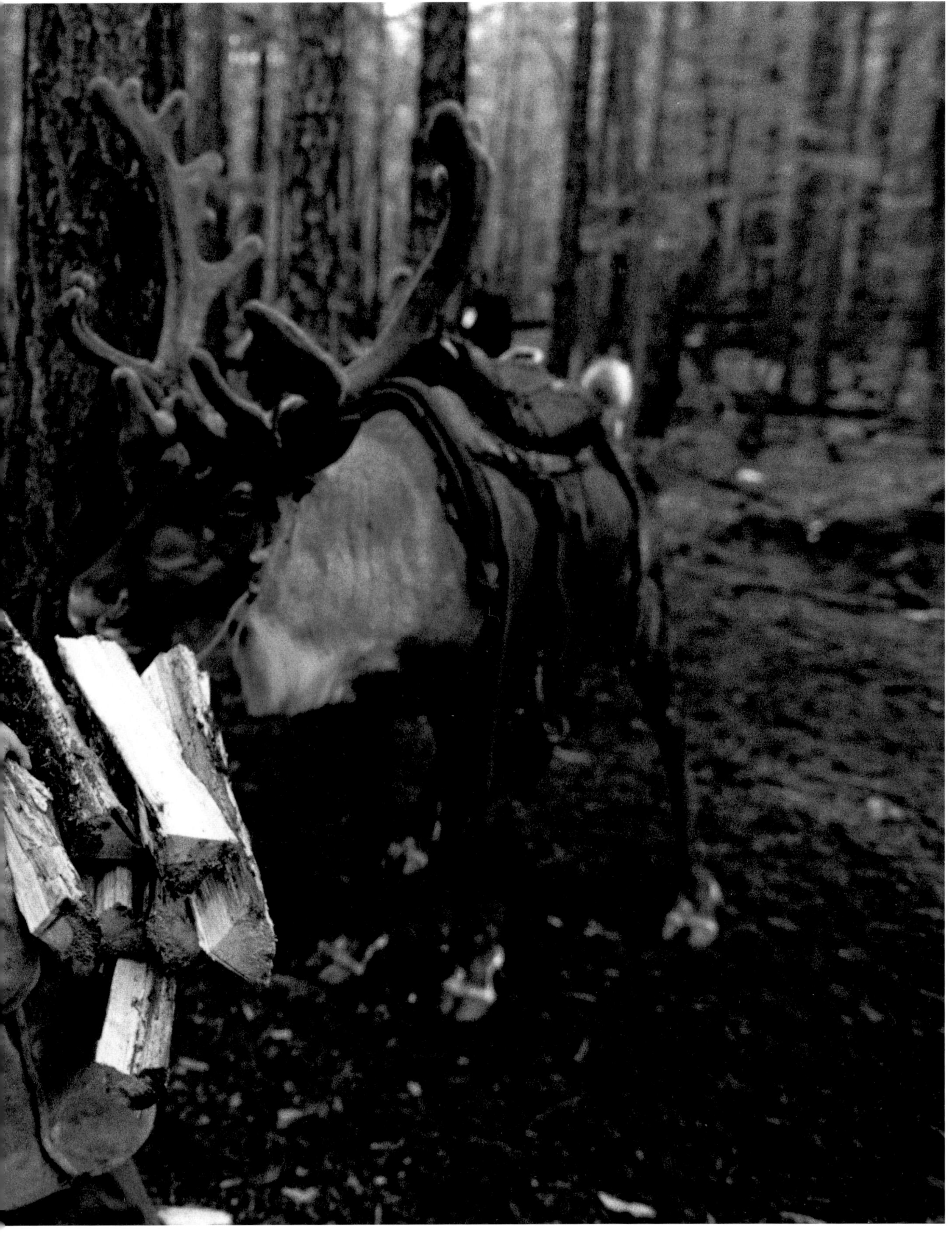

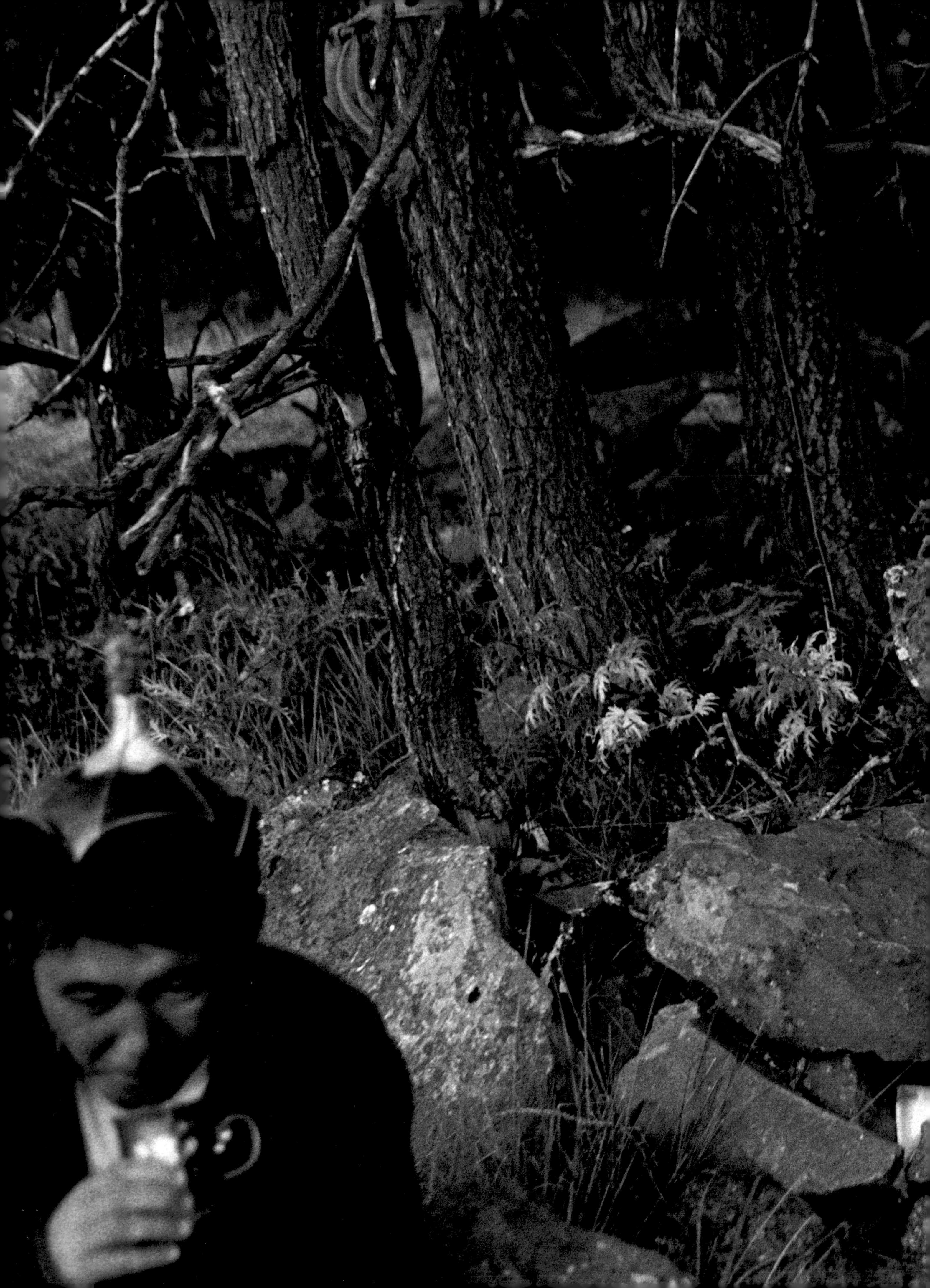

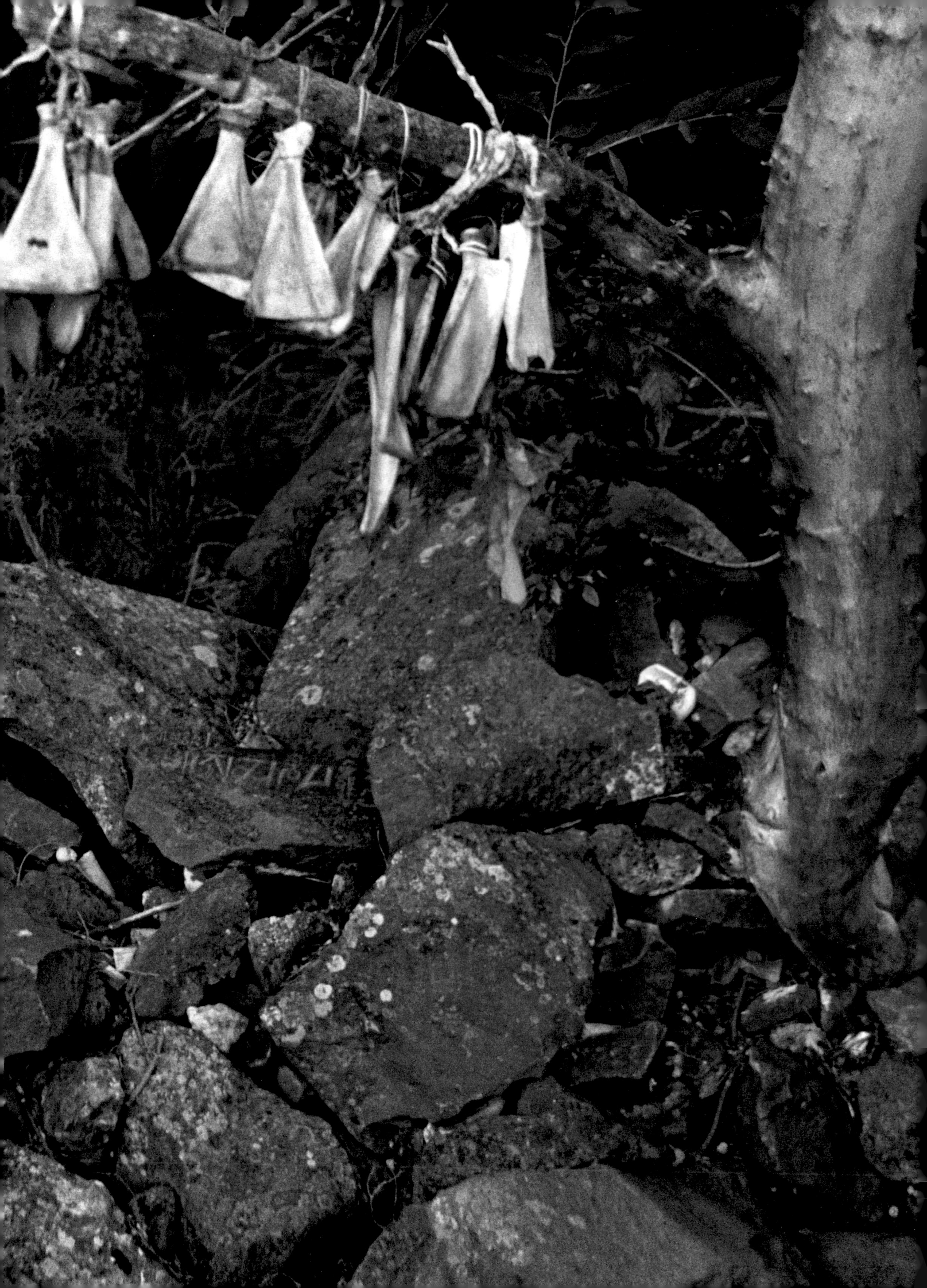

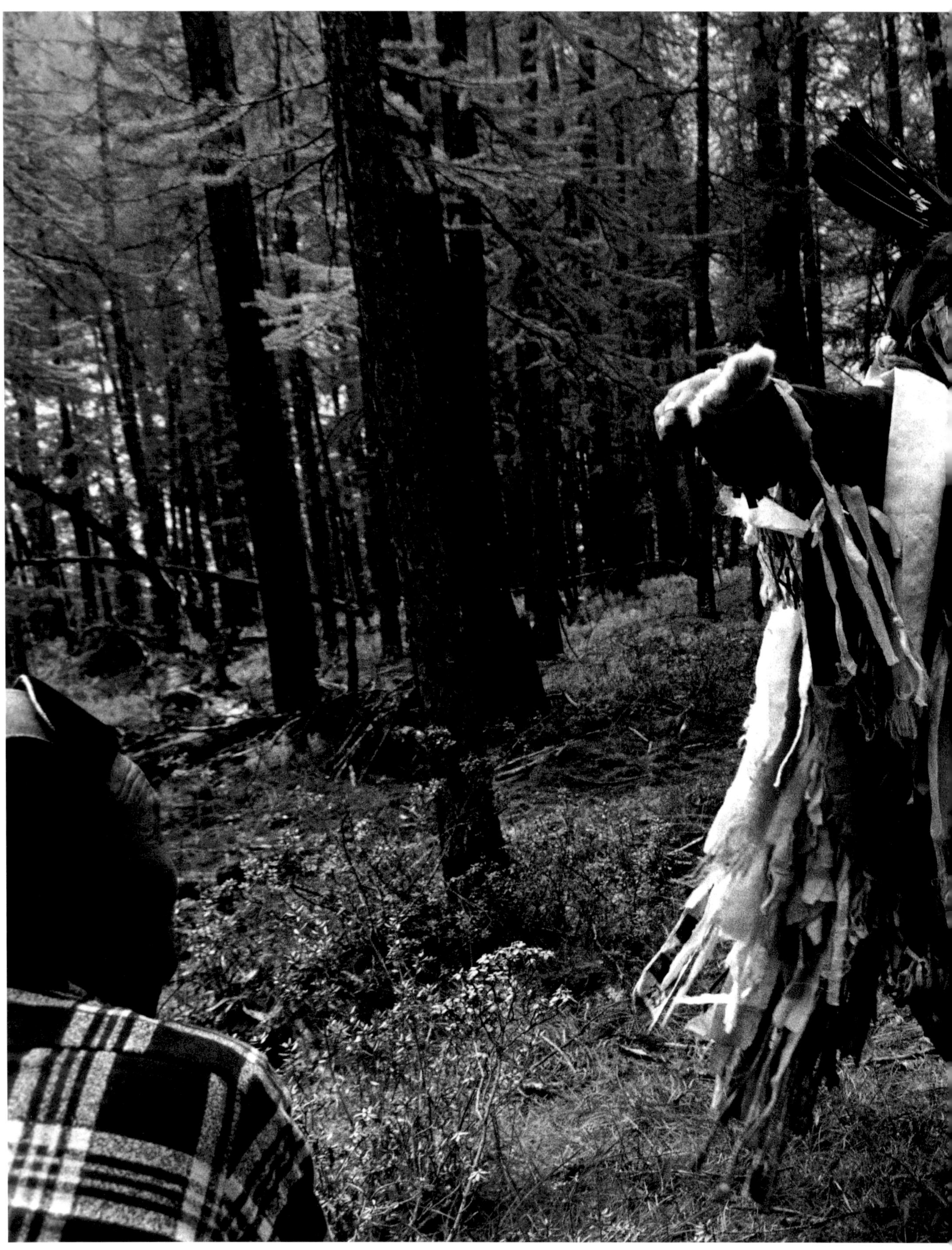

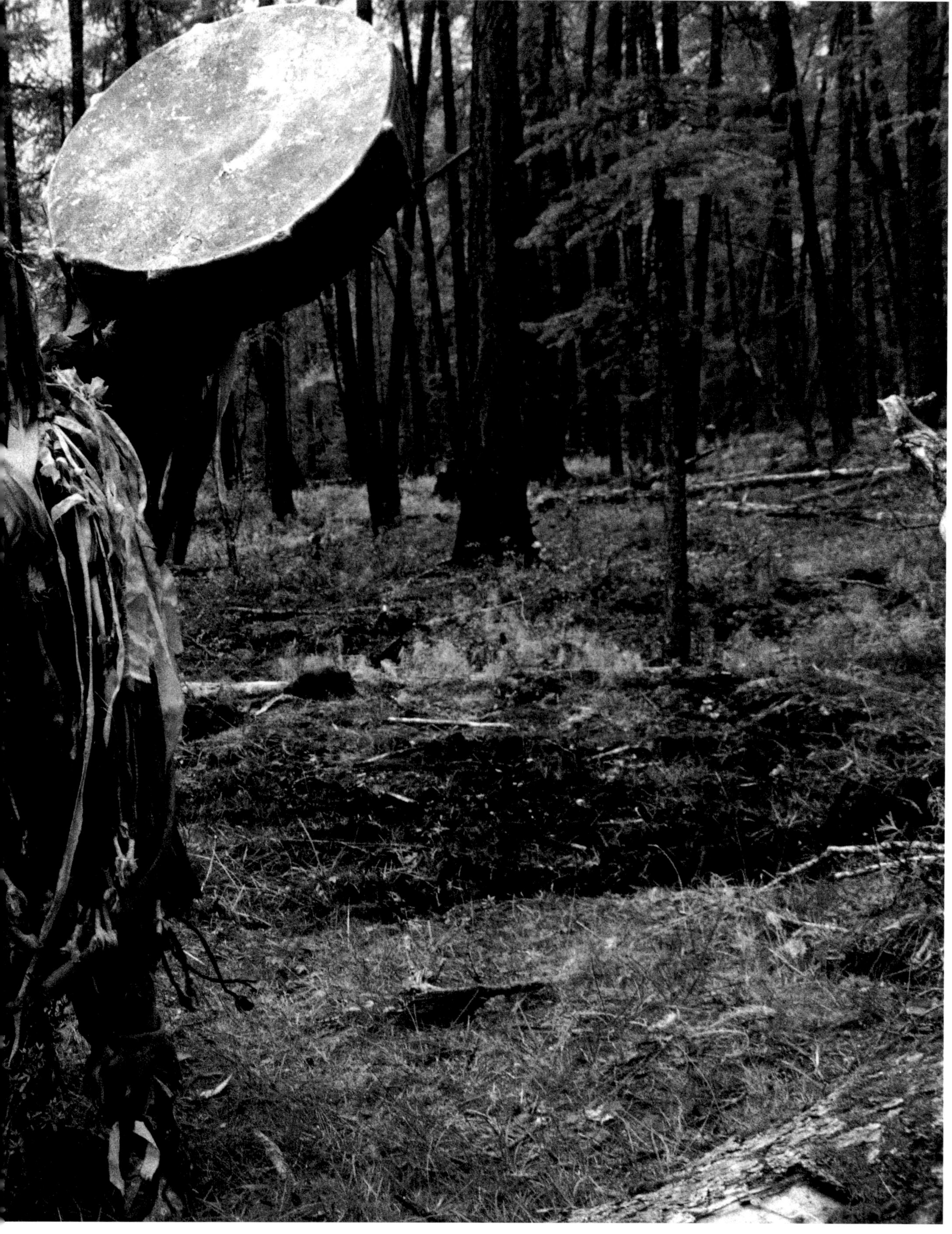

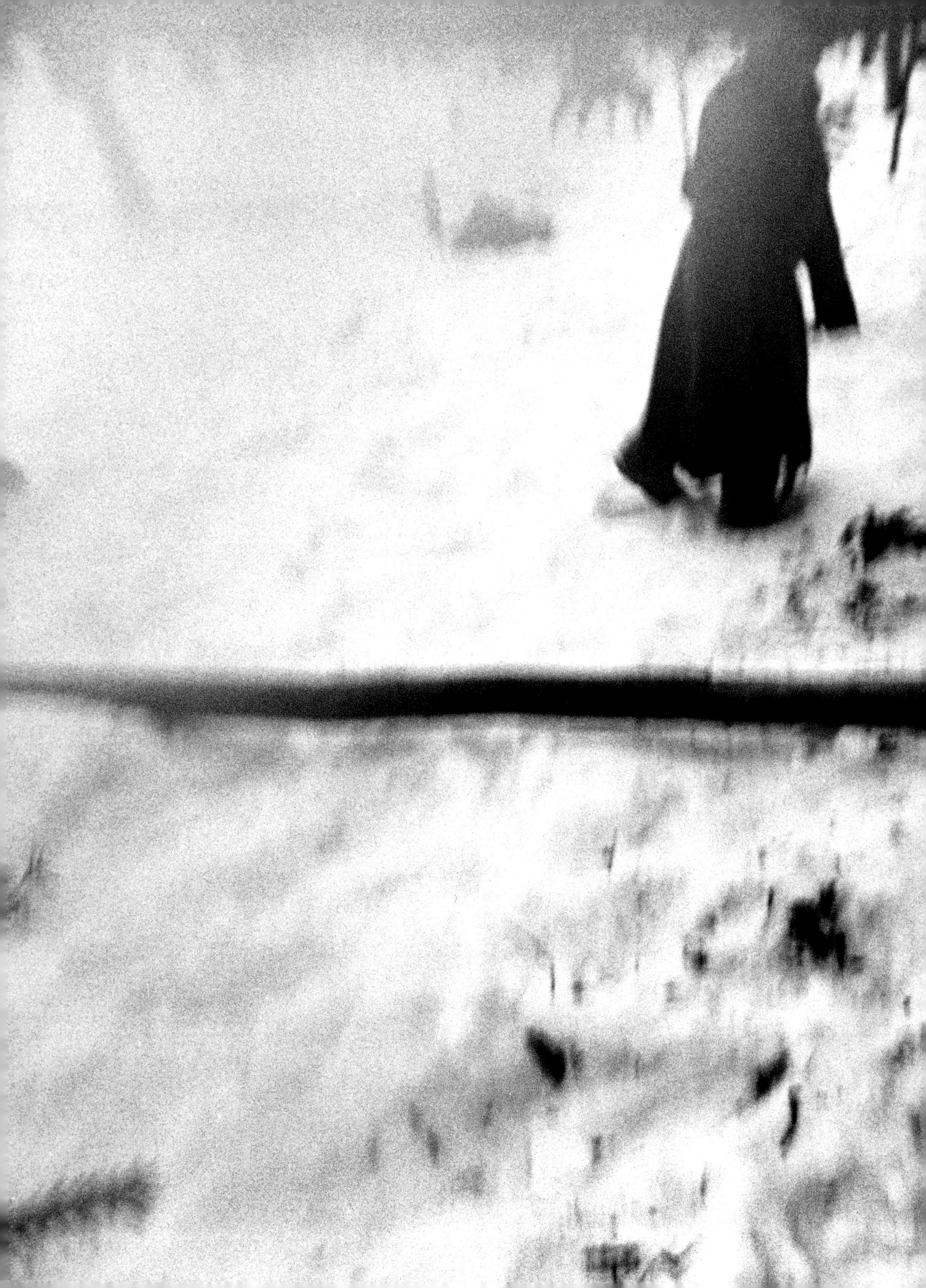

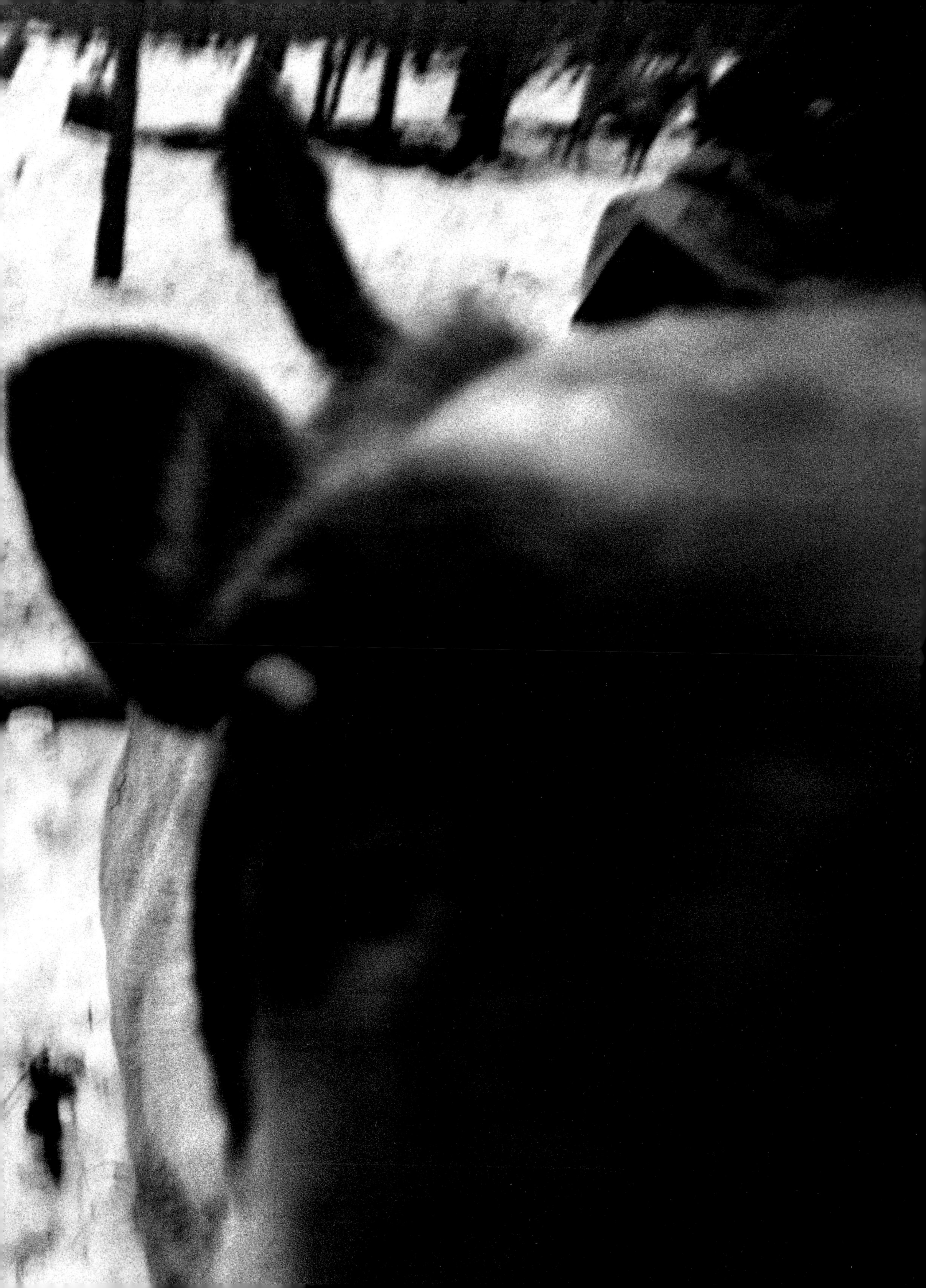

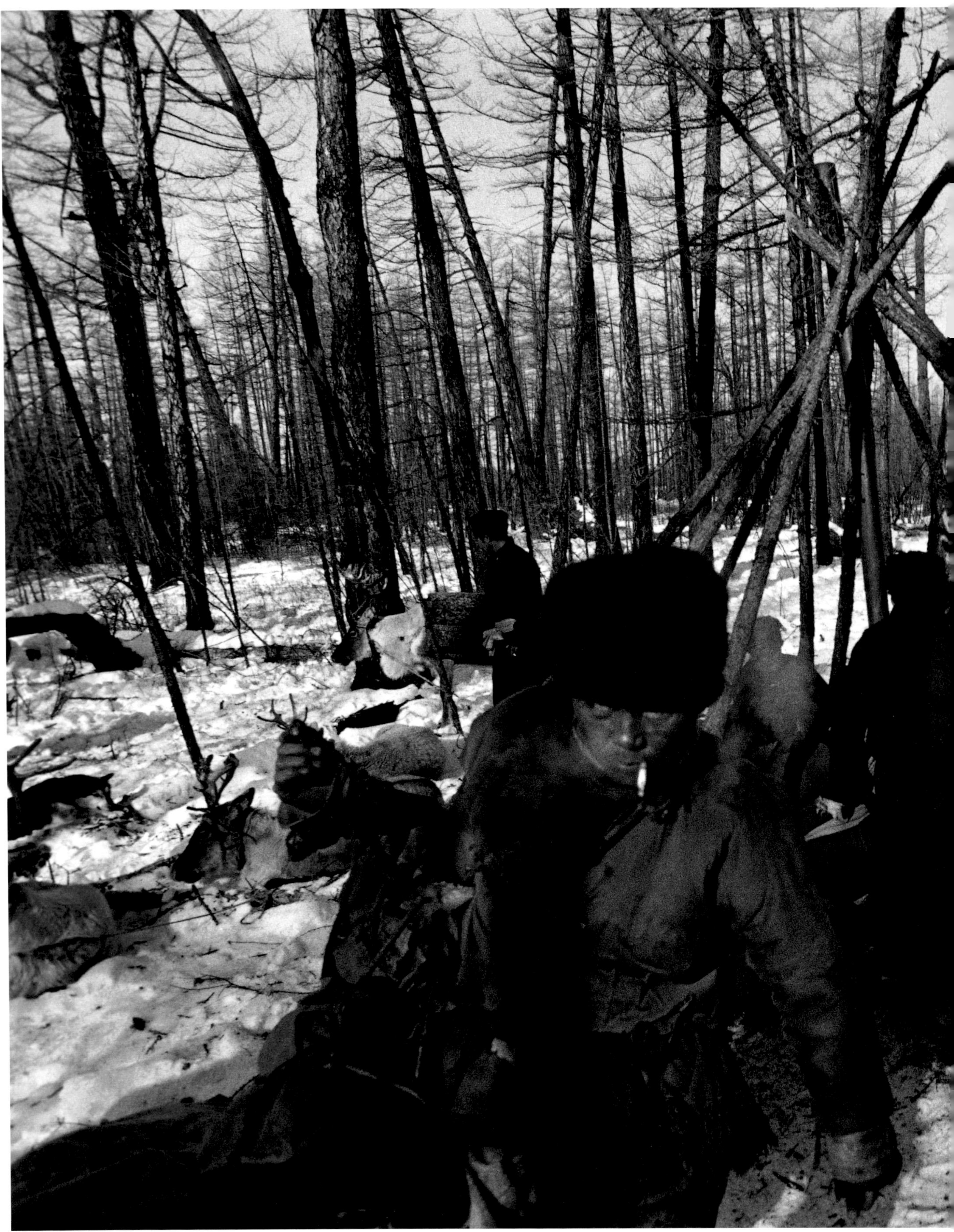

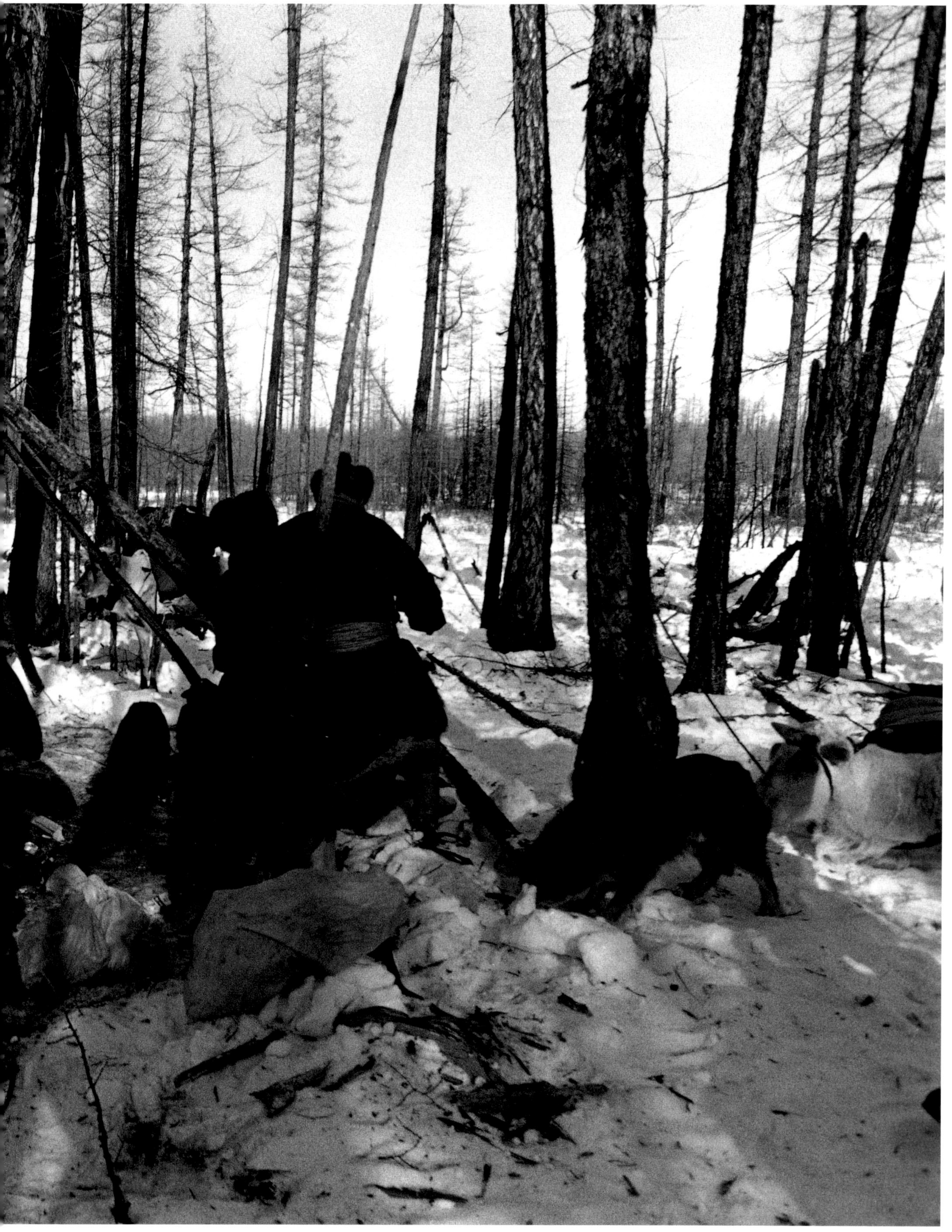

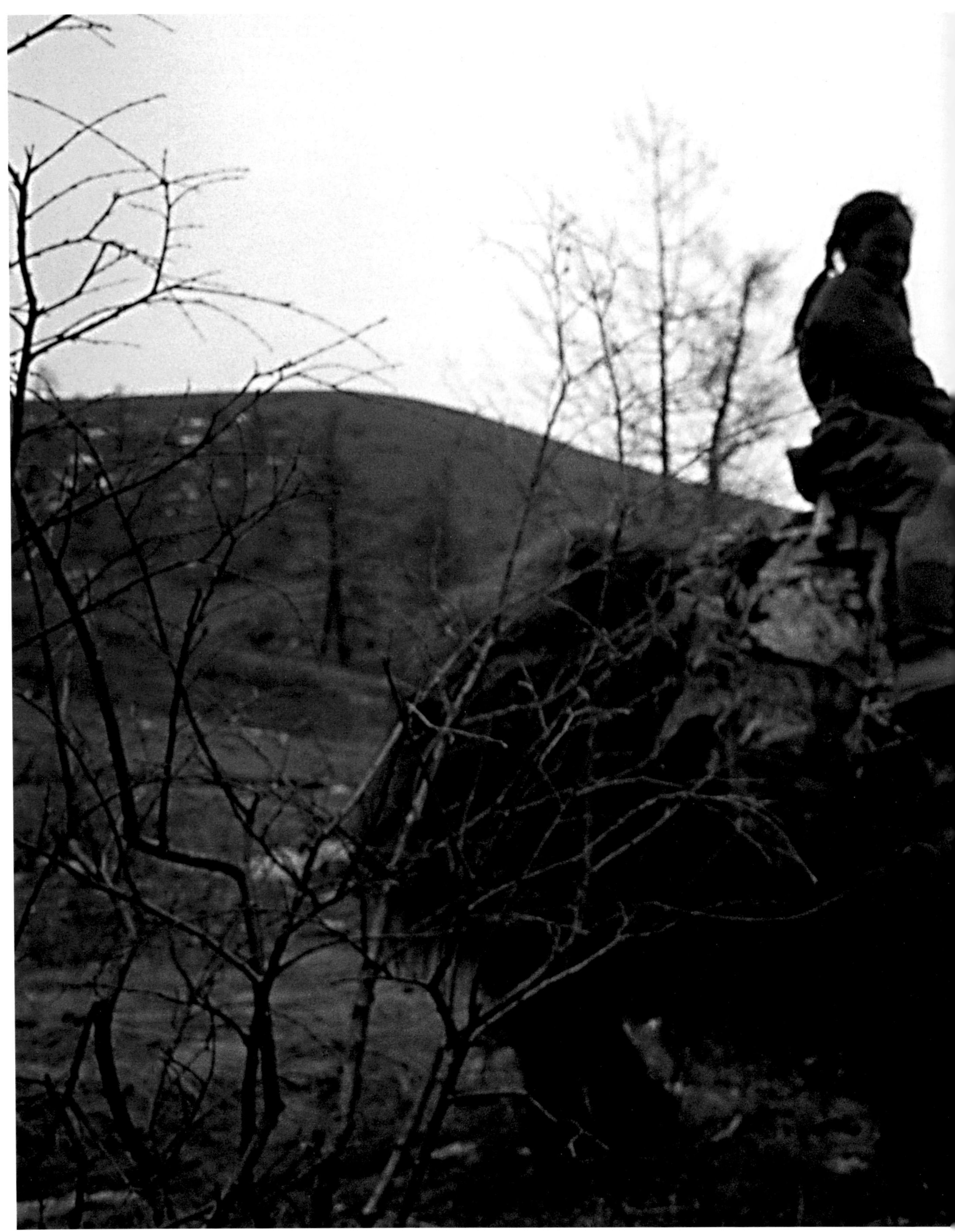

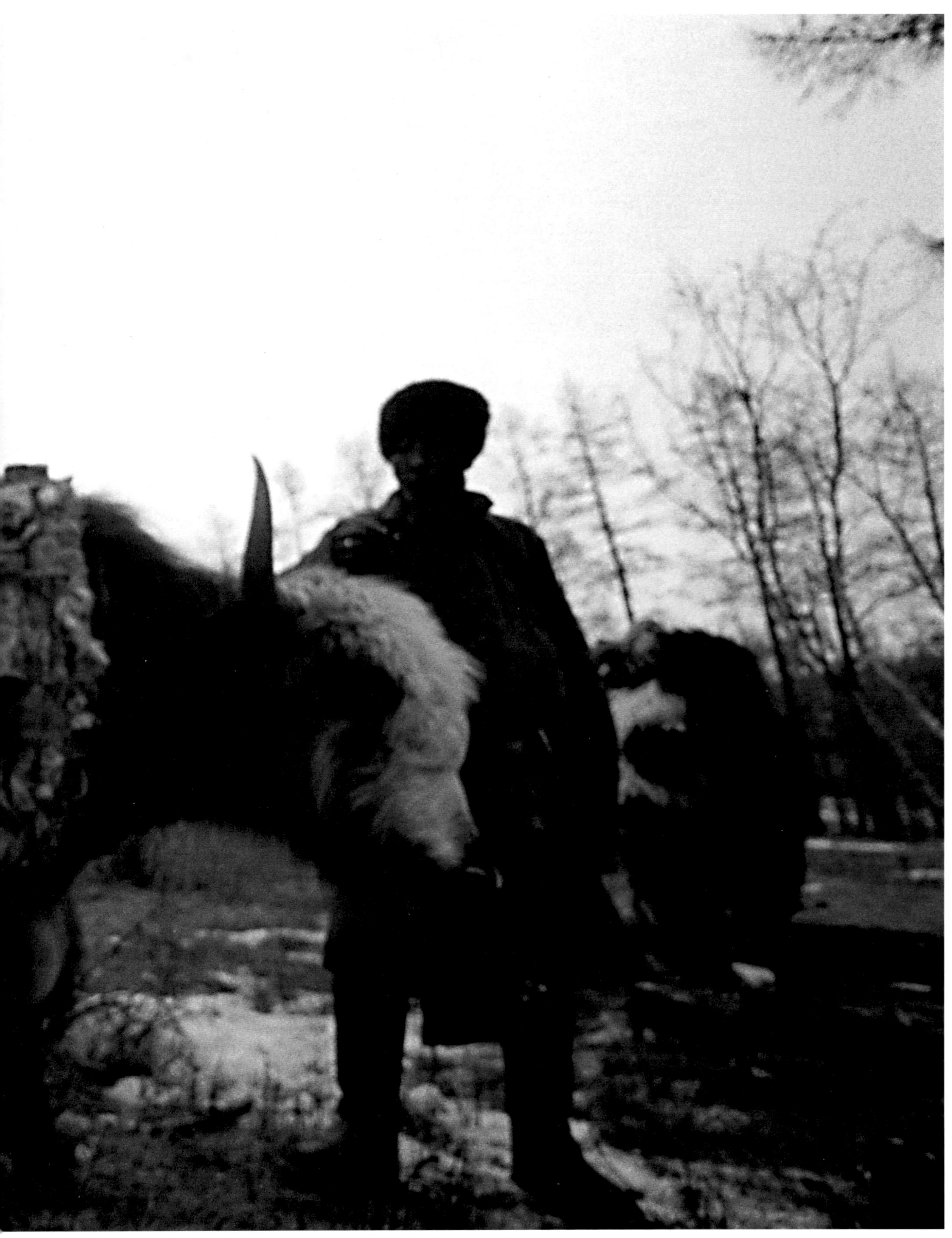

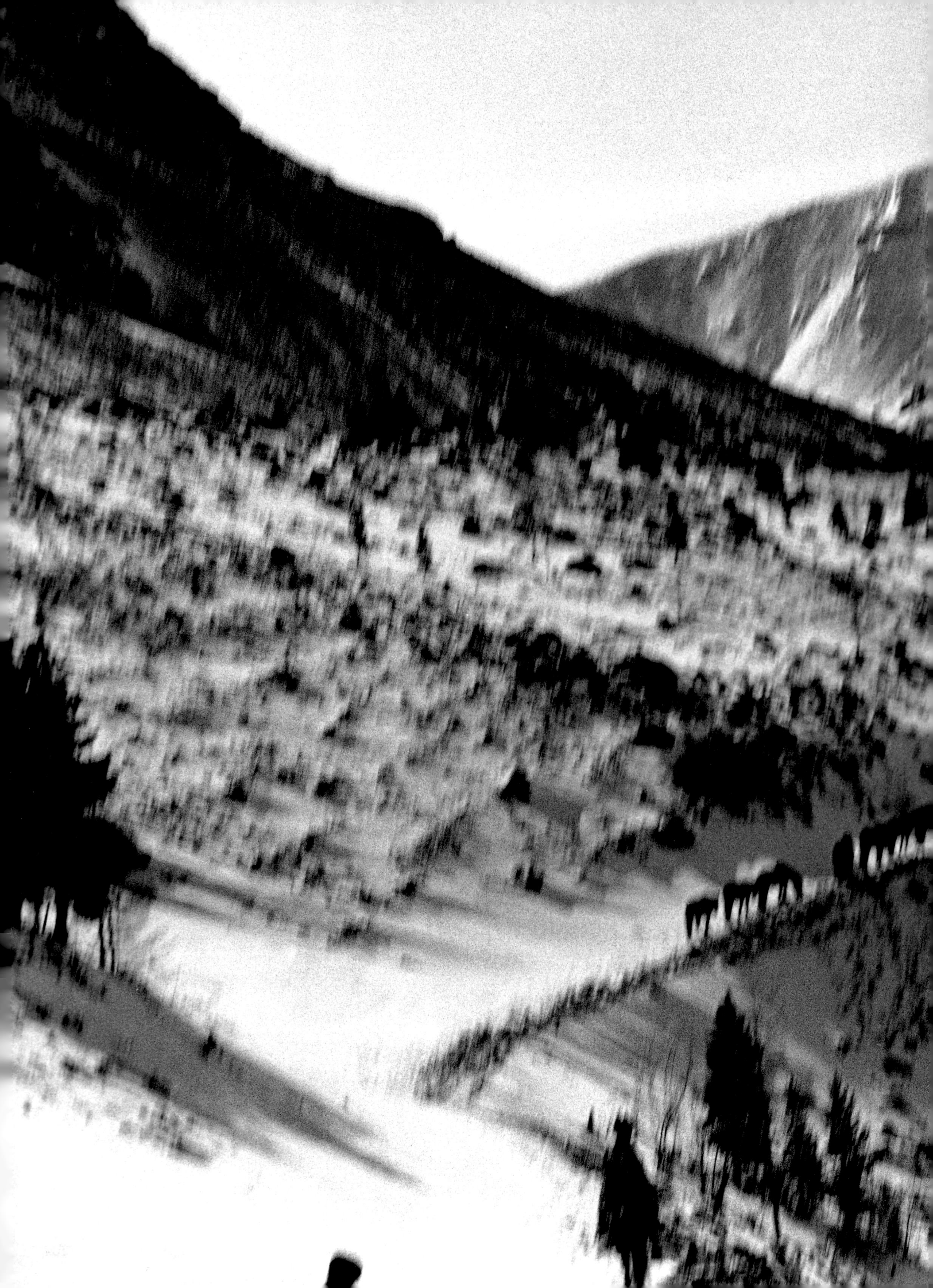

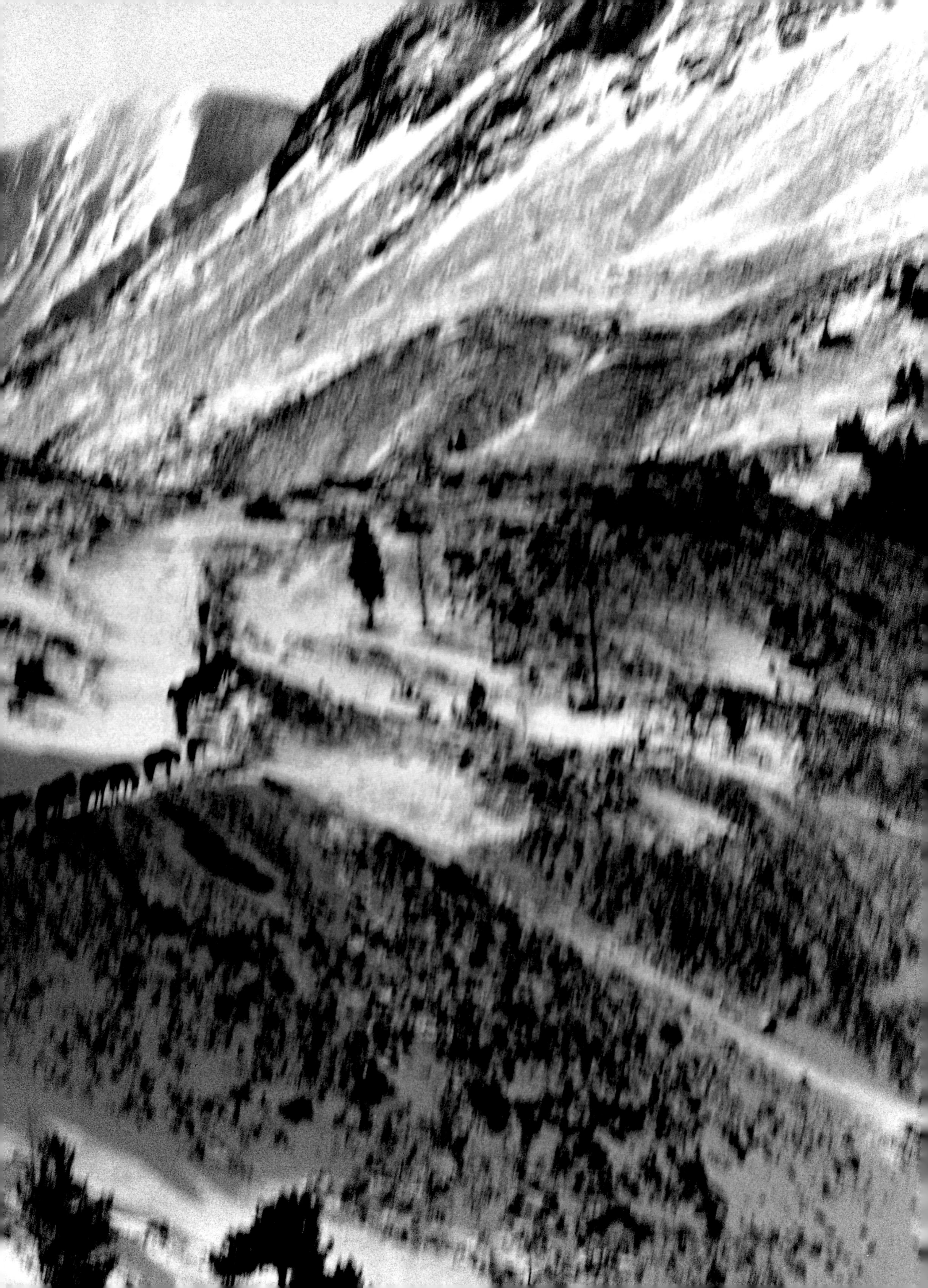

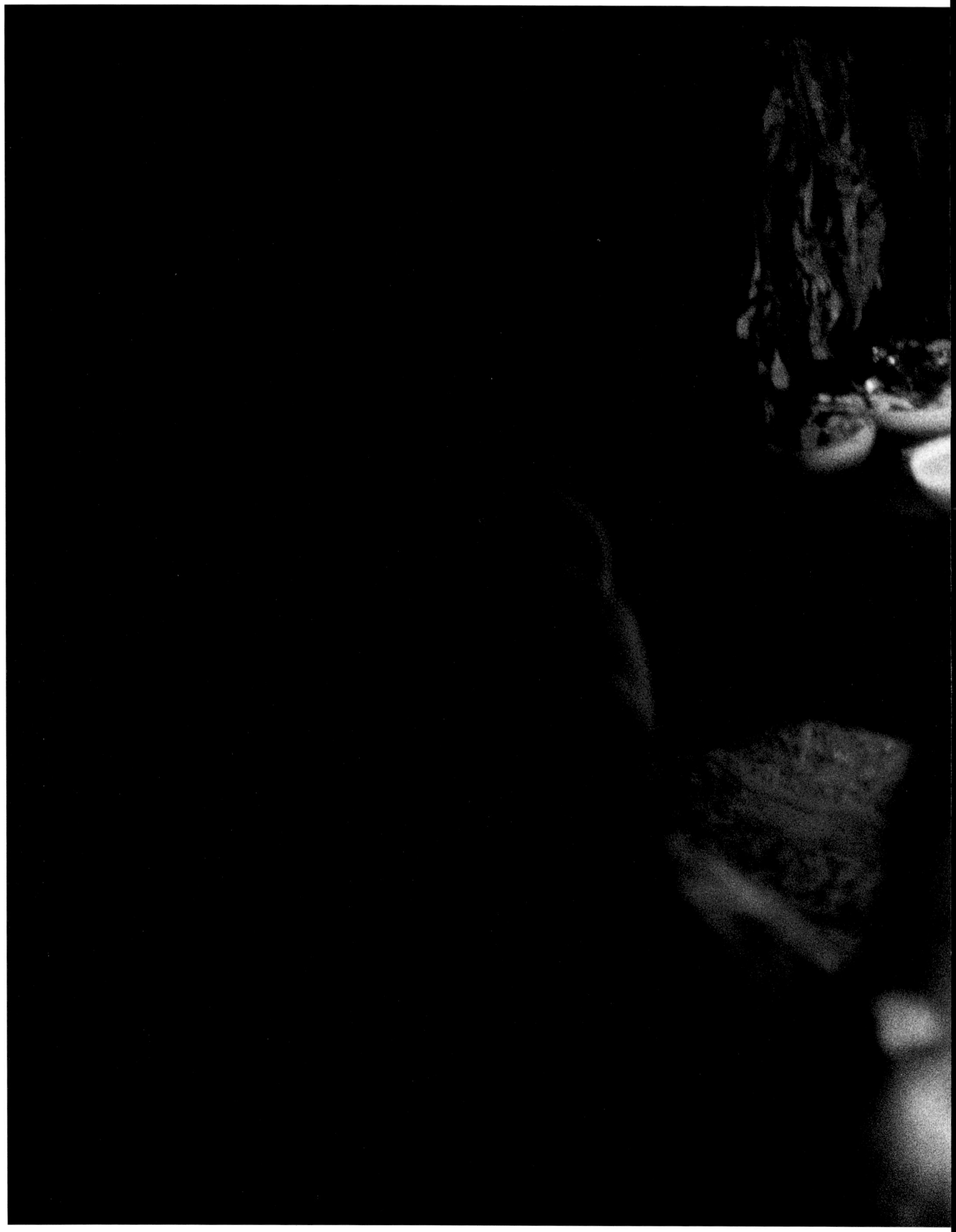

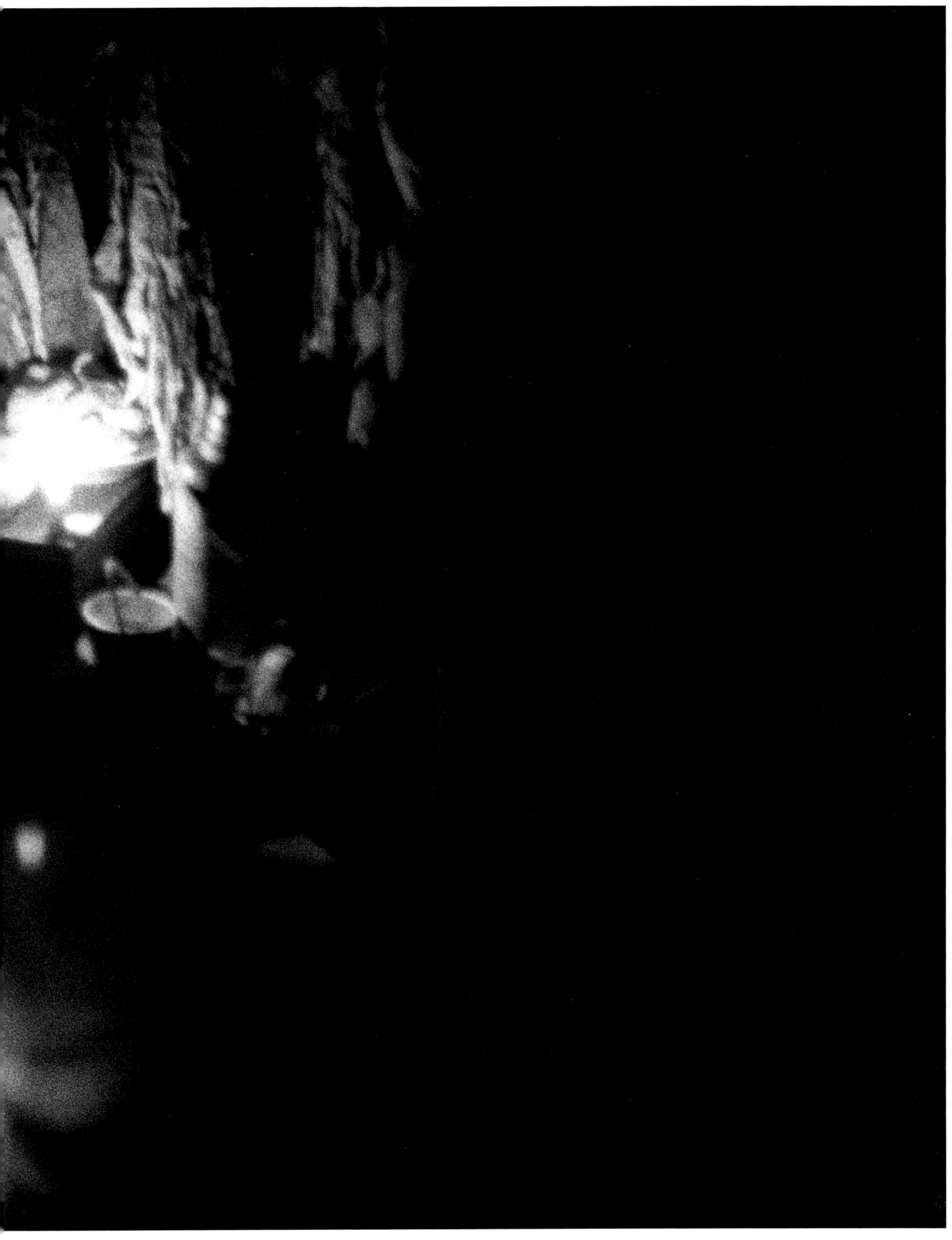

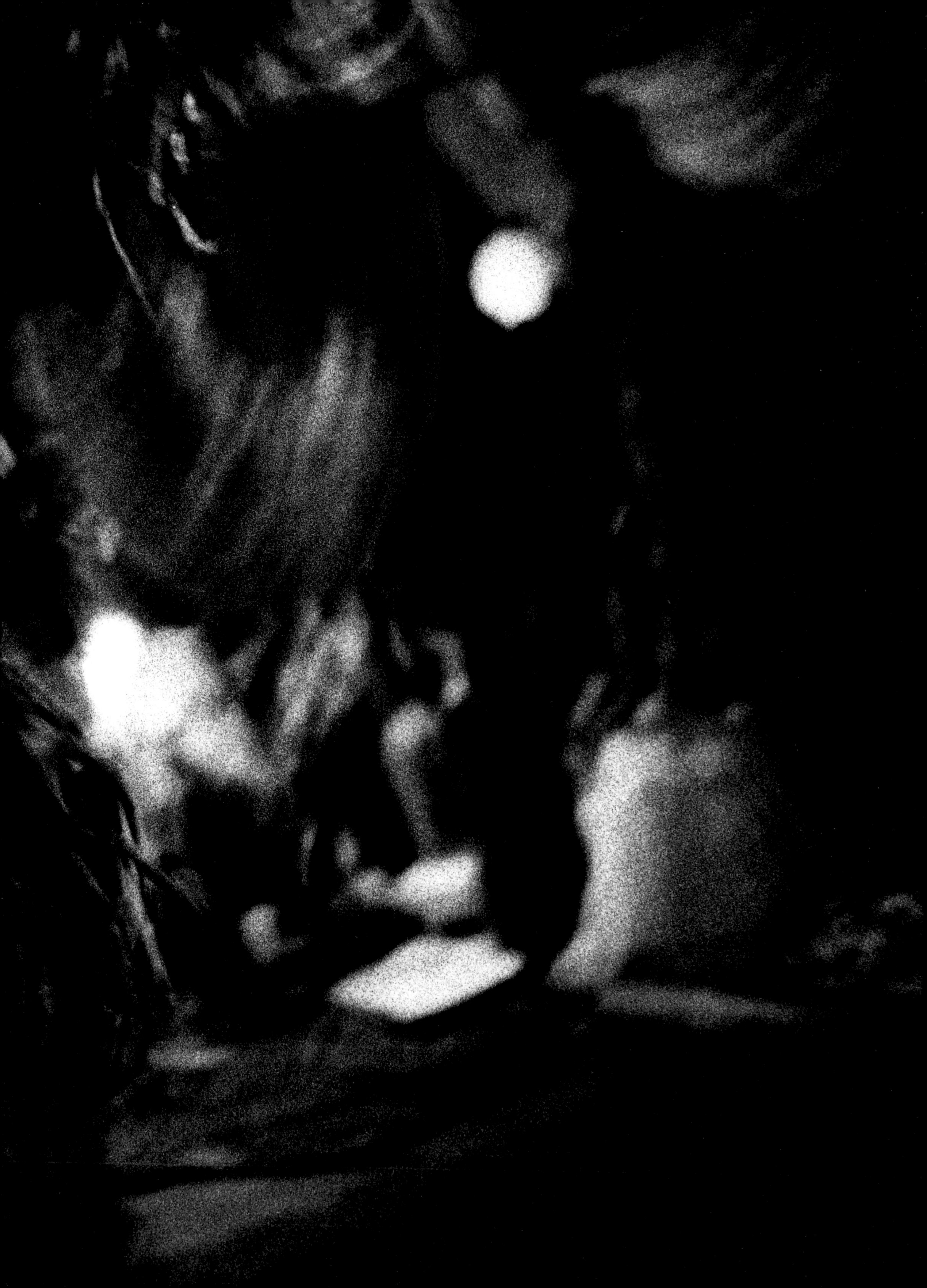

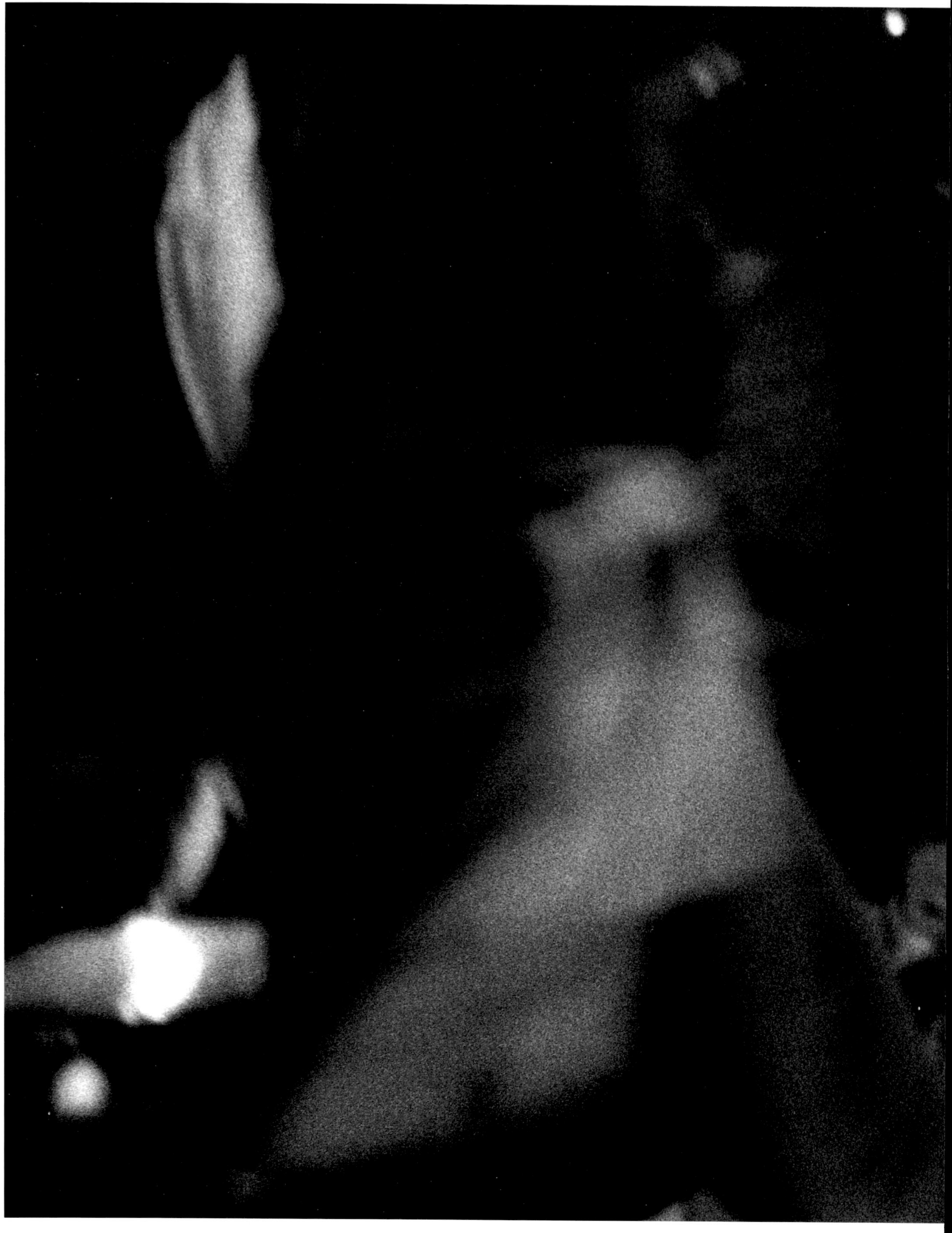

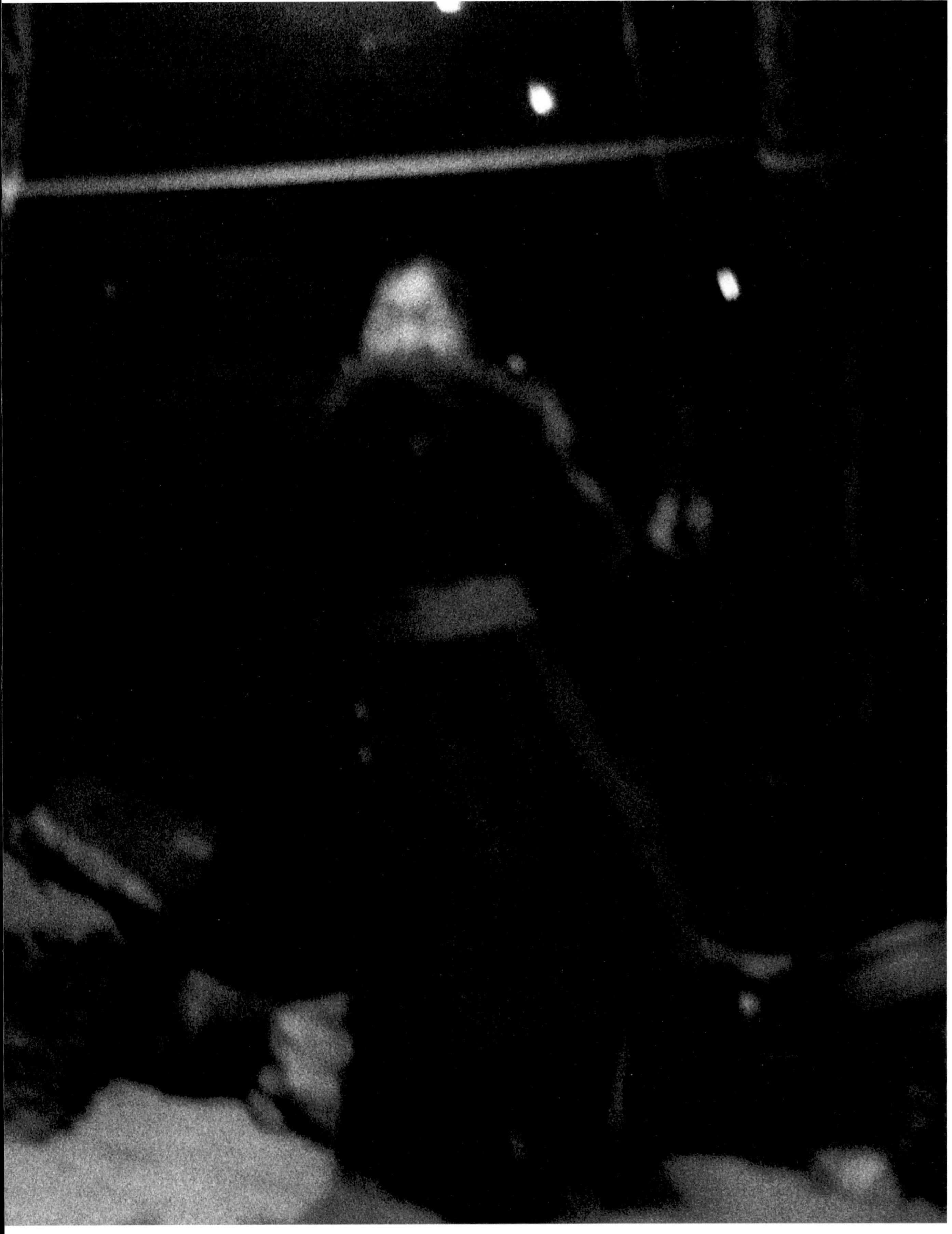

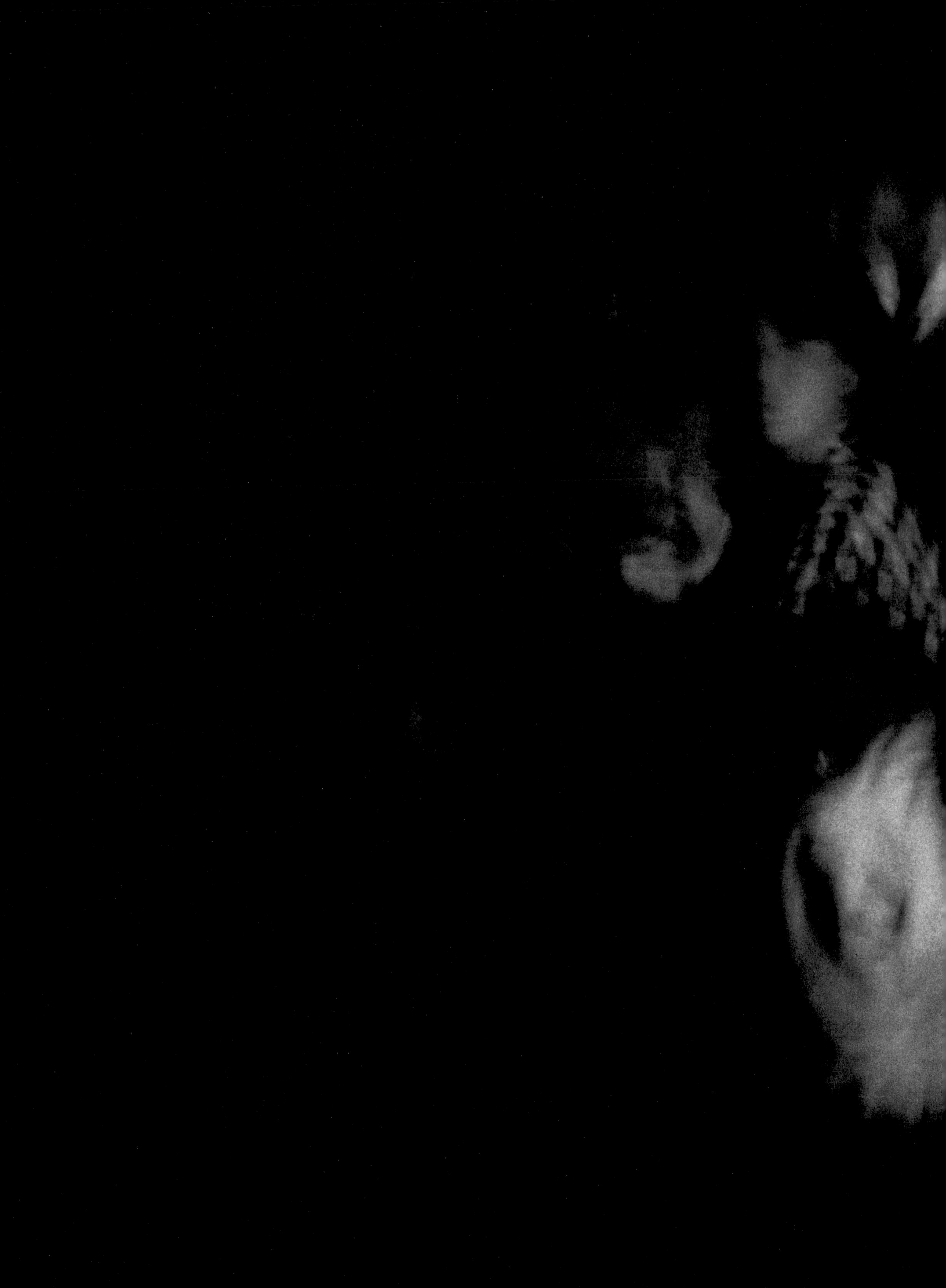

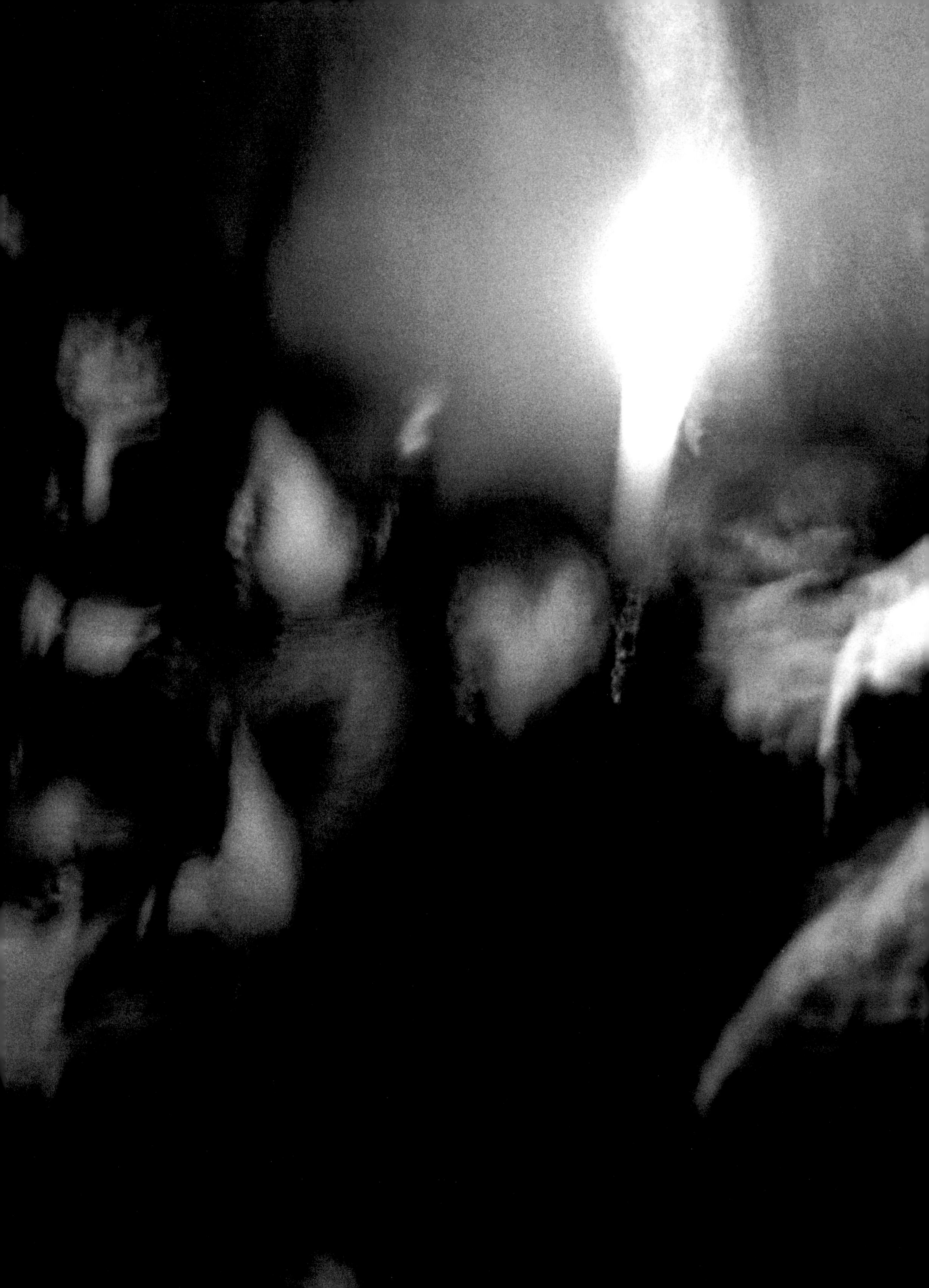

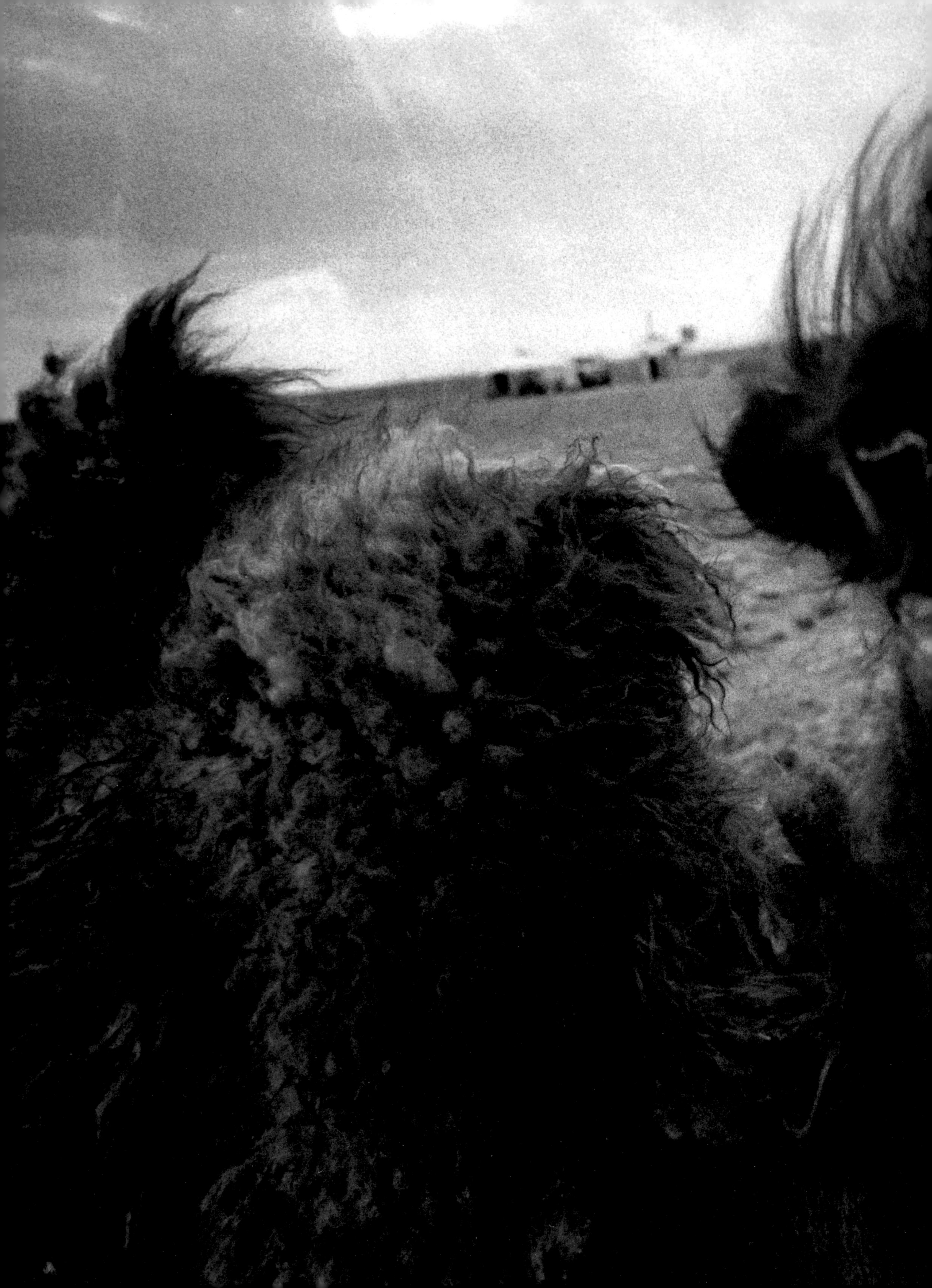

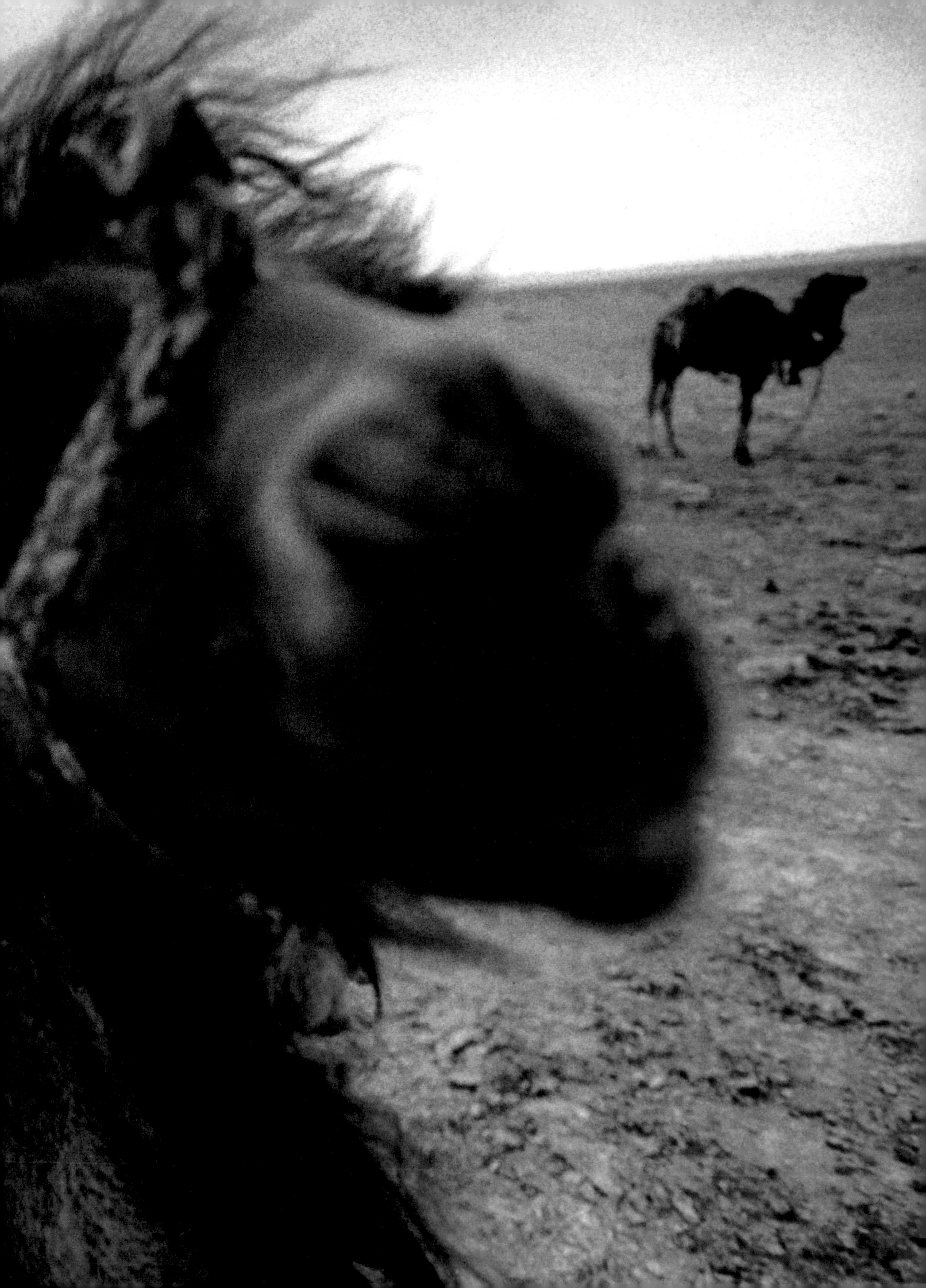

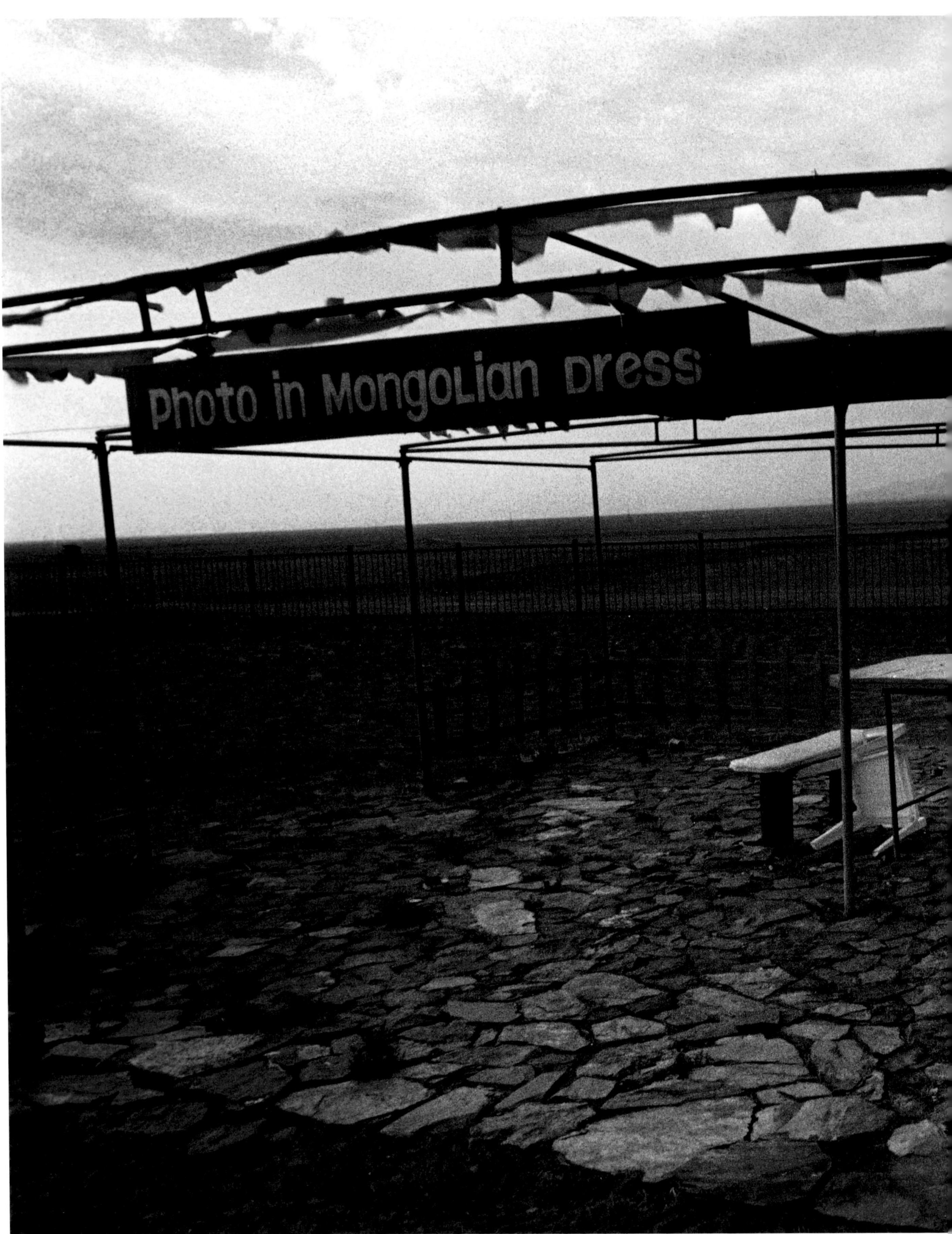
Photo in MongoLian Dress

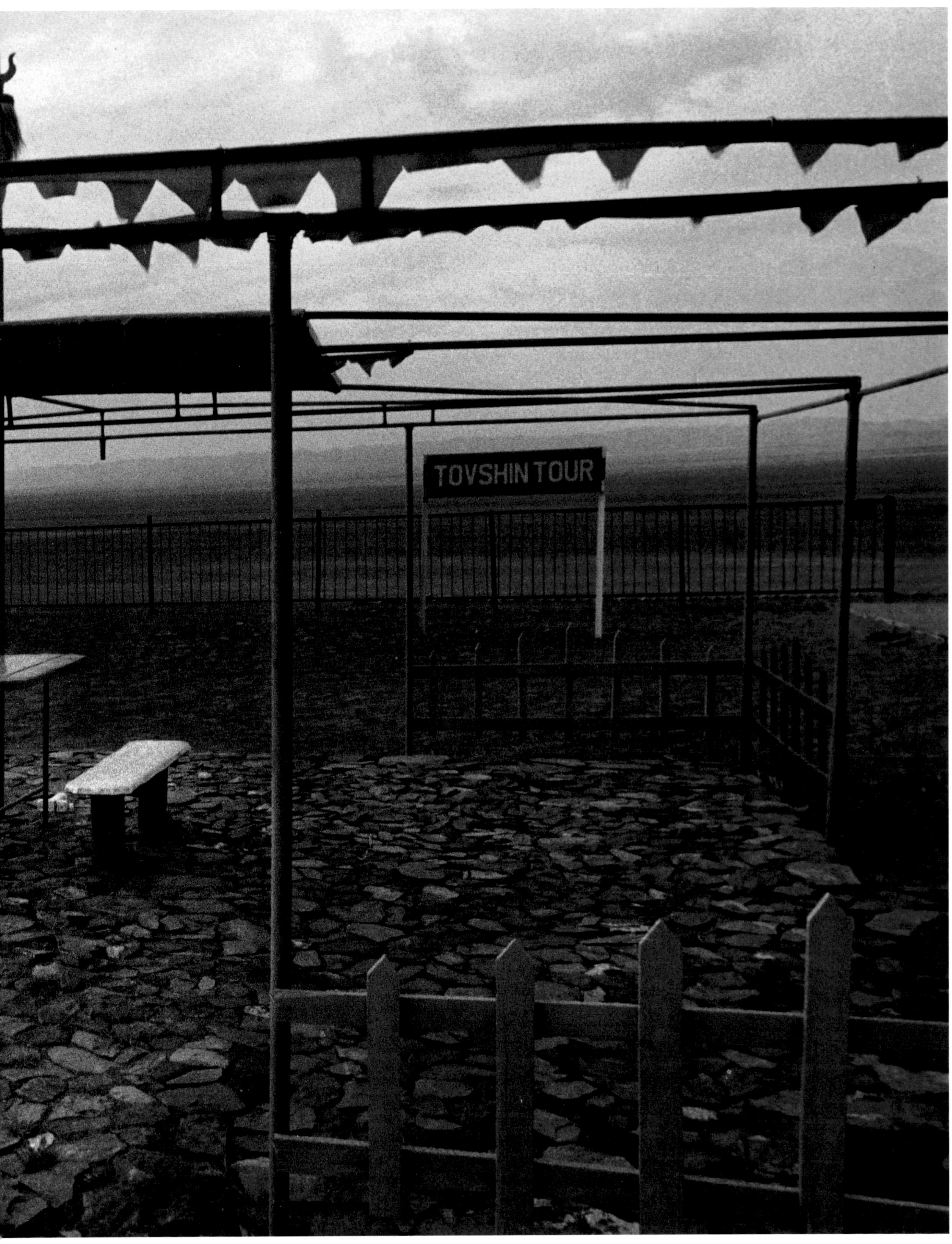
TOVSHIN TOUR

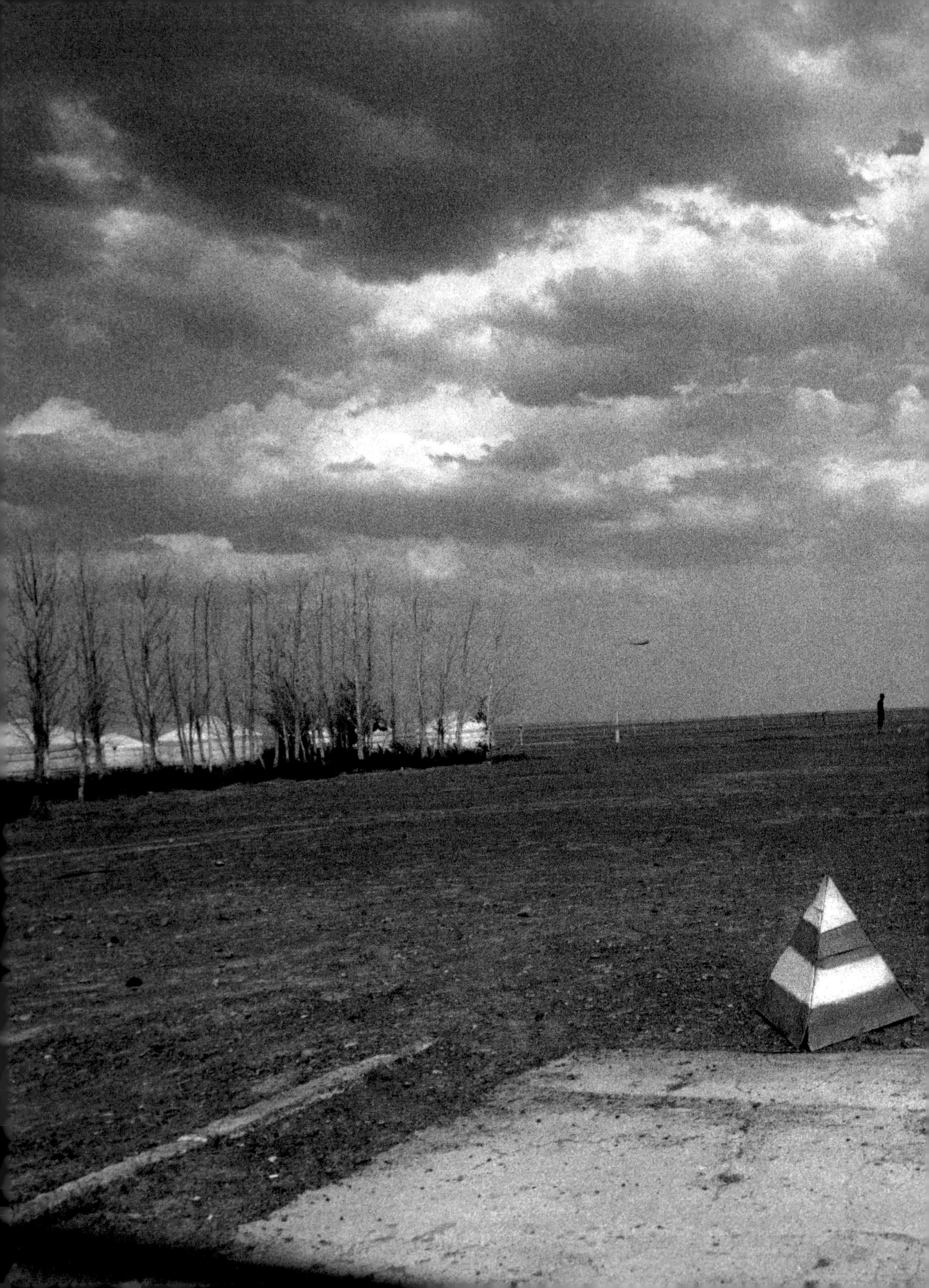

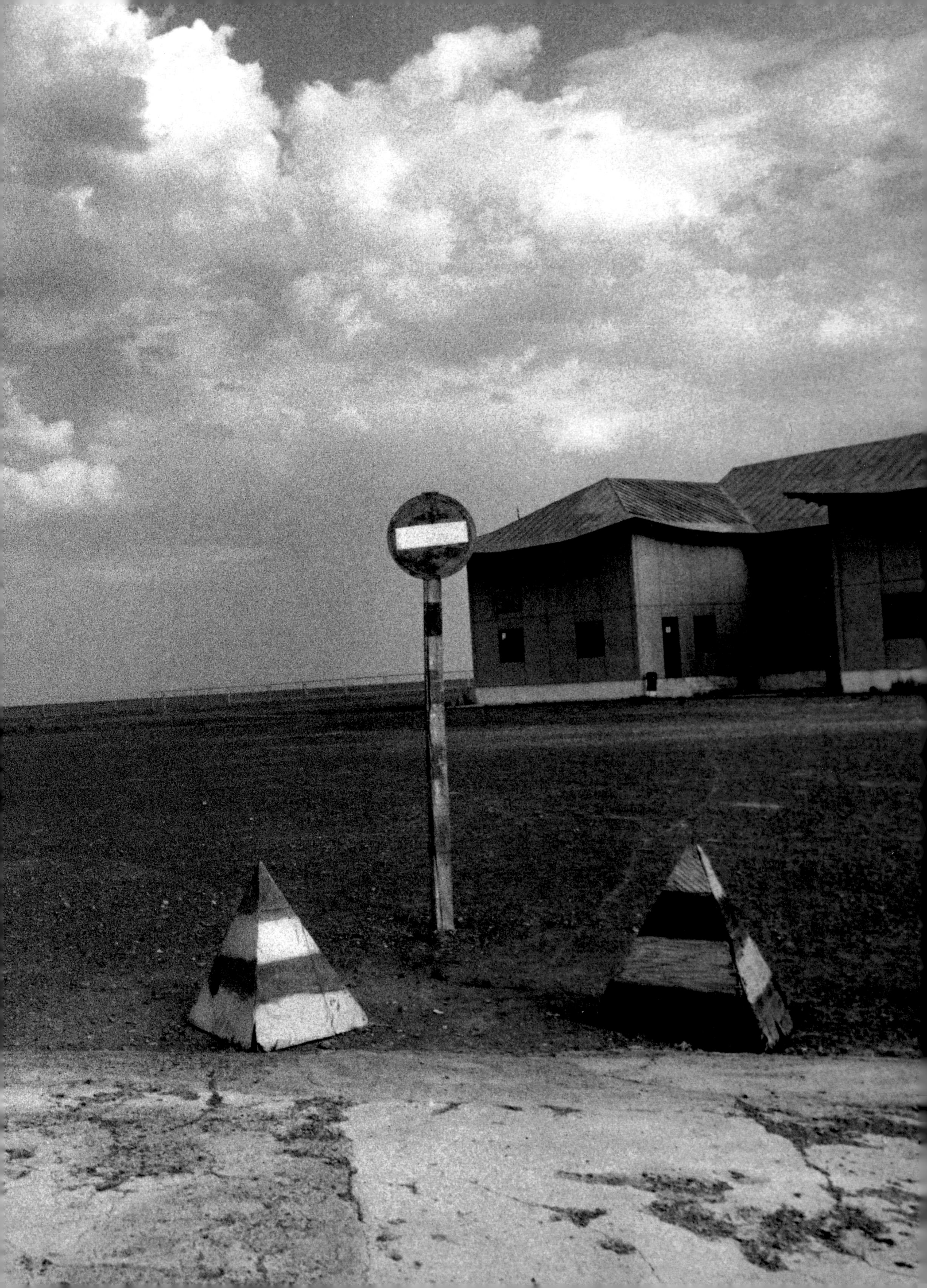

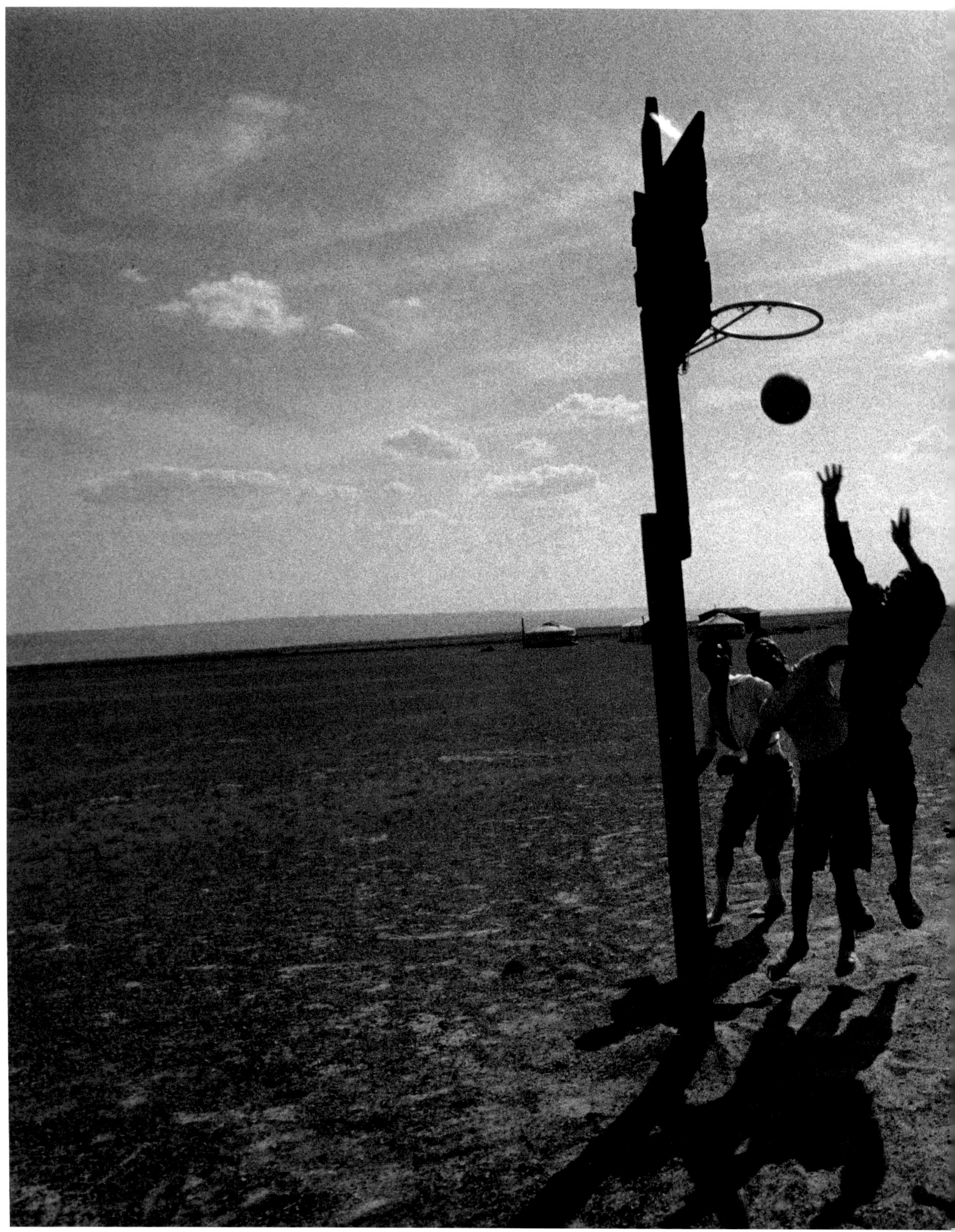

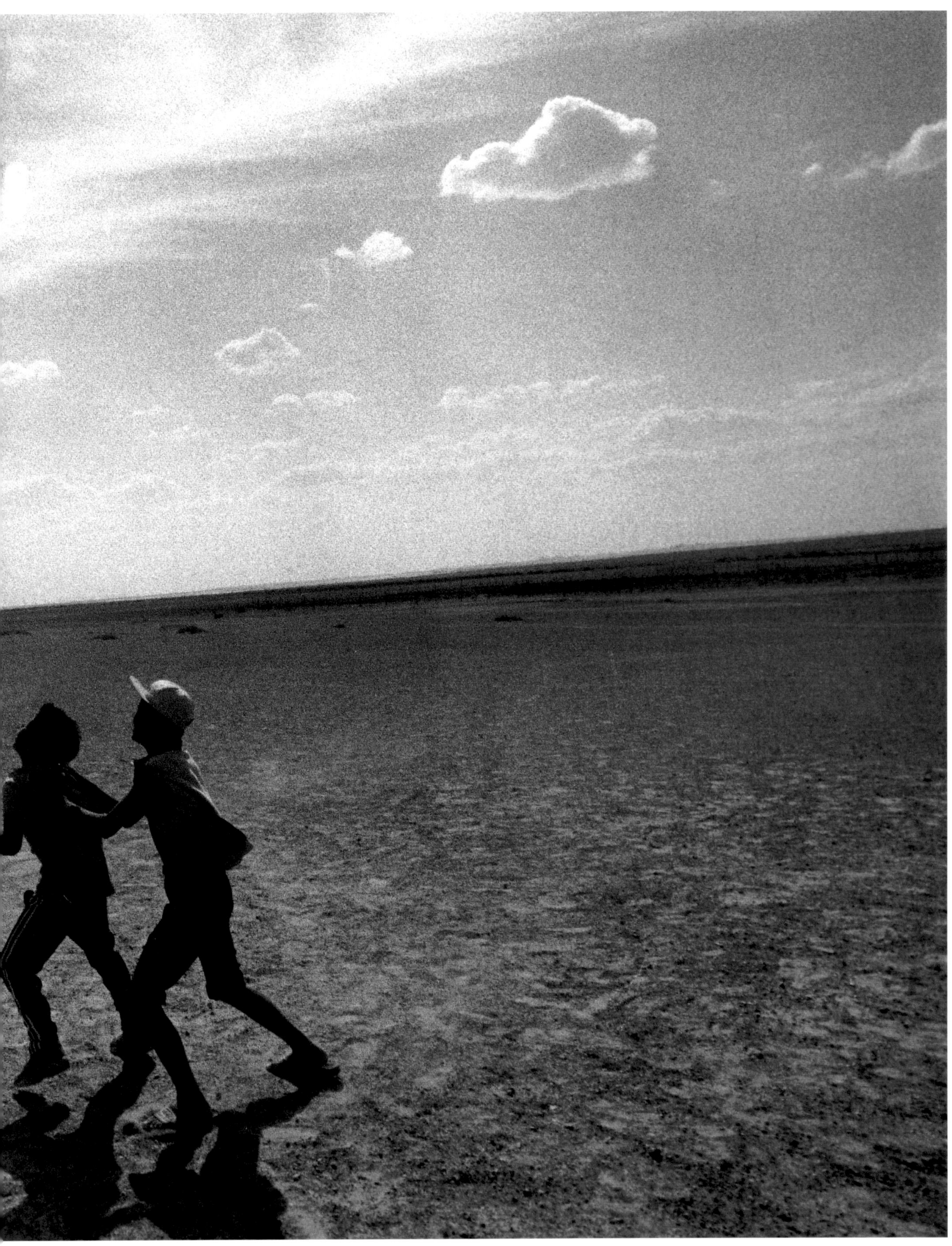

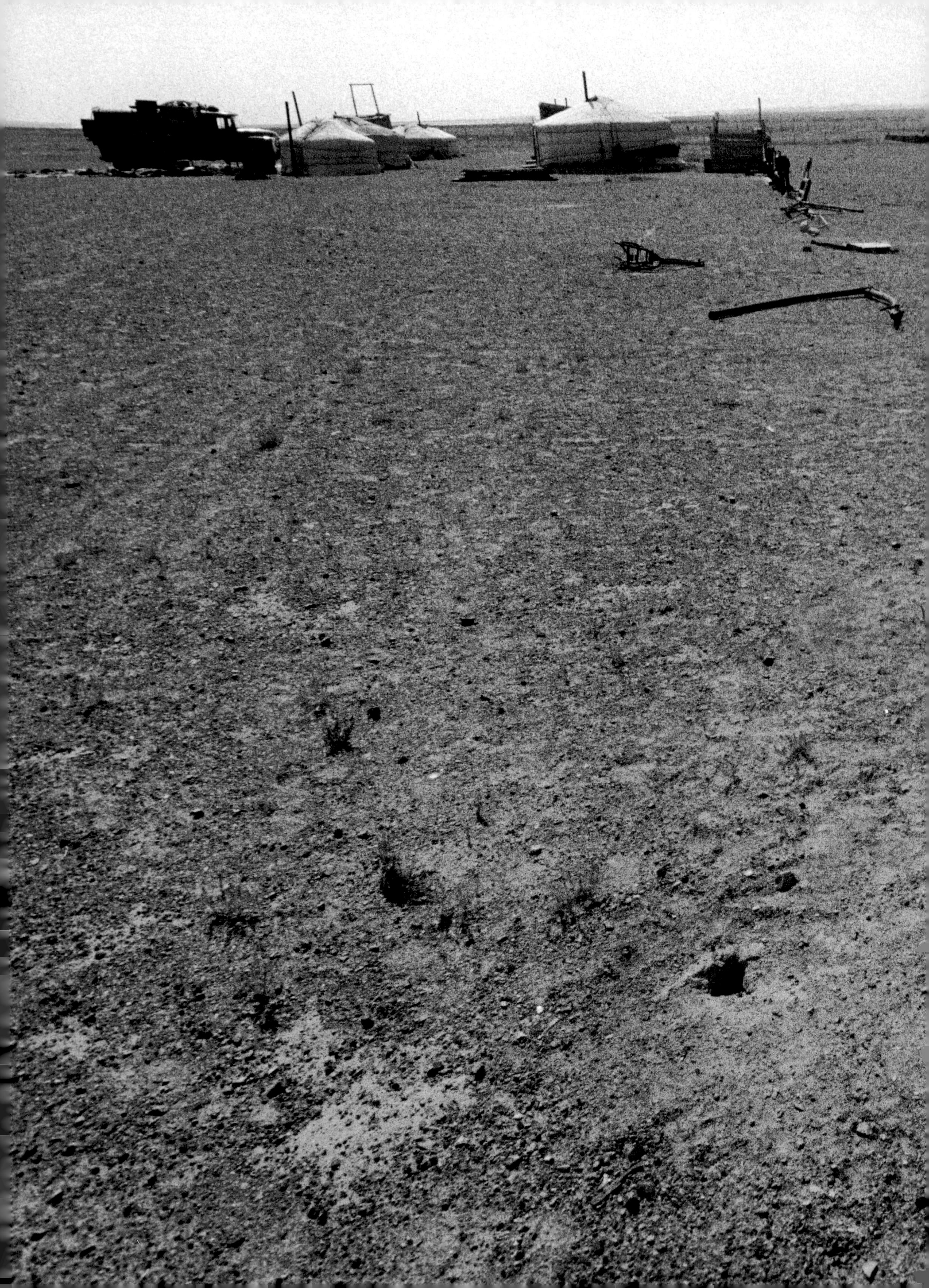

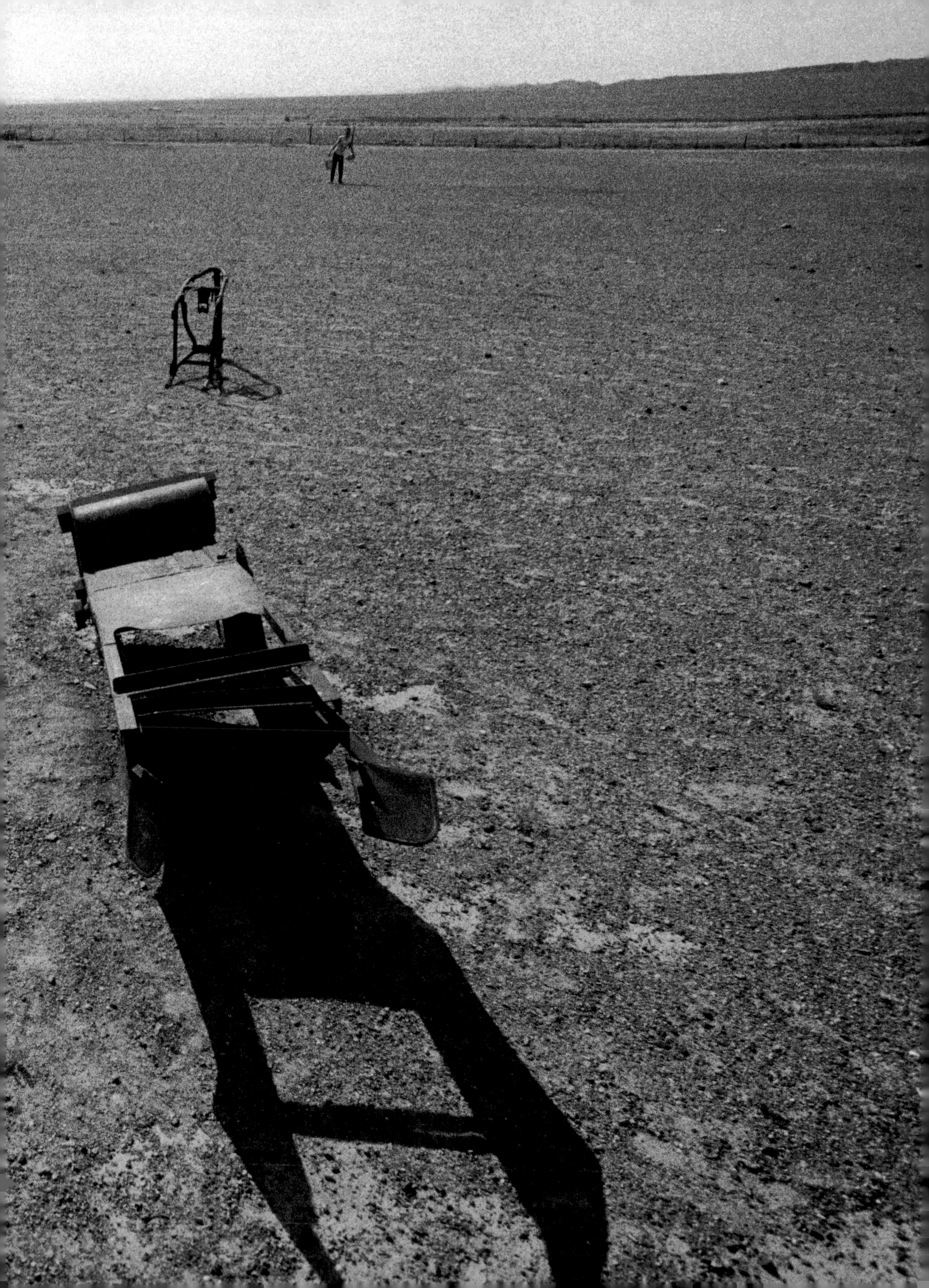

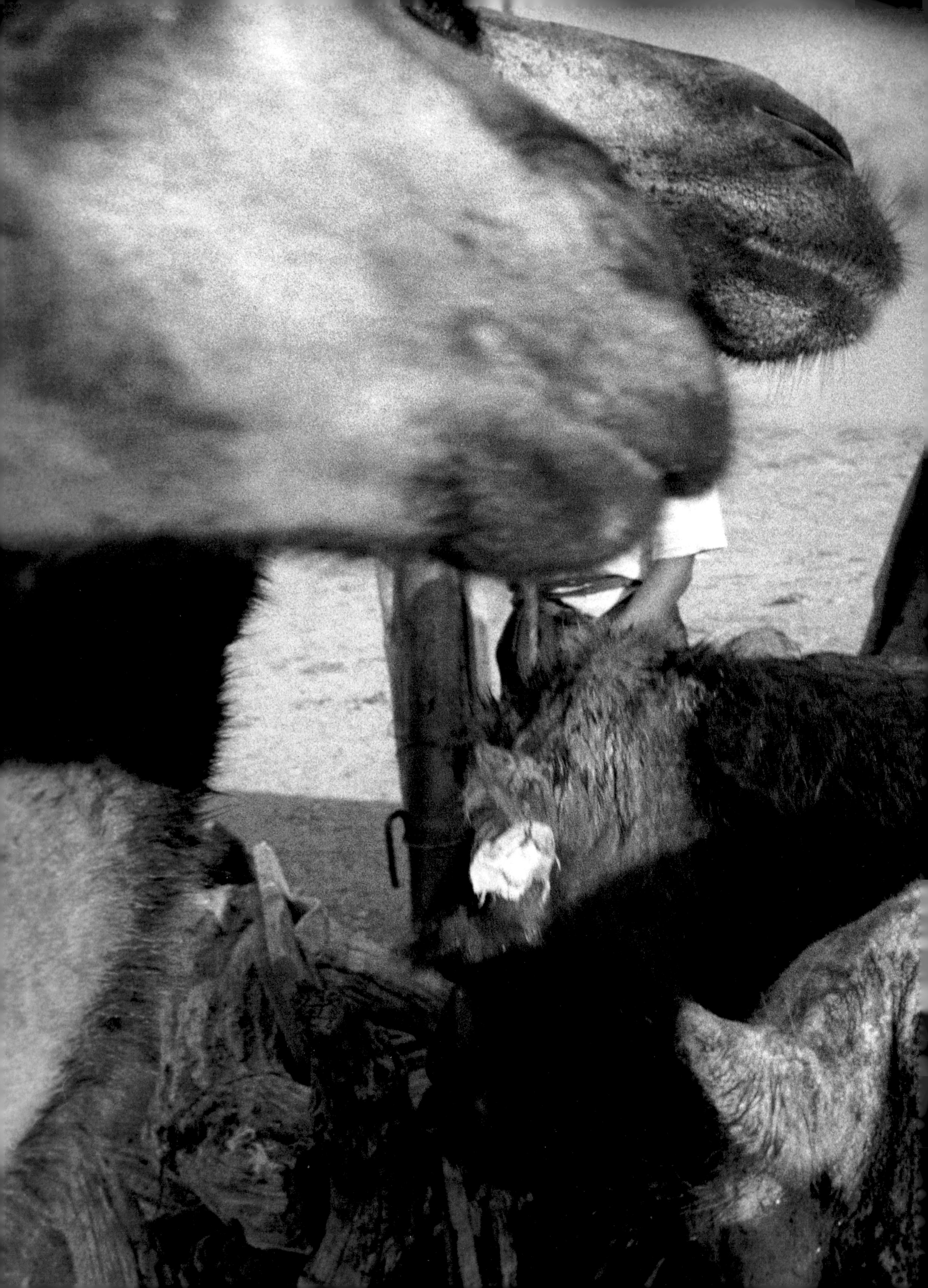

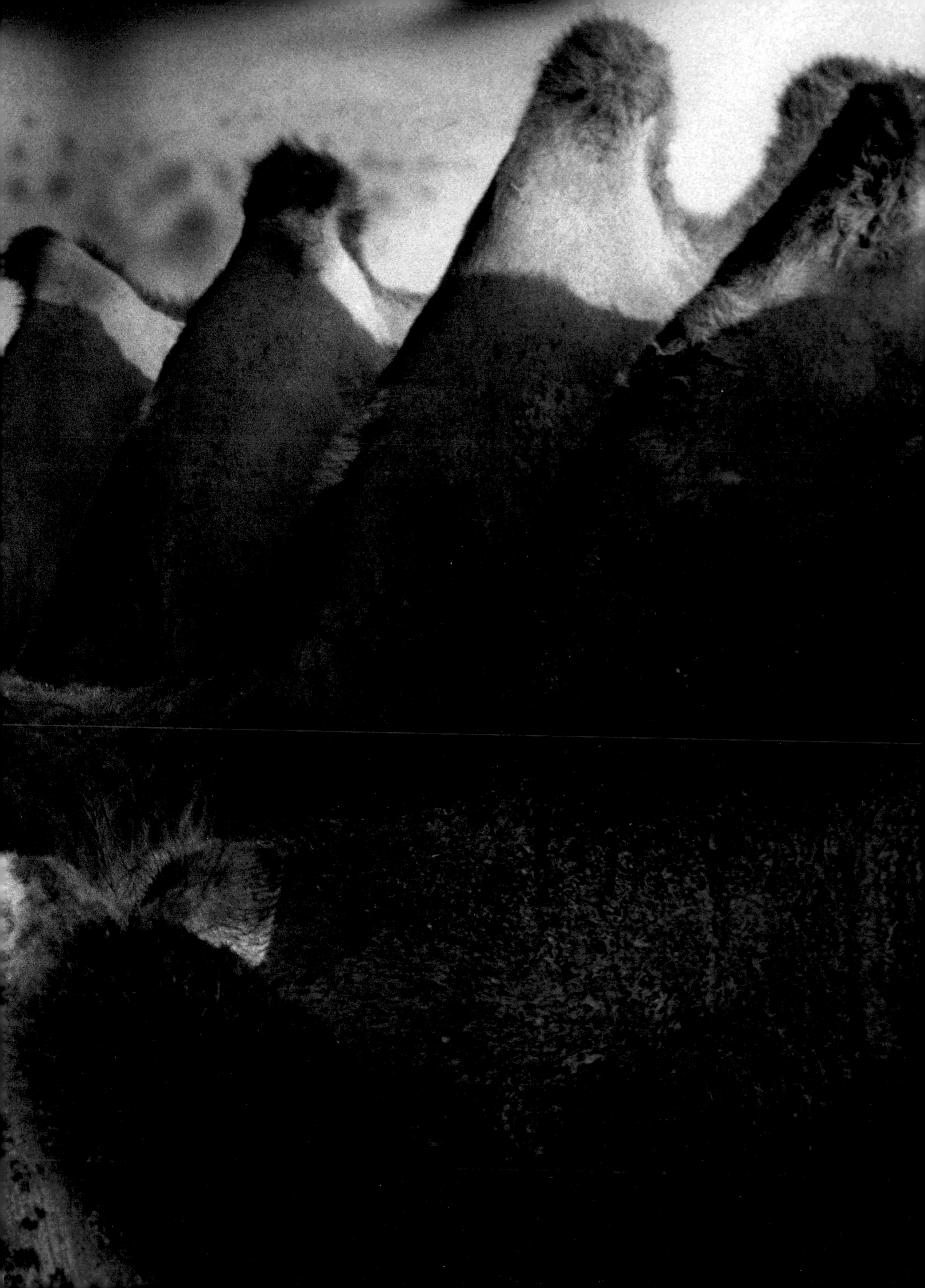

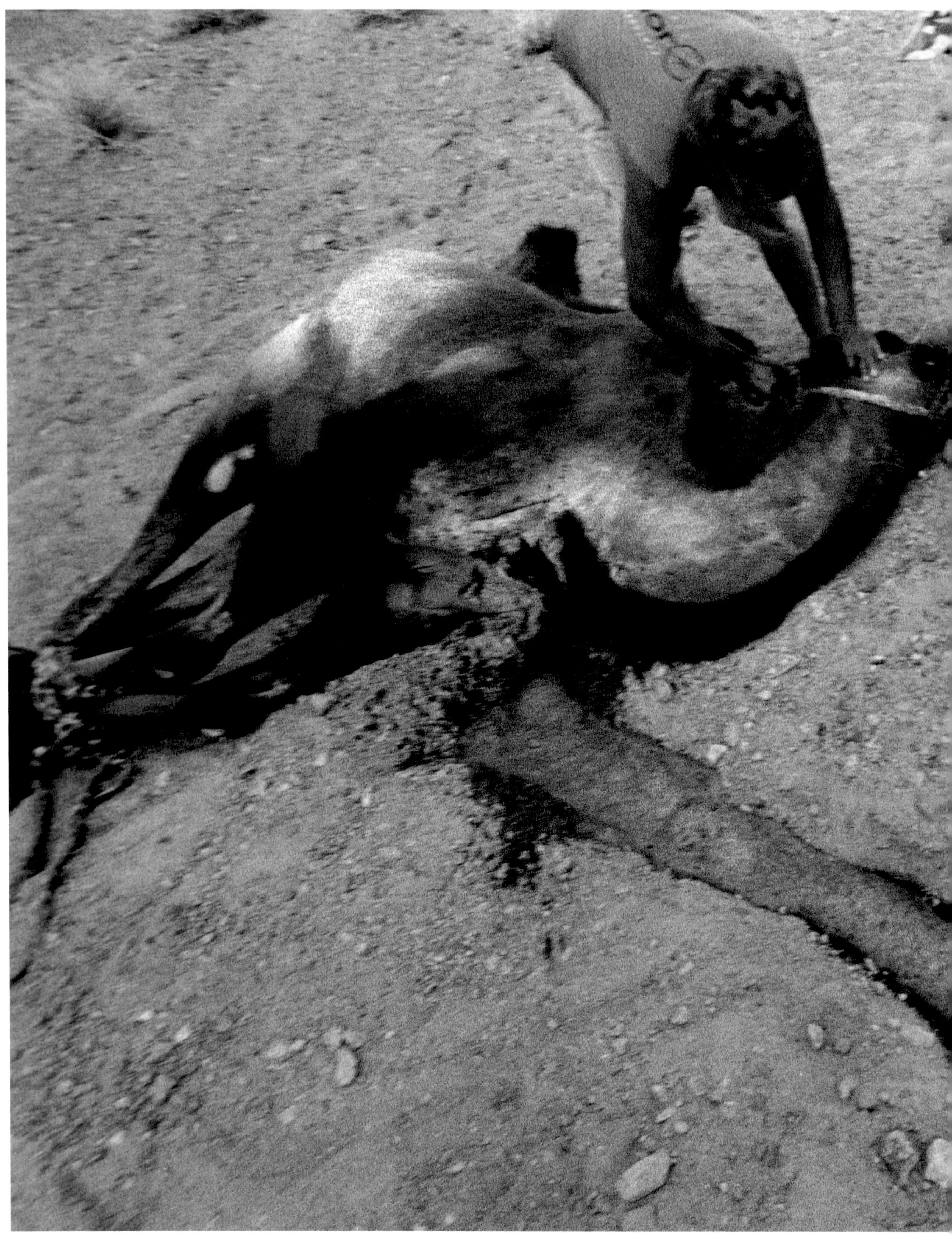

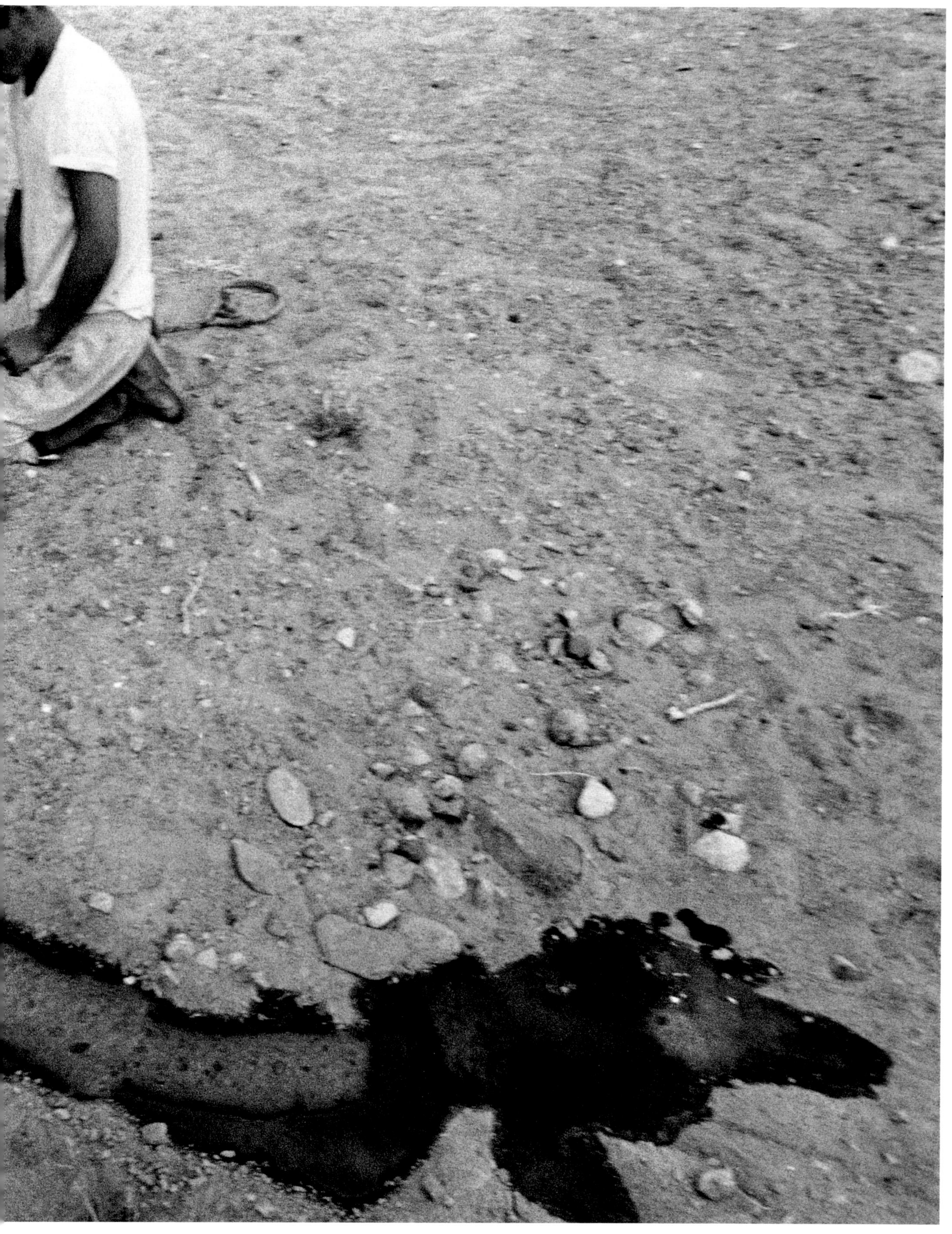

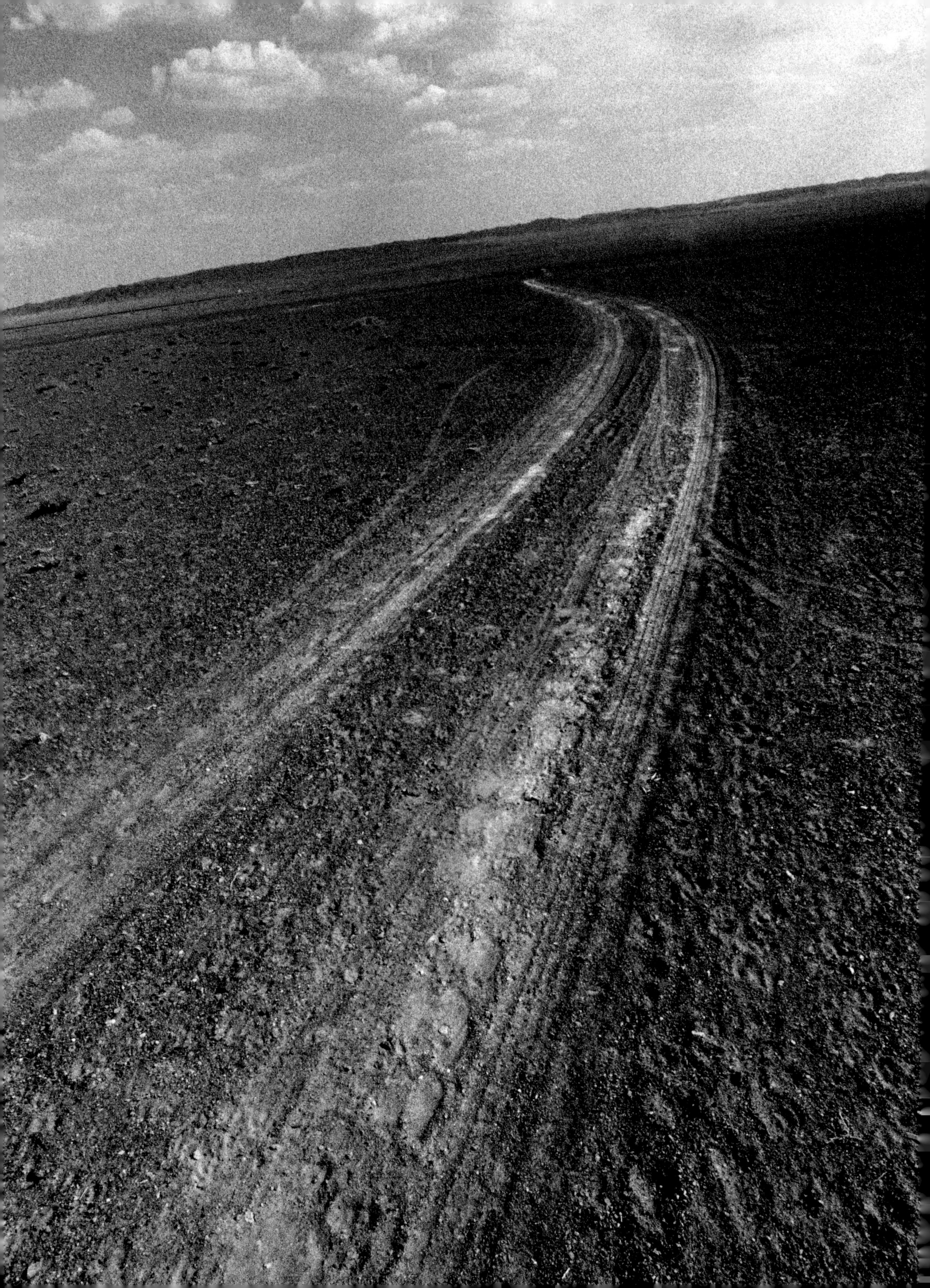

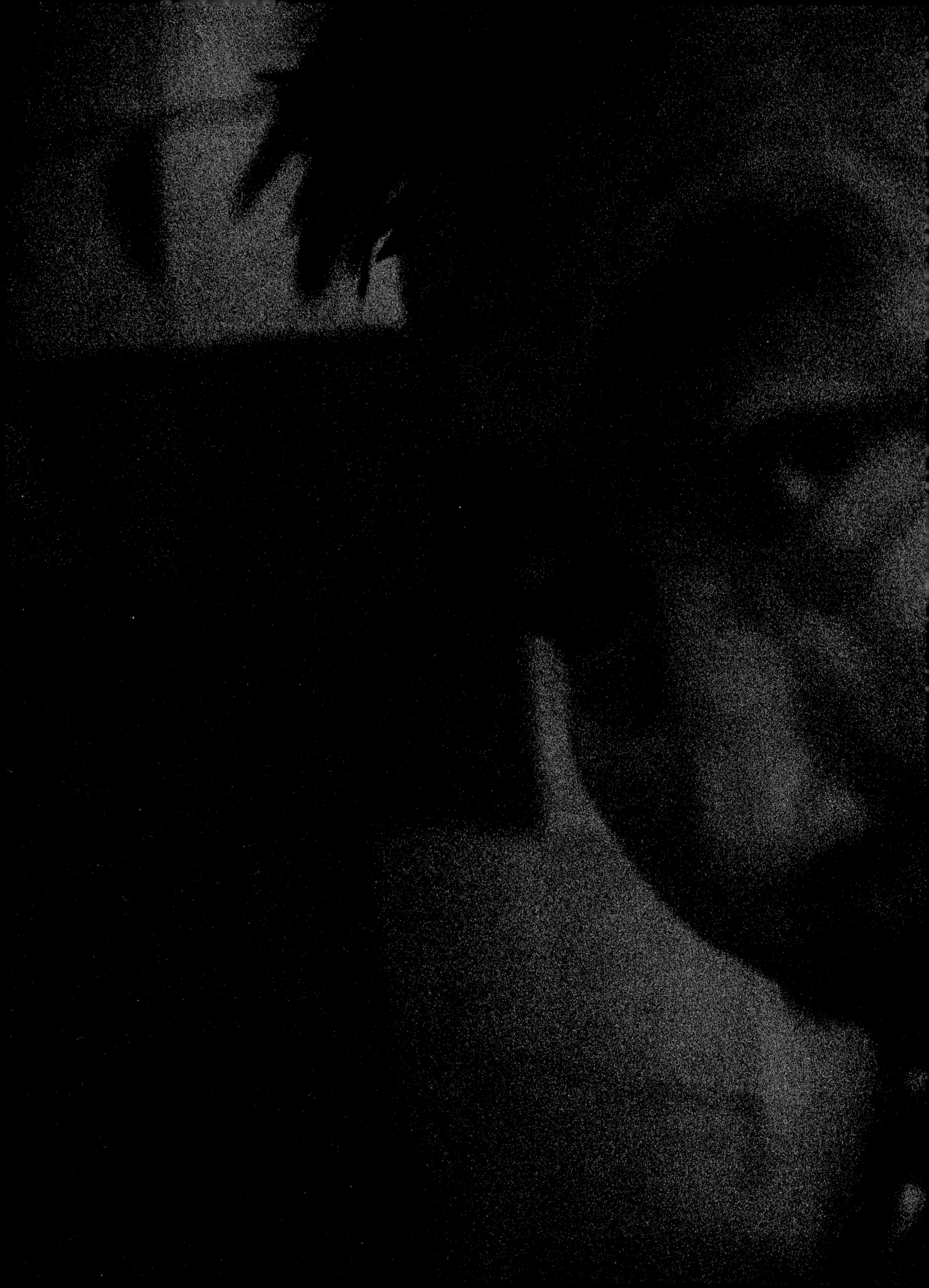

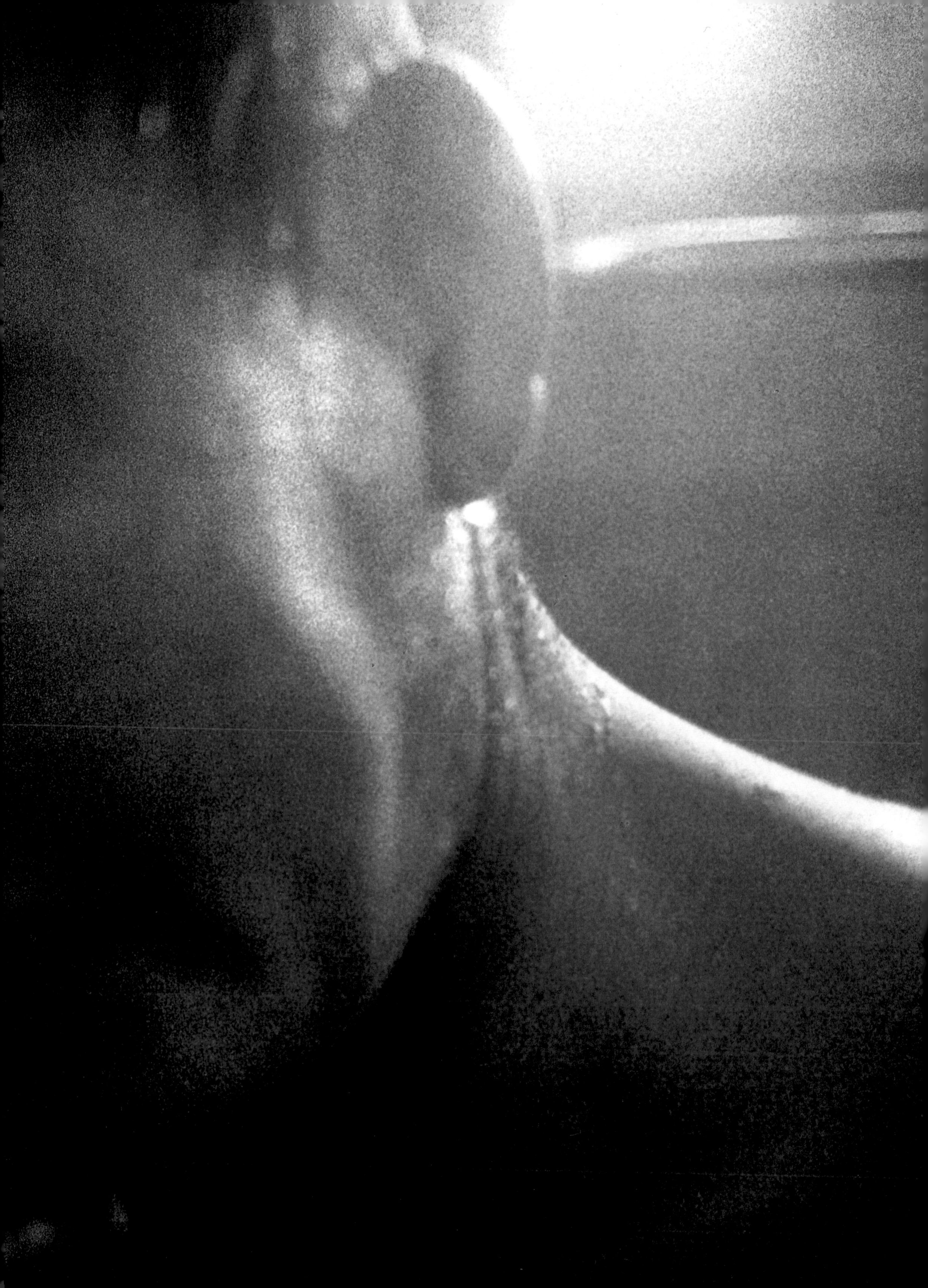

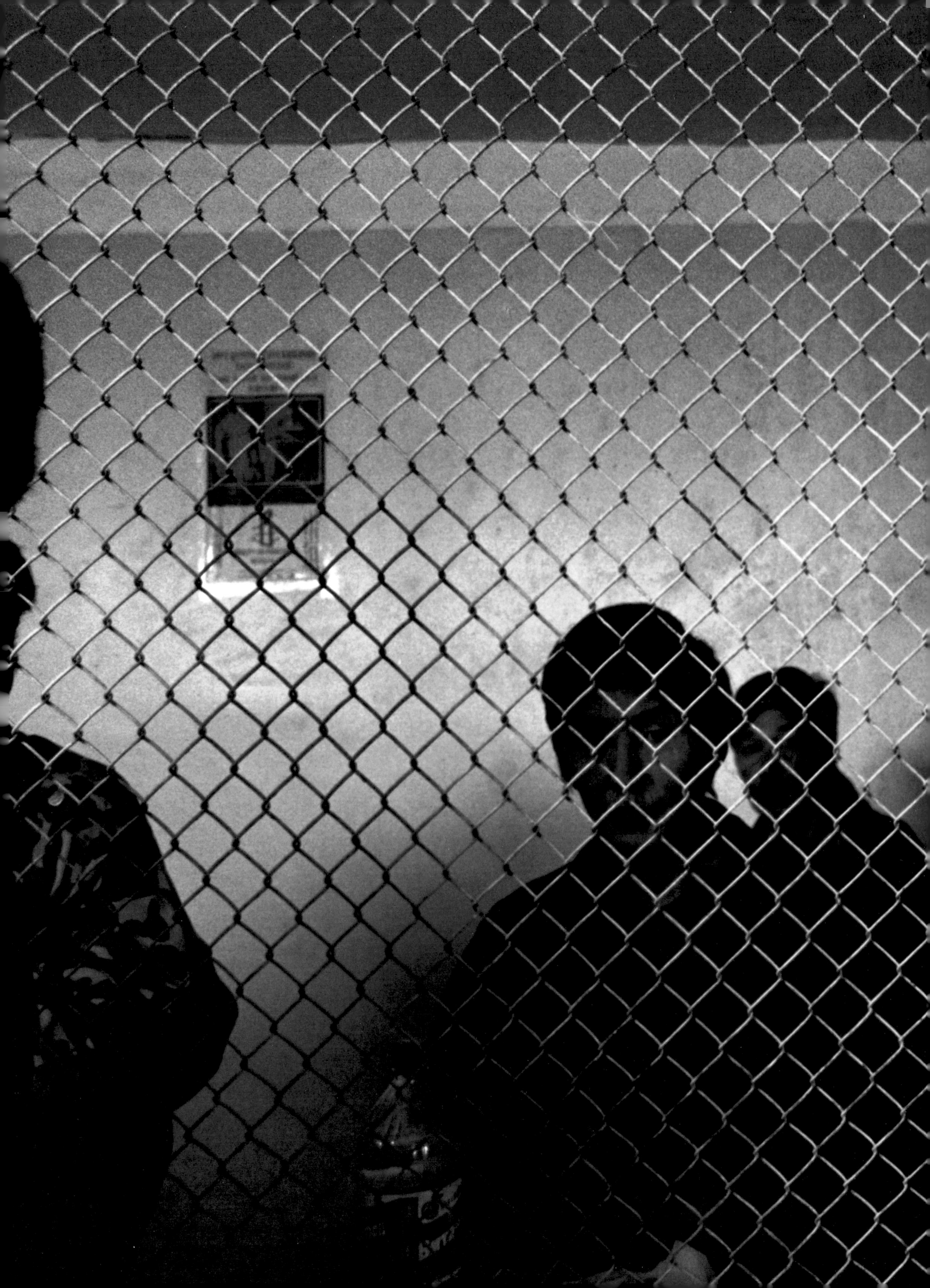

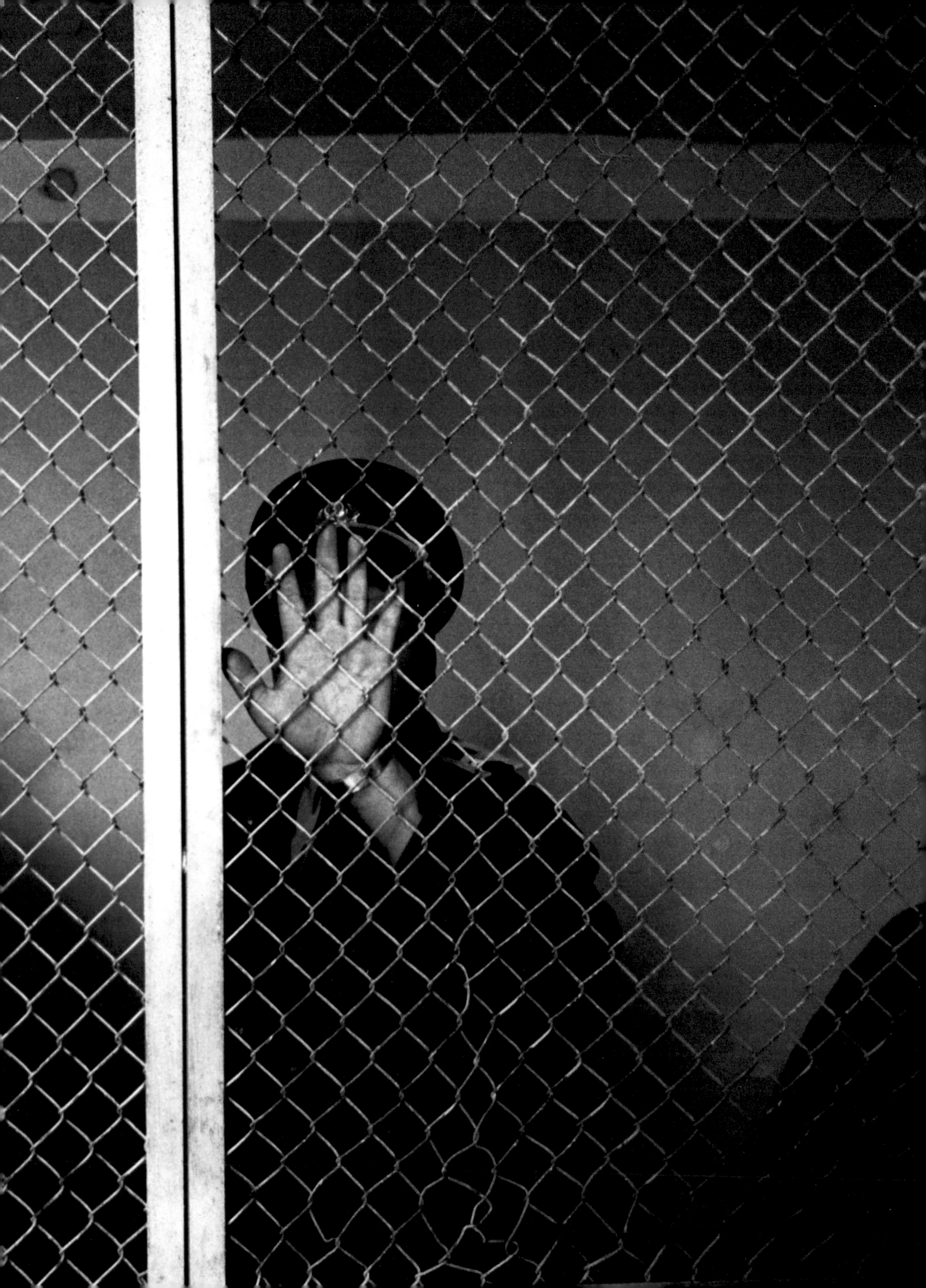

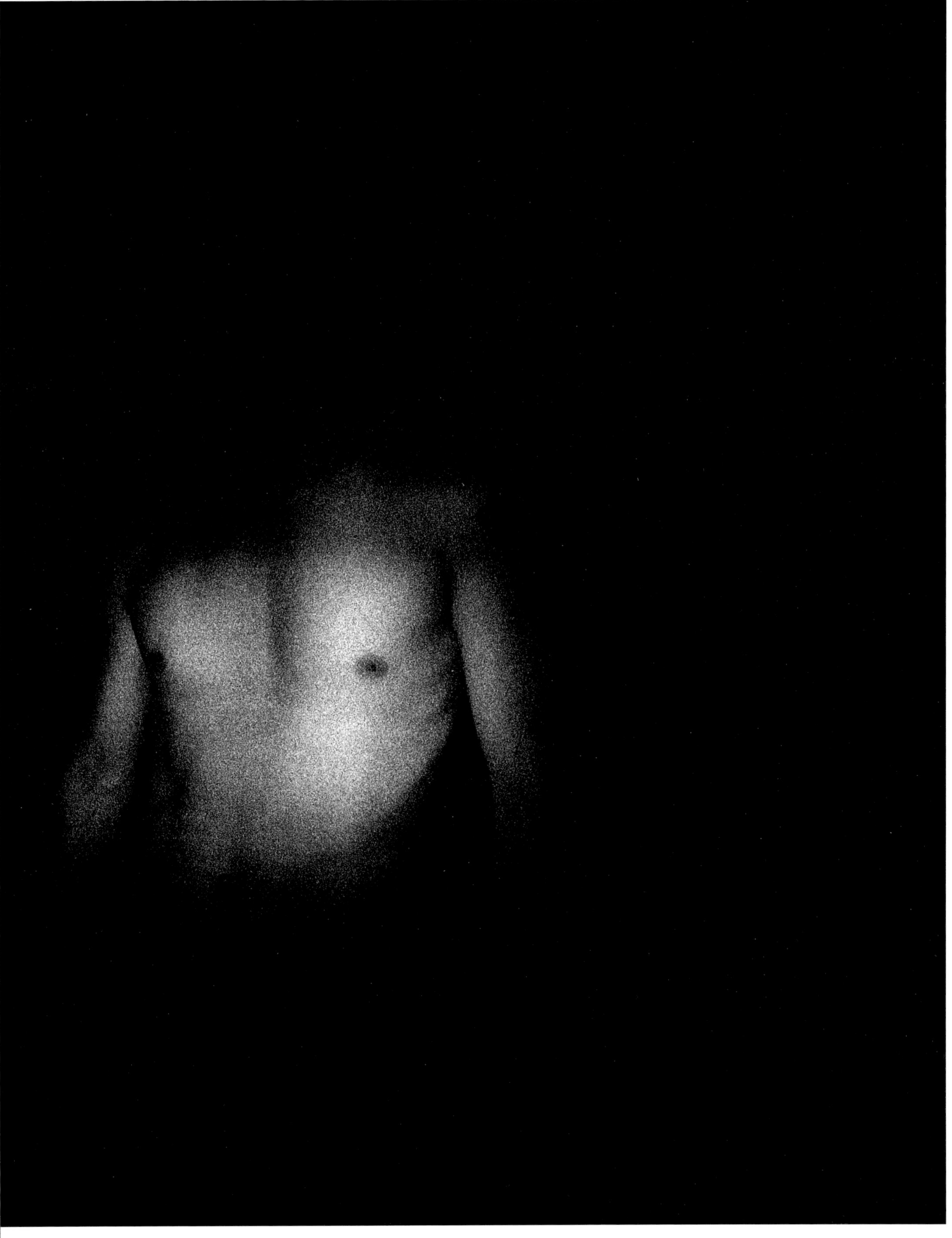

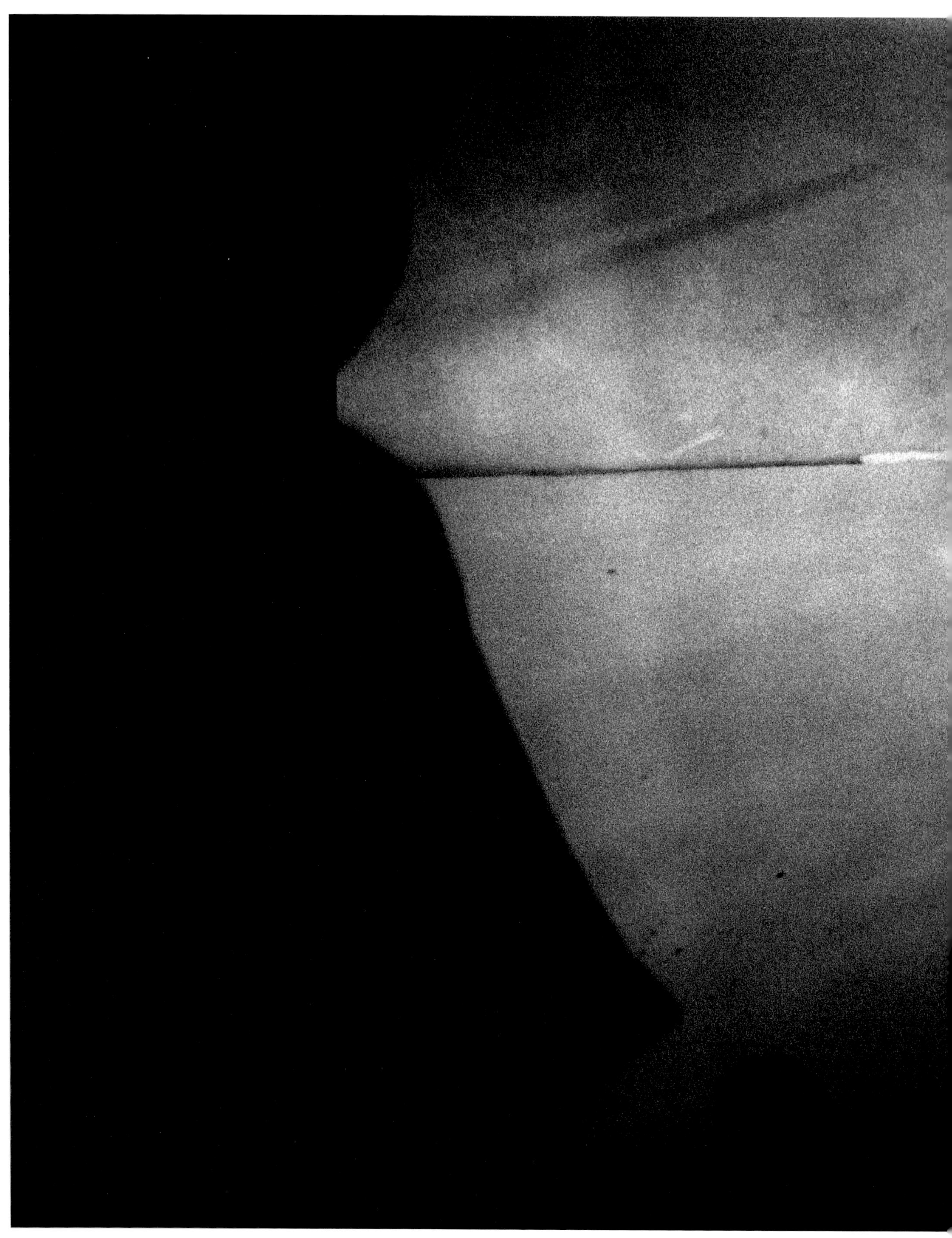

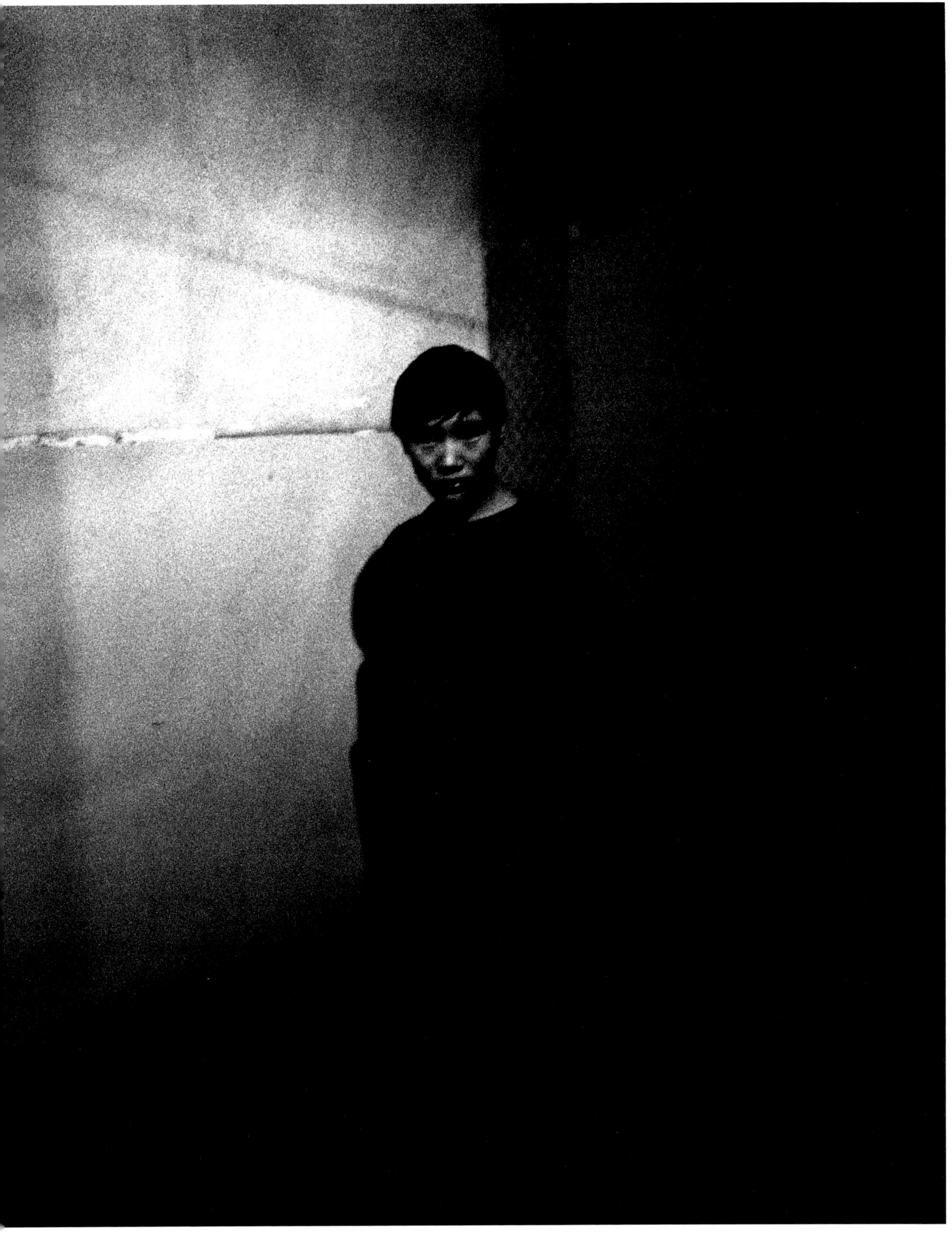

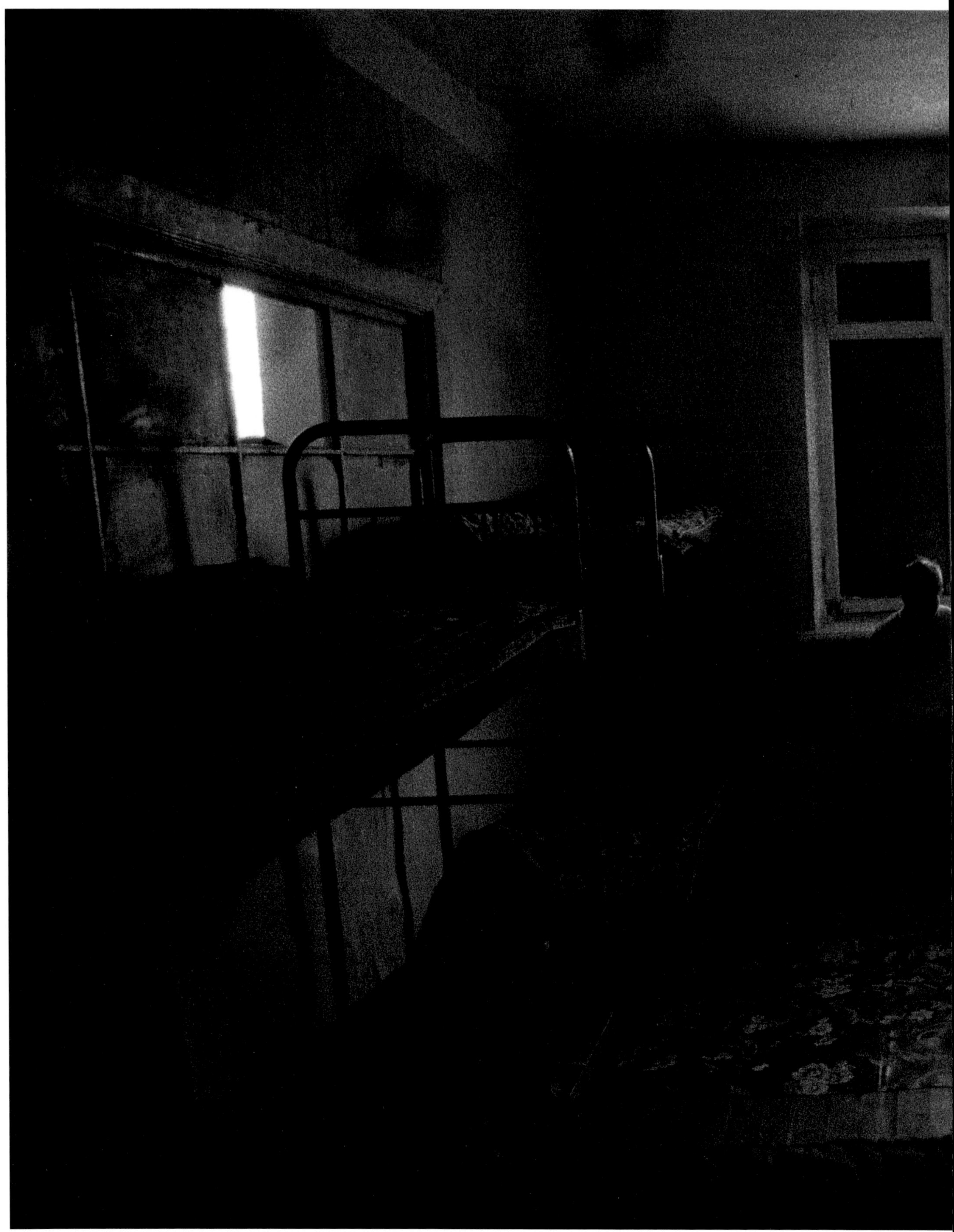

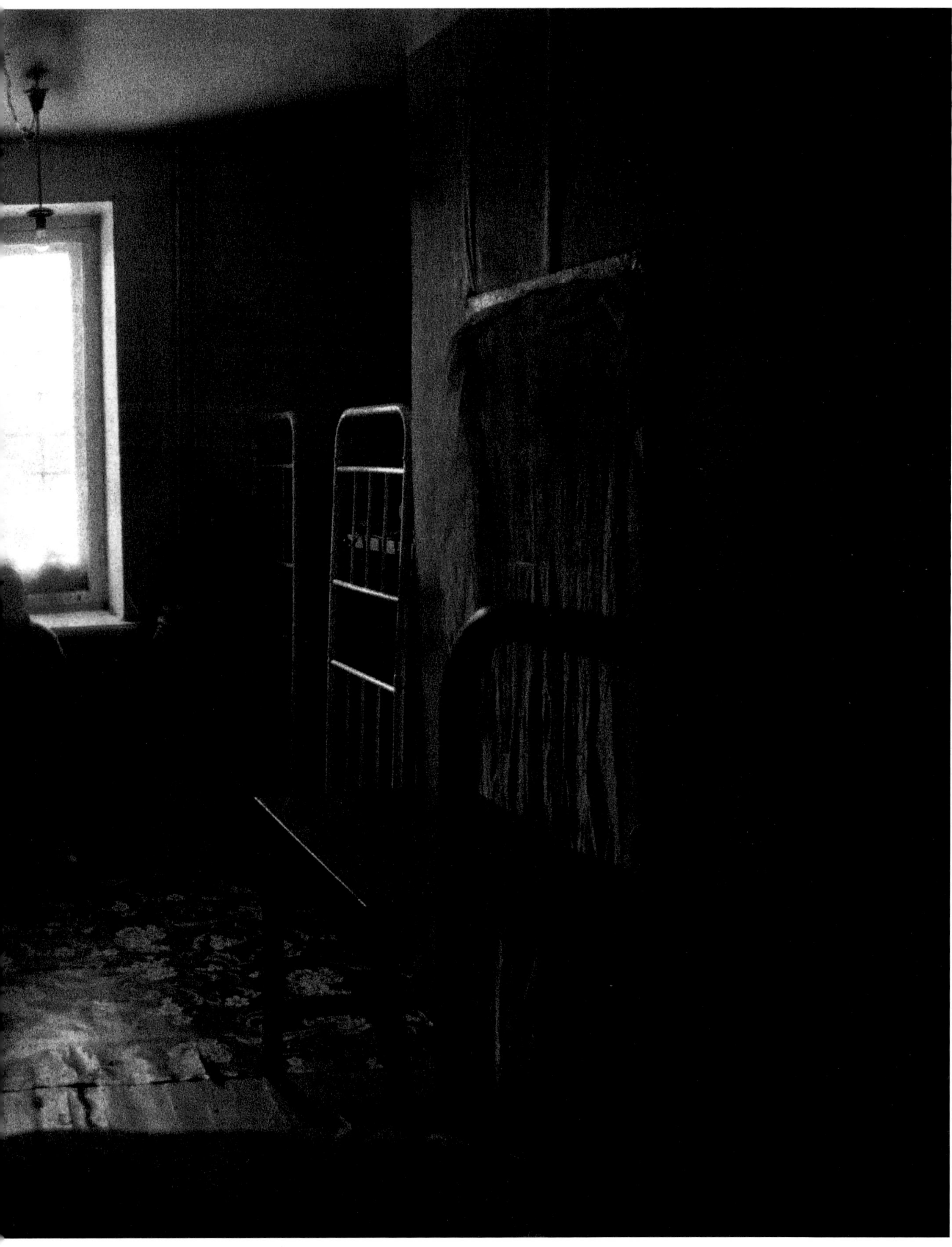

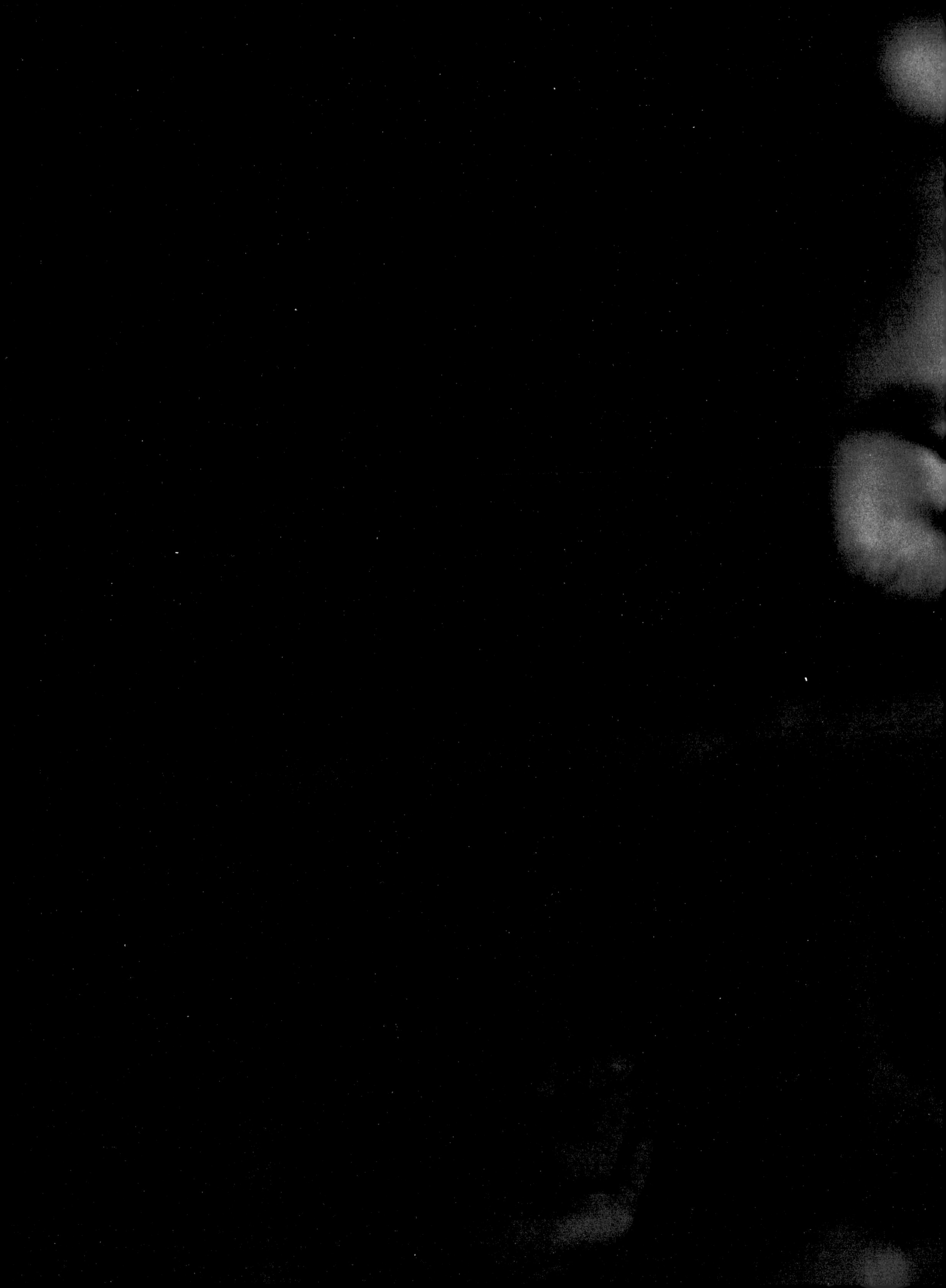

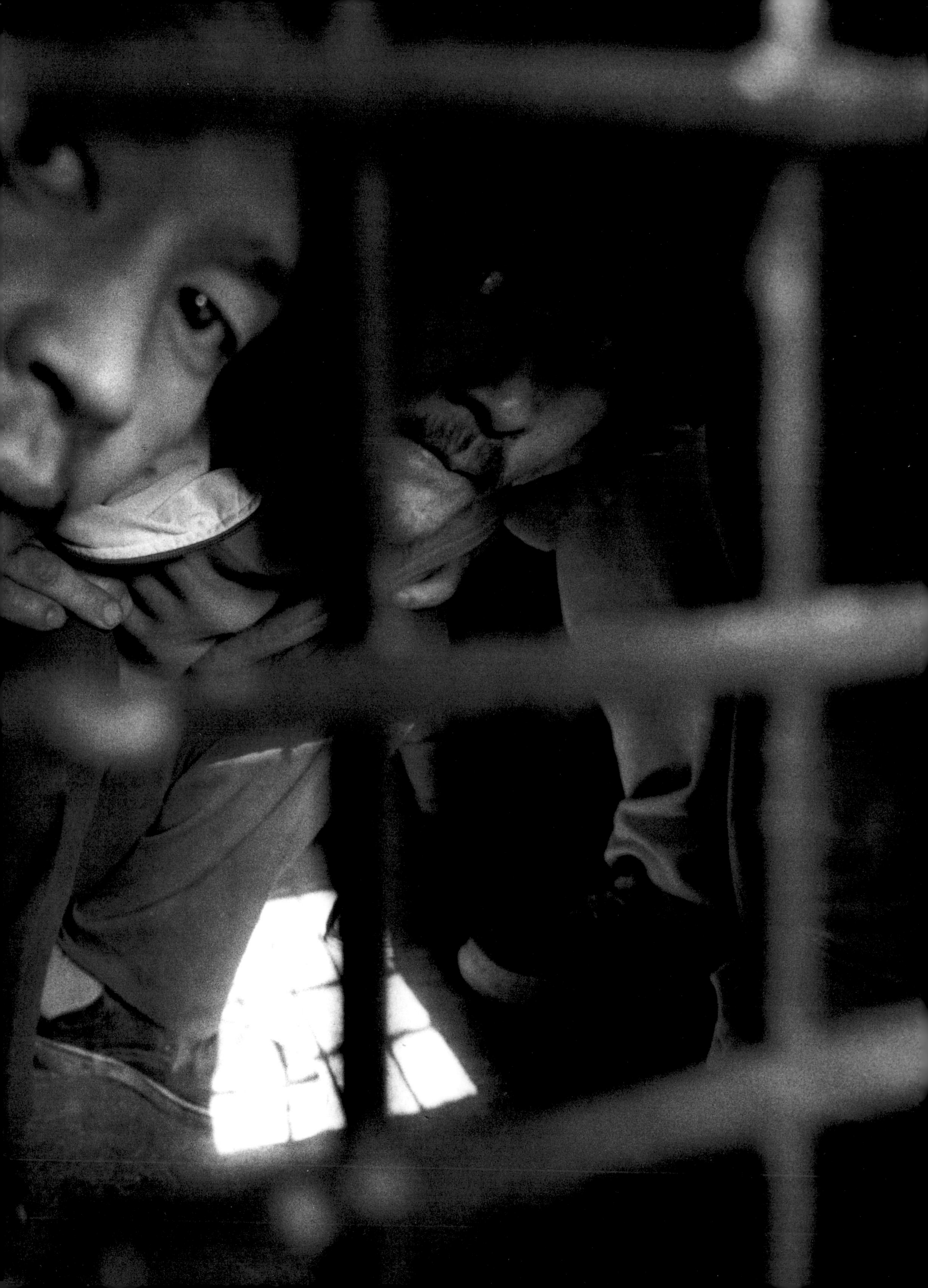

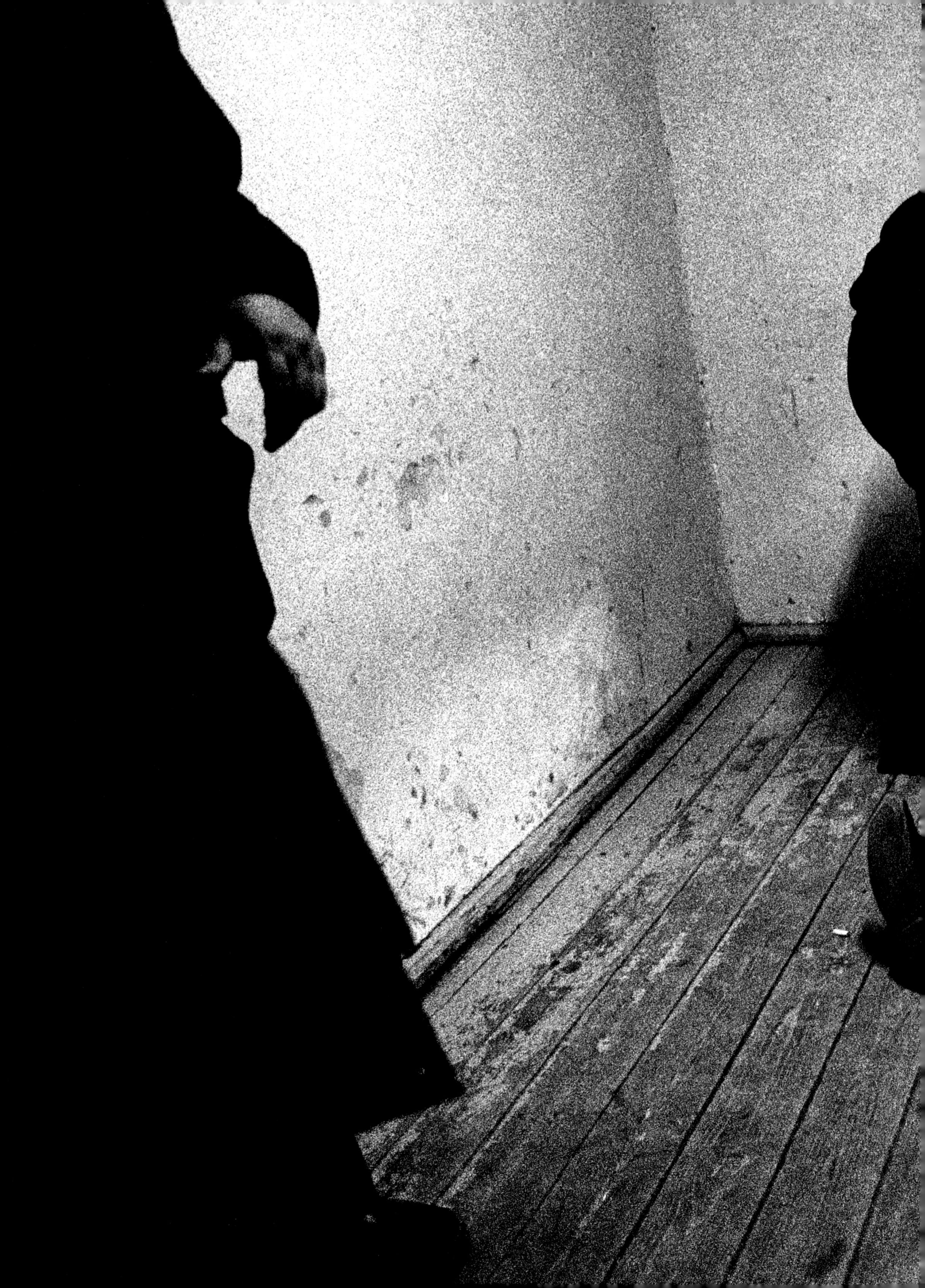

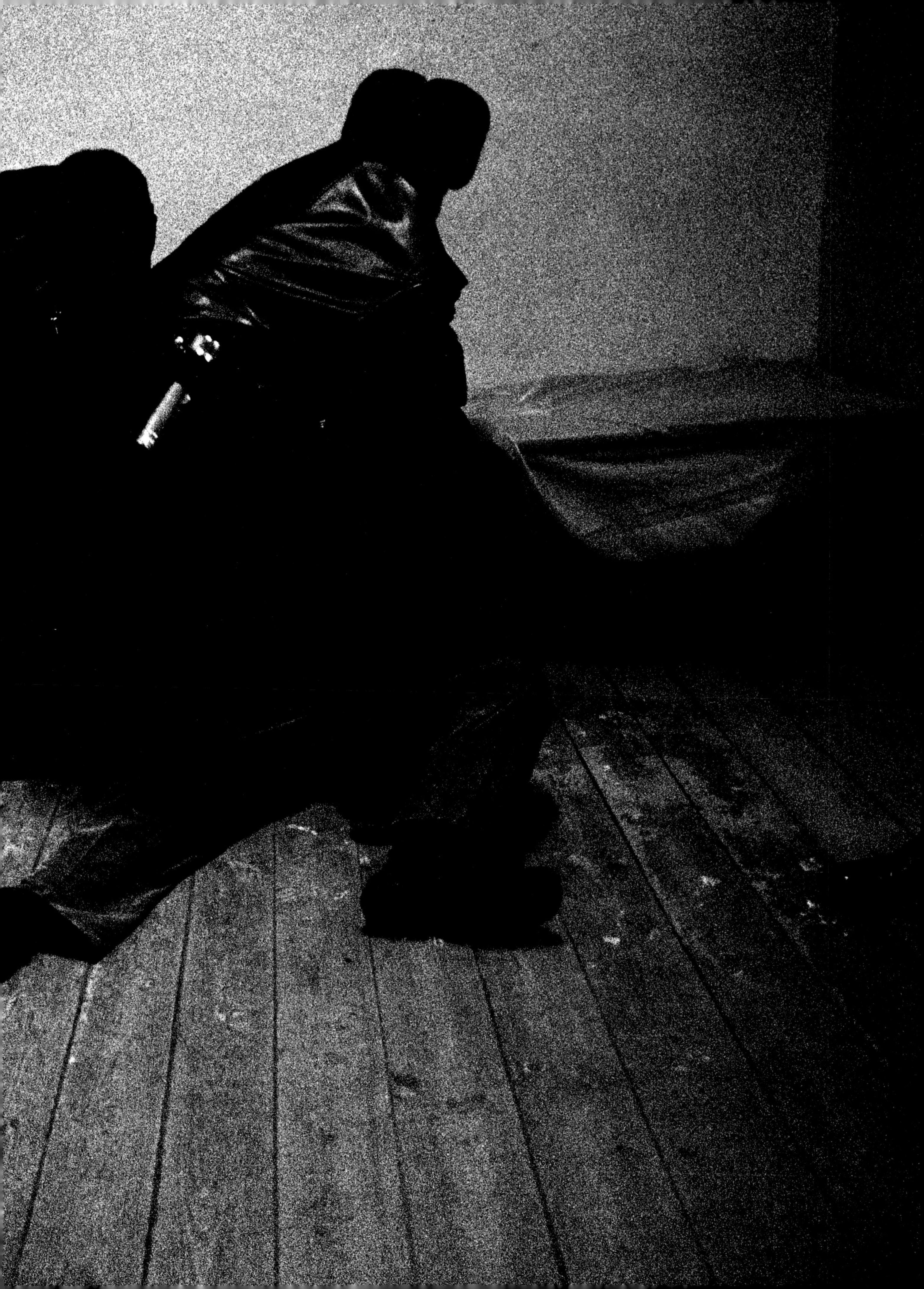

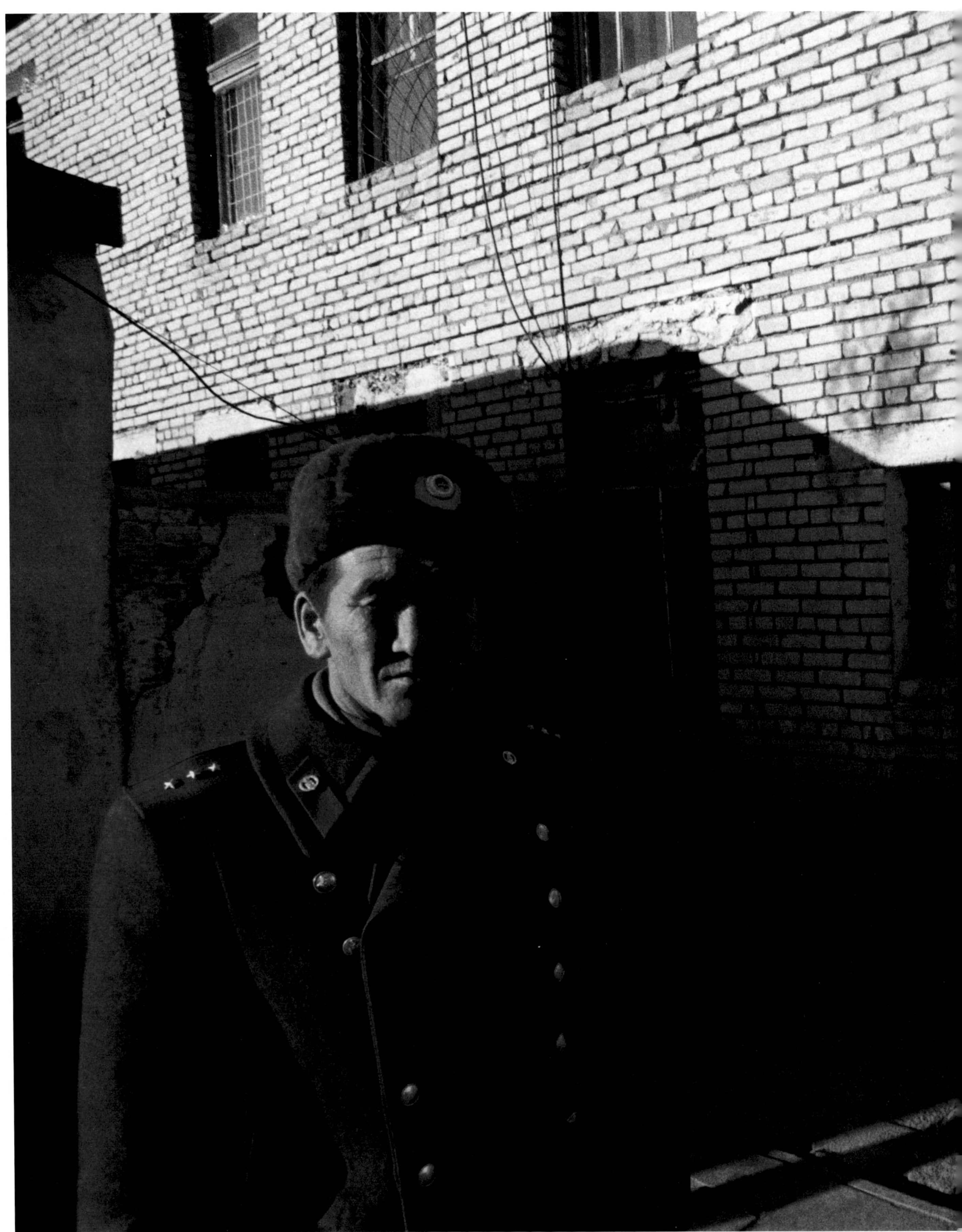

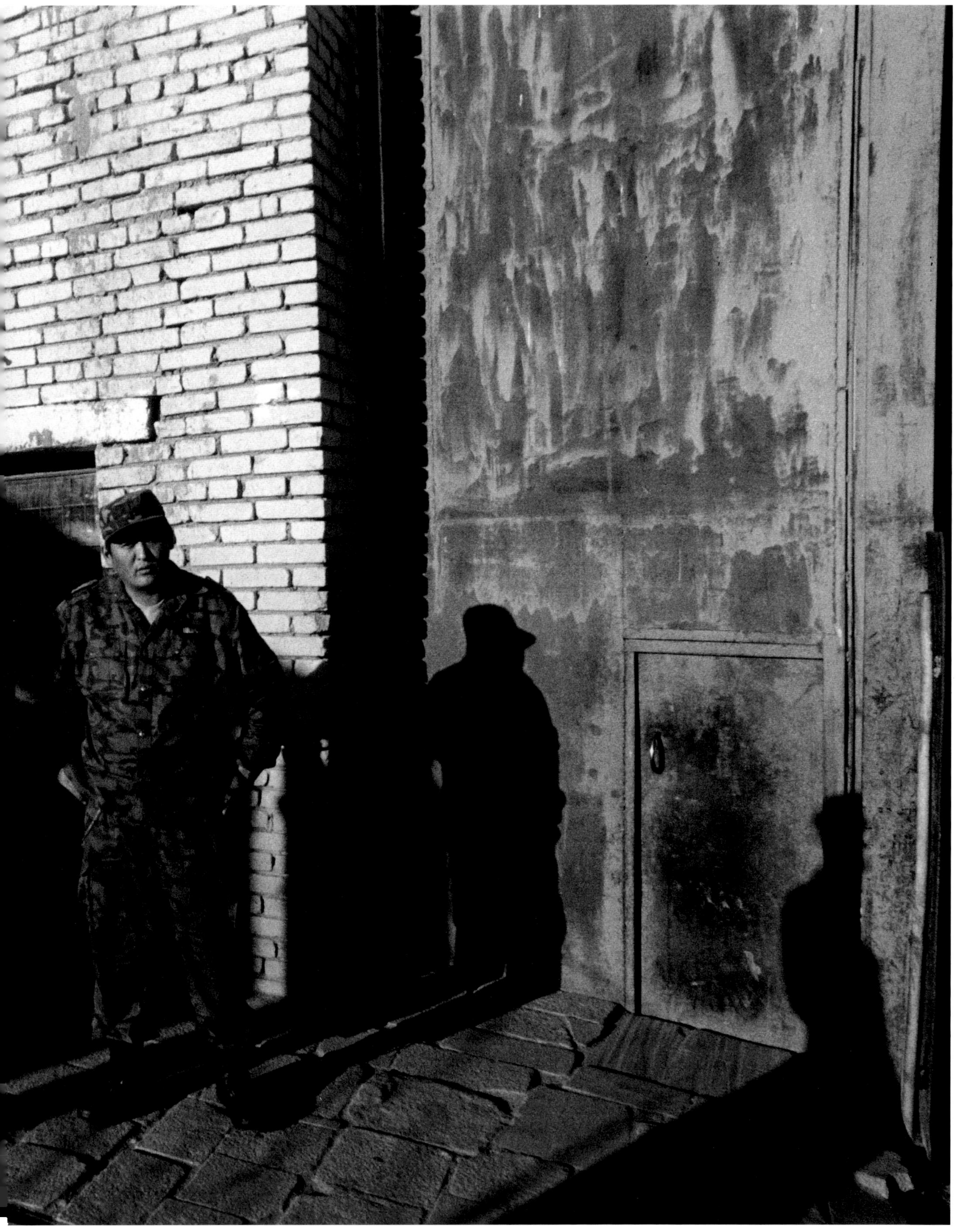

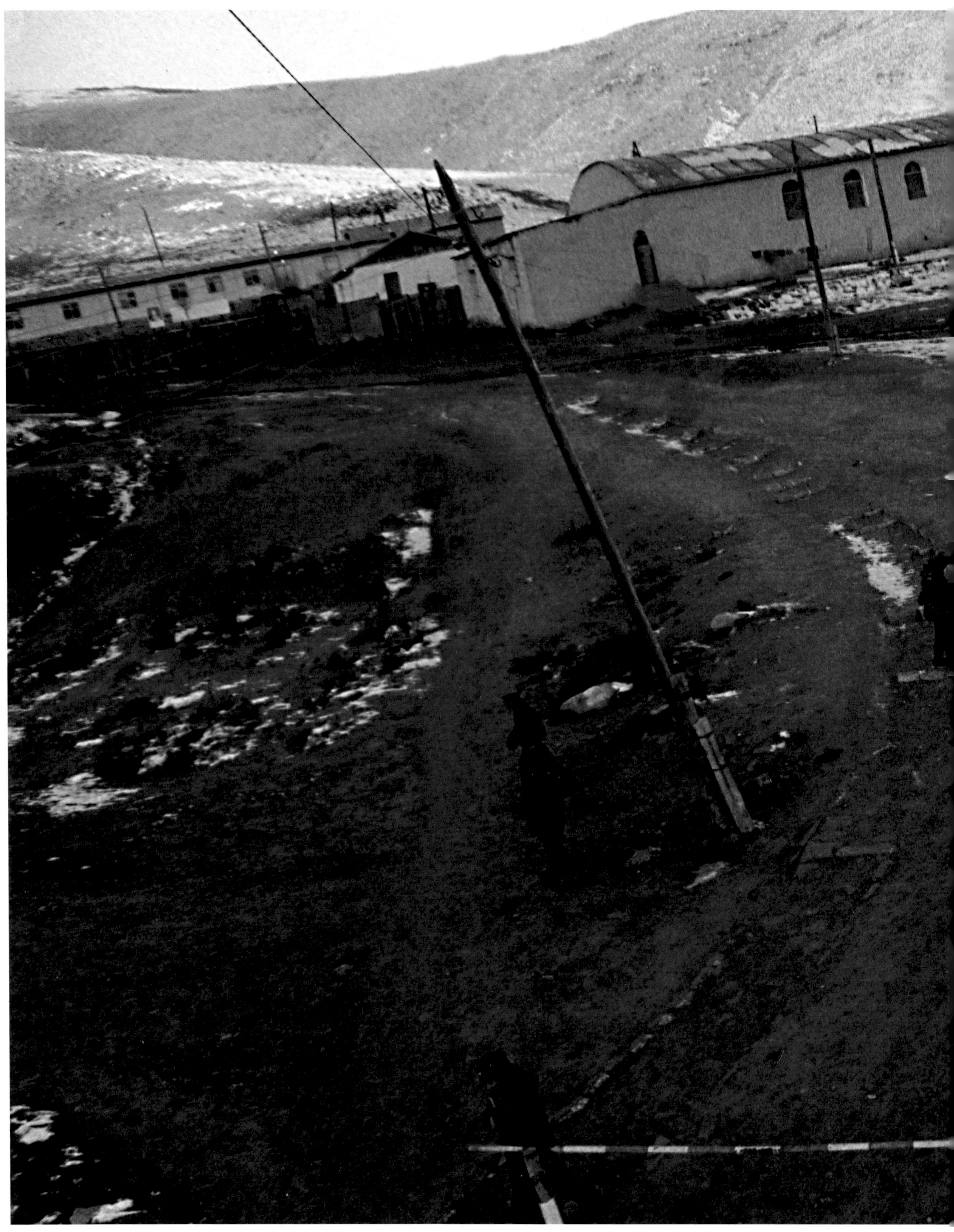

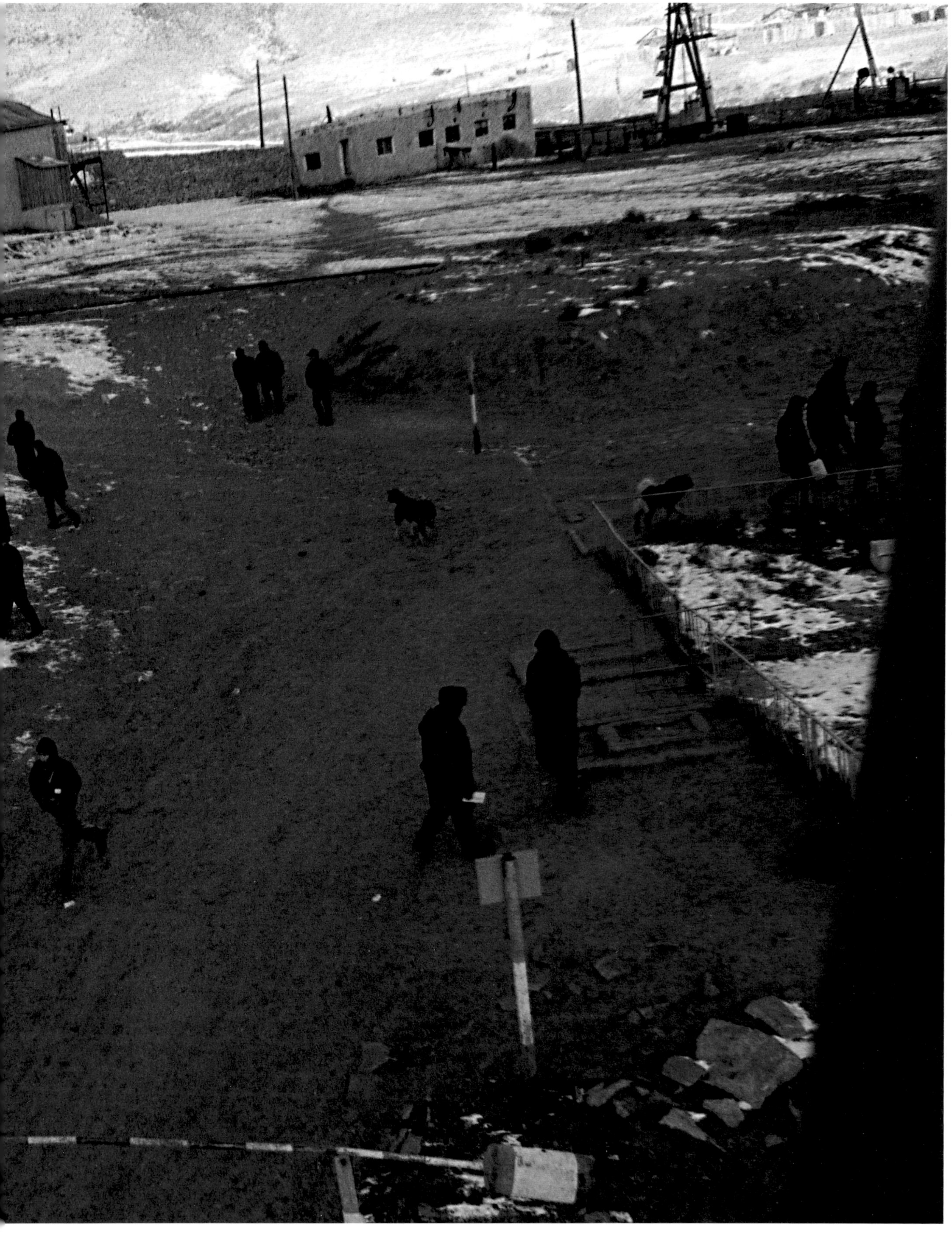

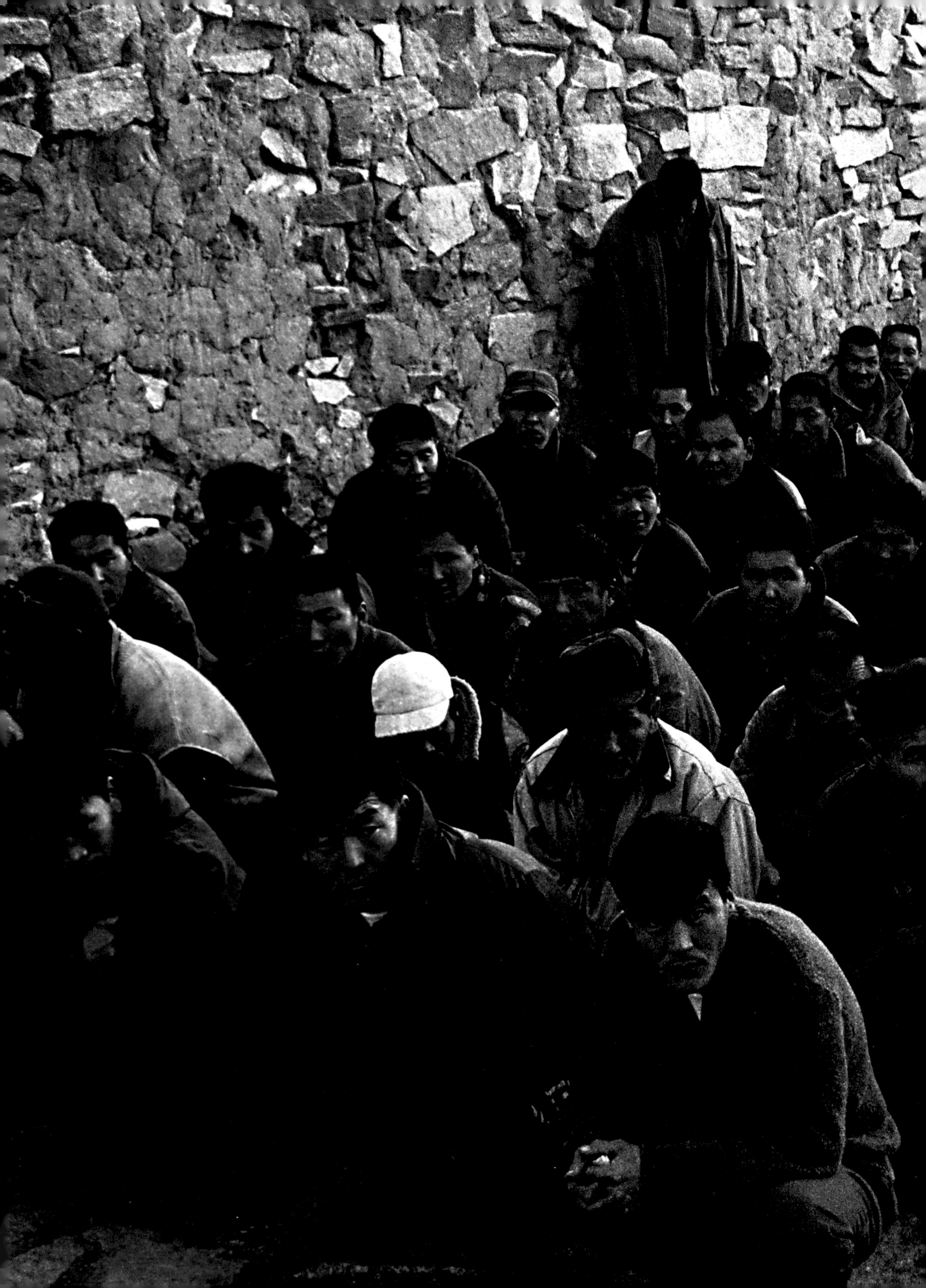

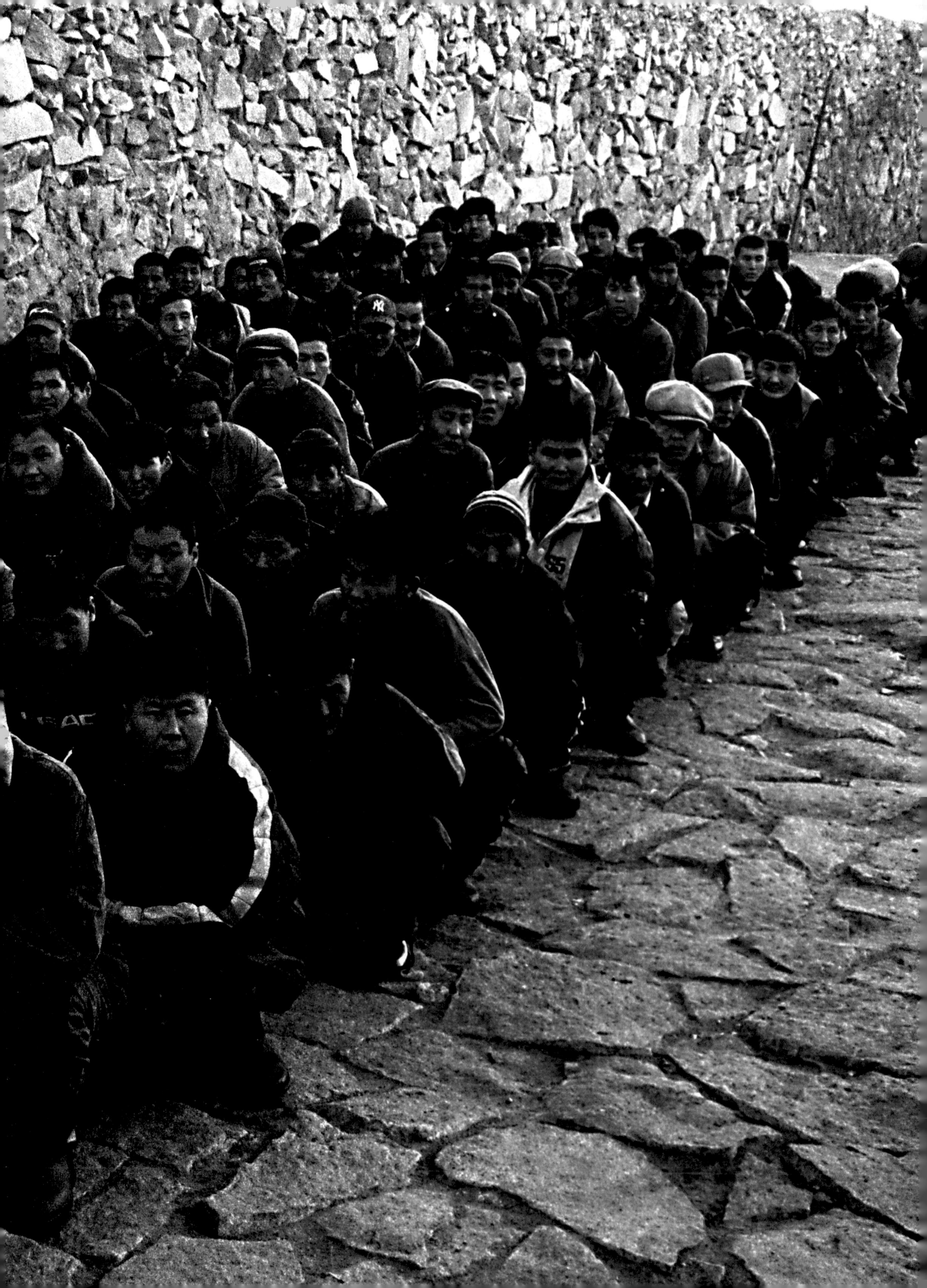

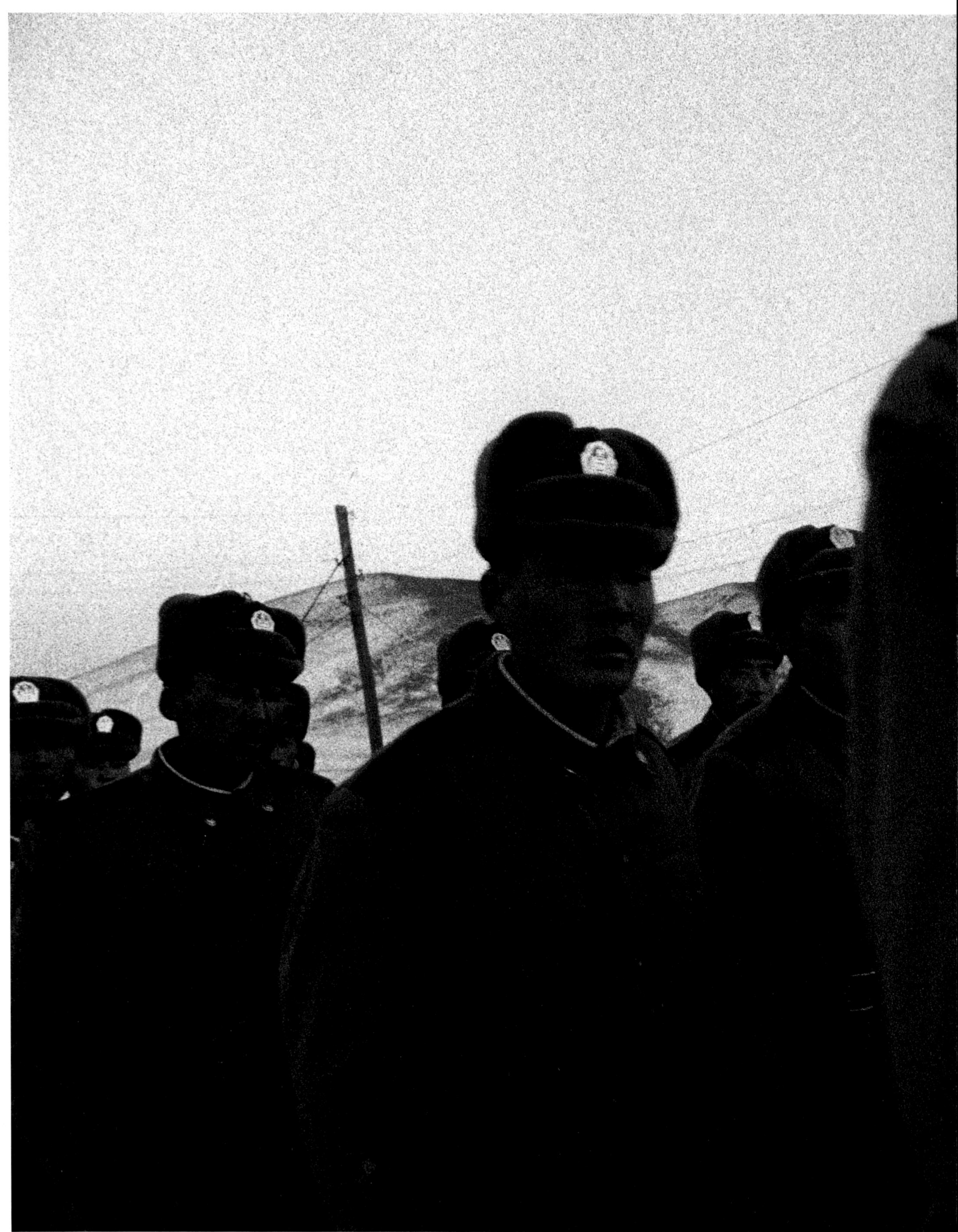

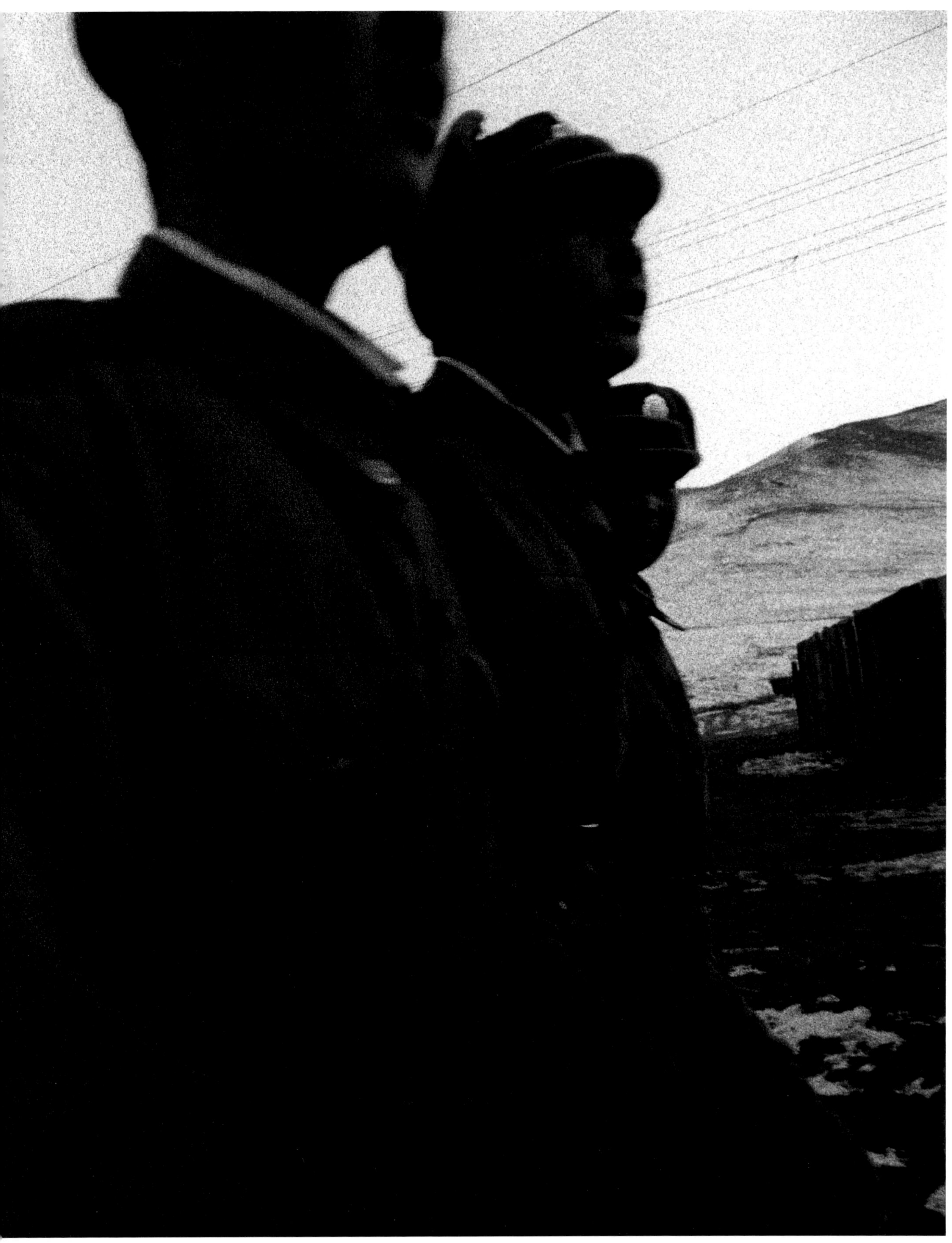

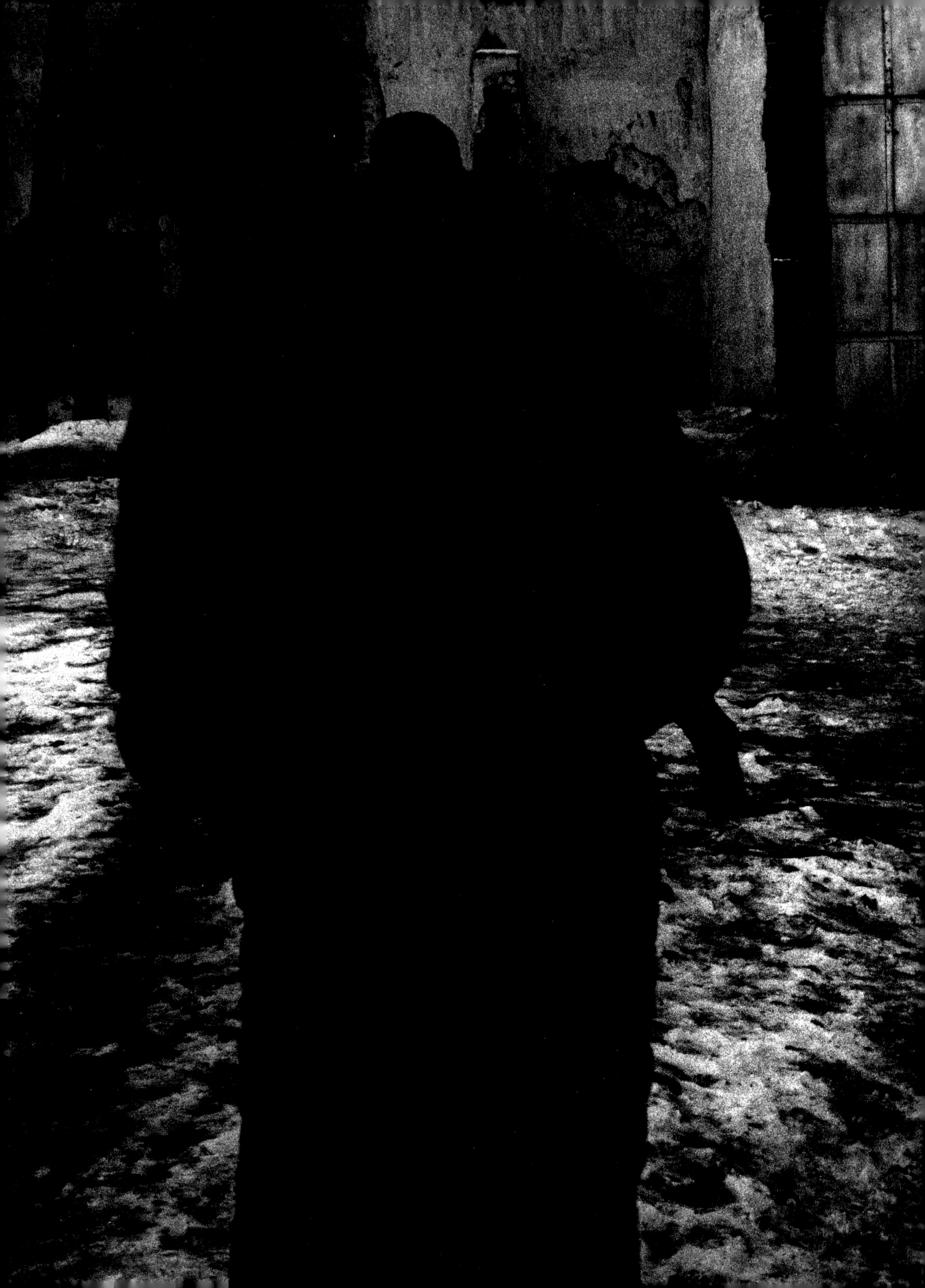

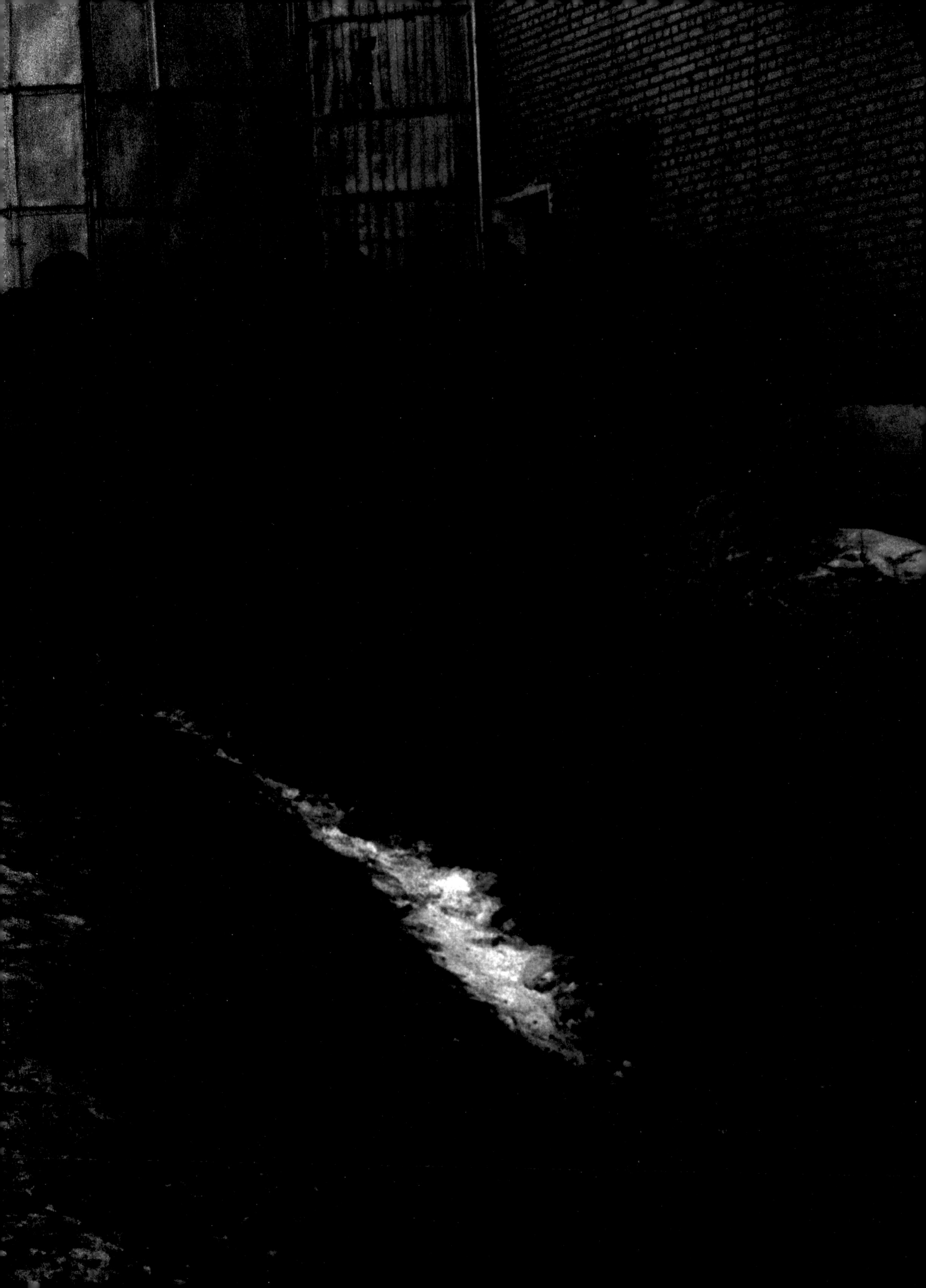

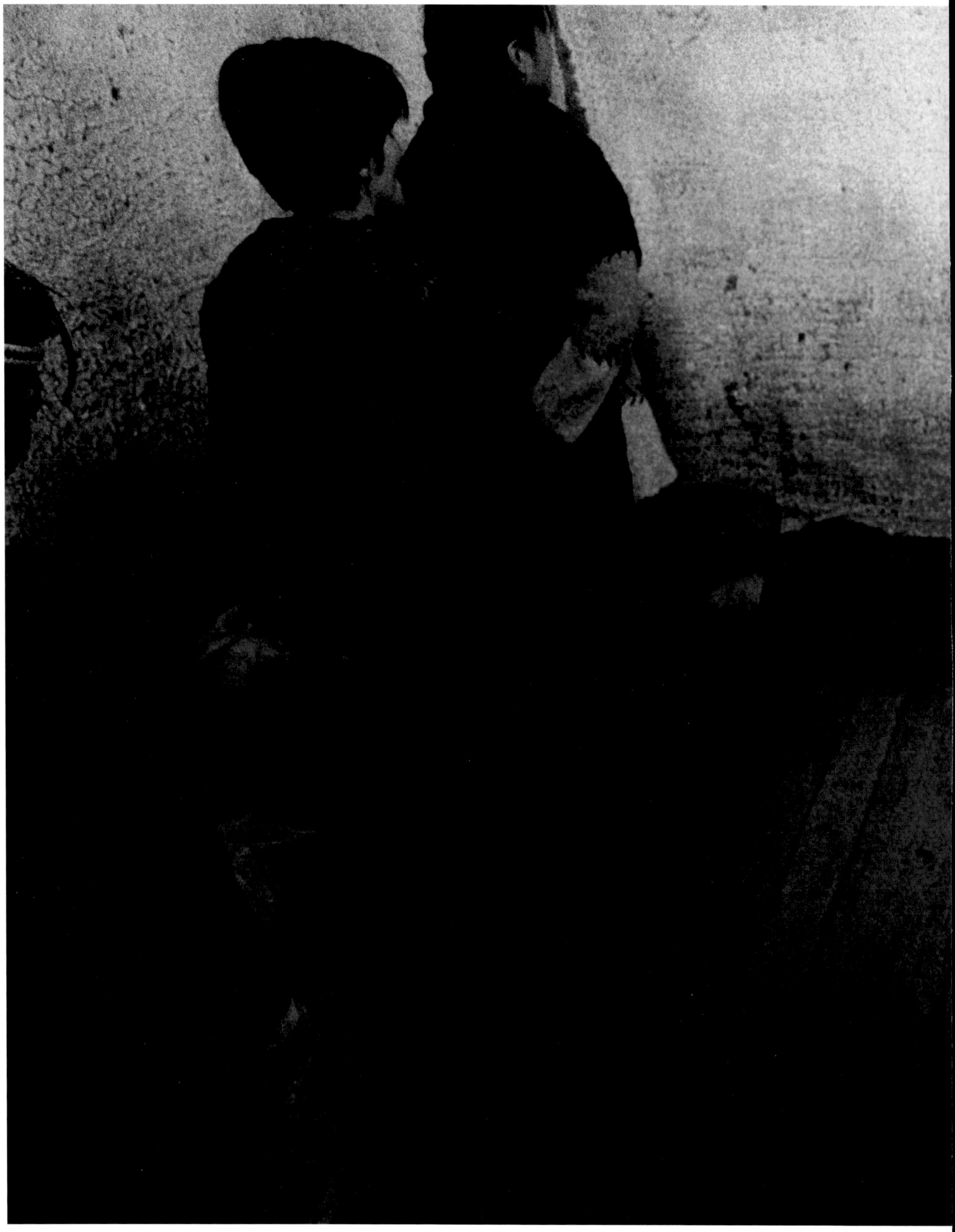

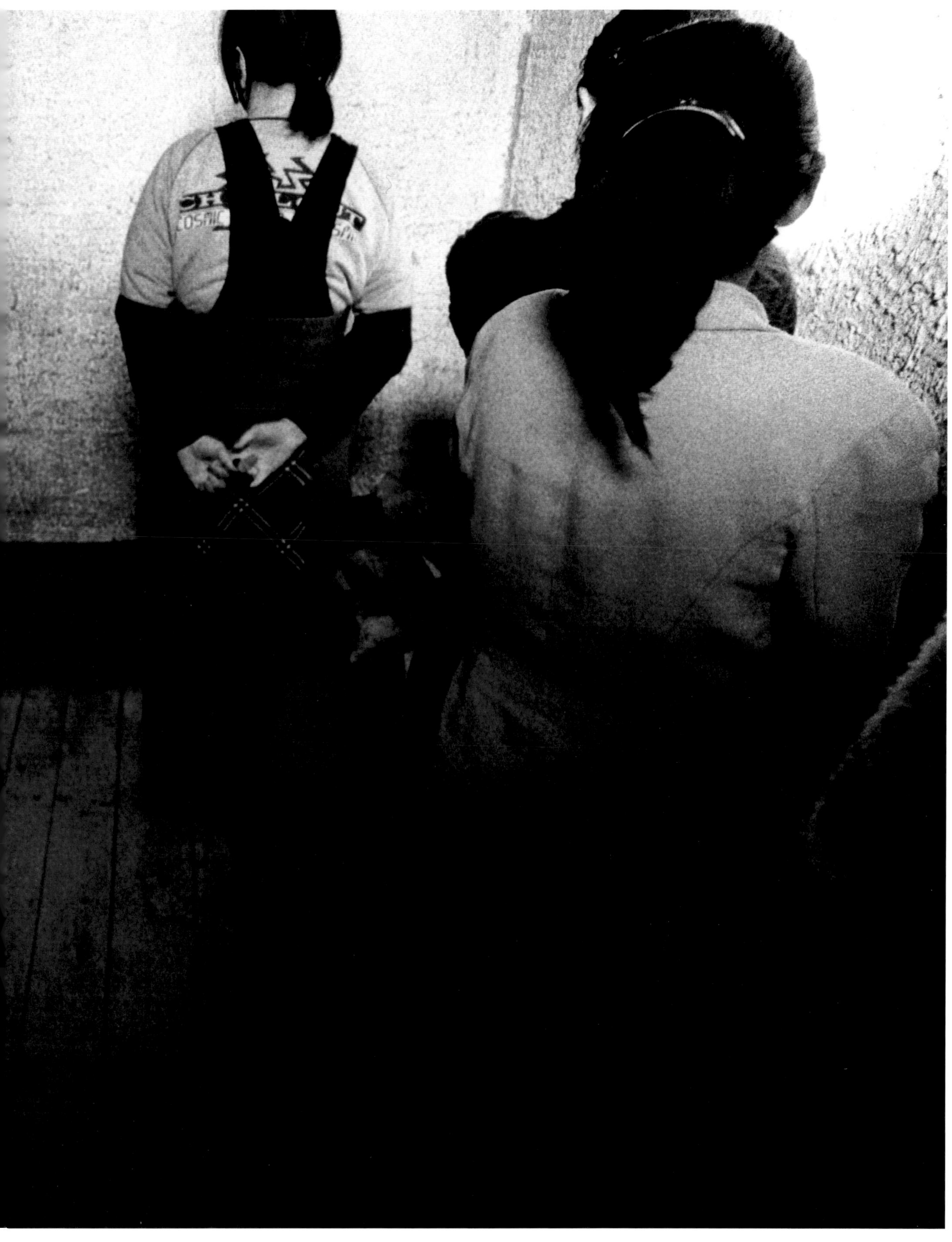
COSMIC

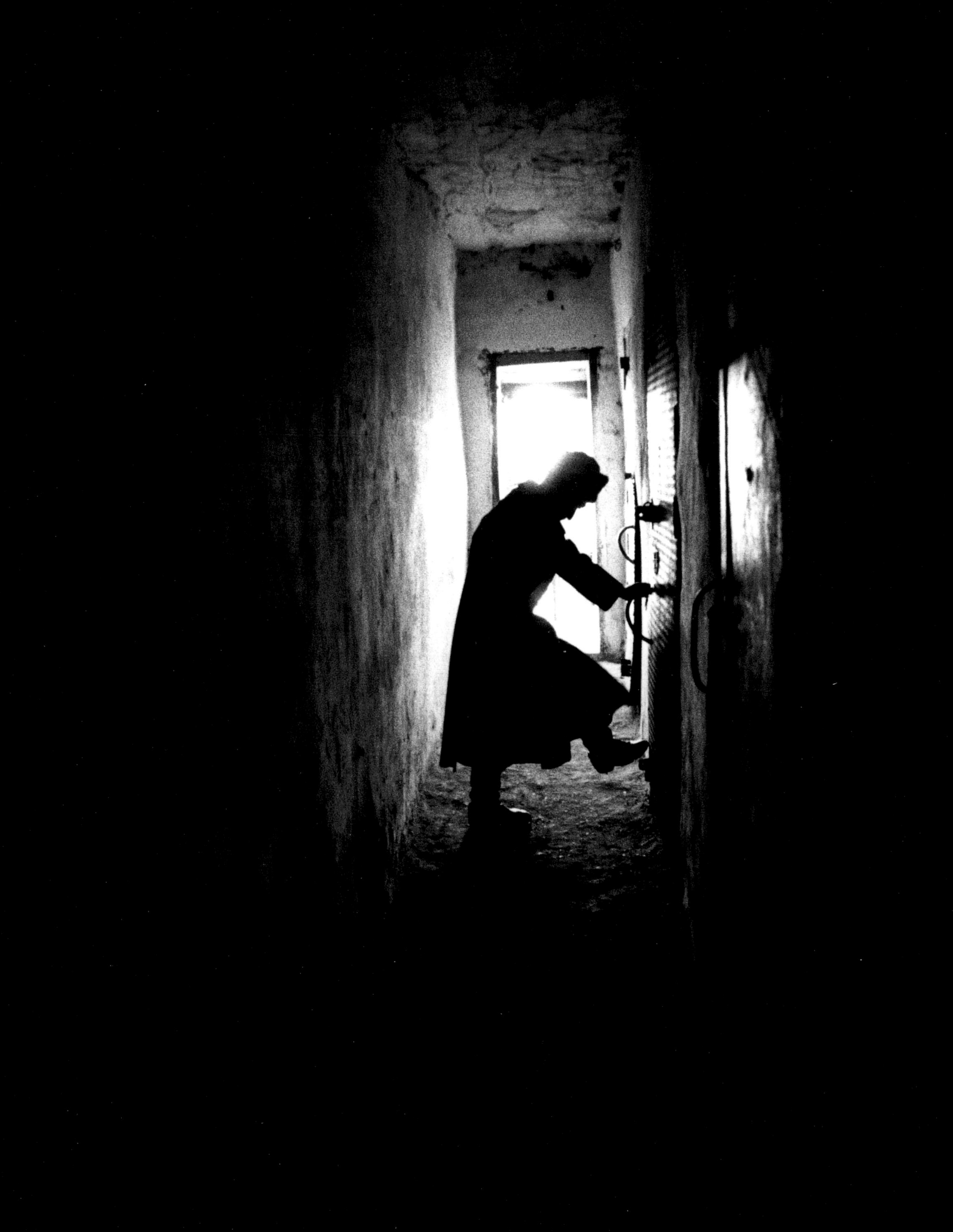

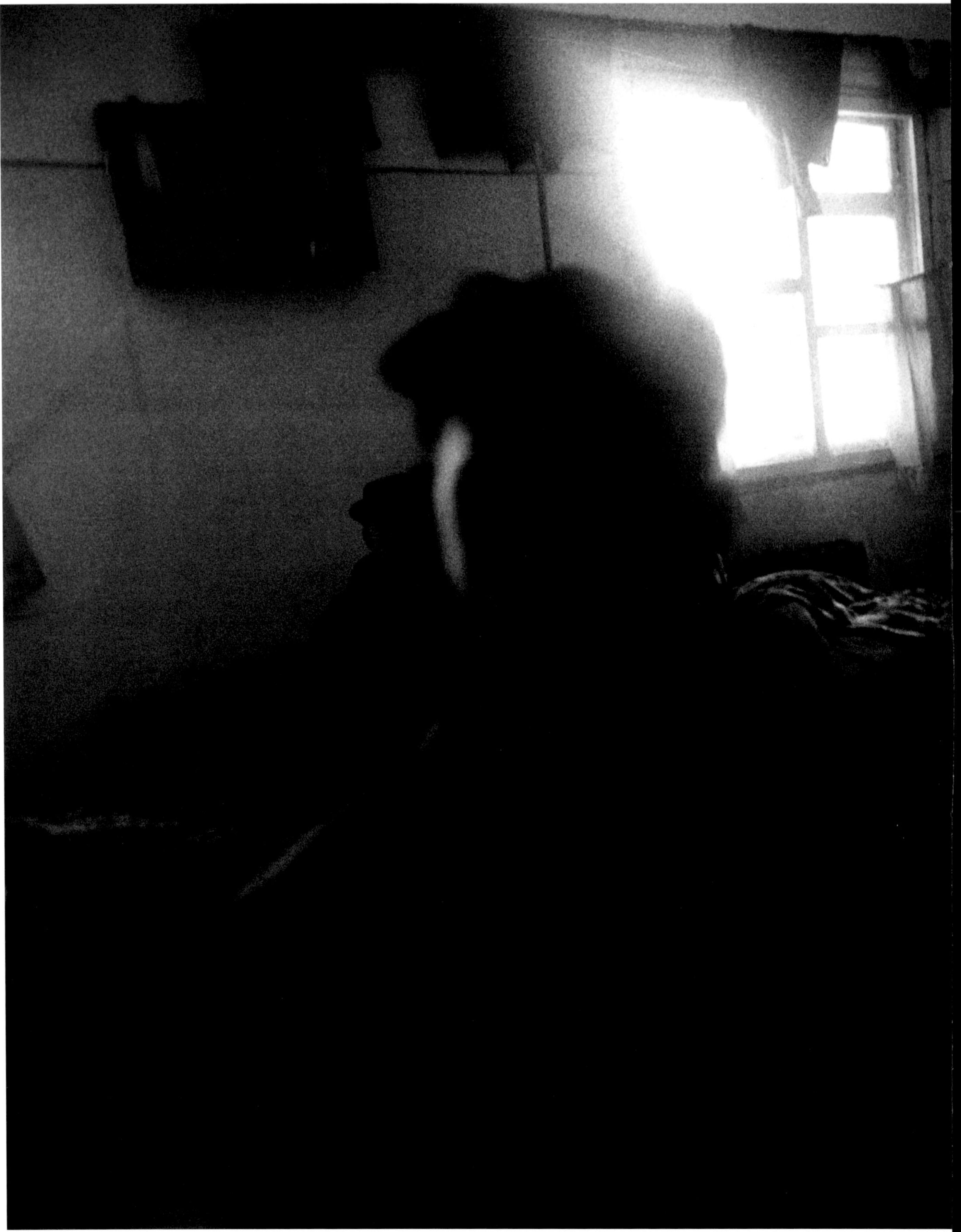

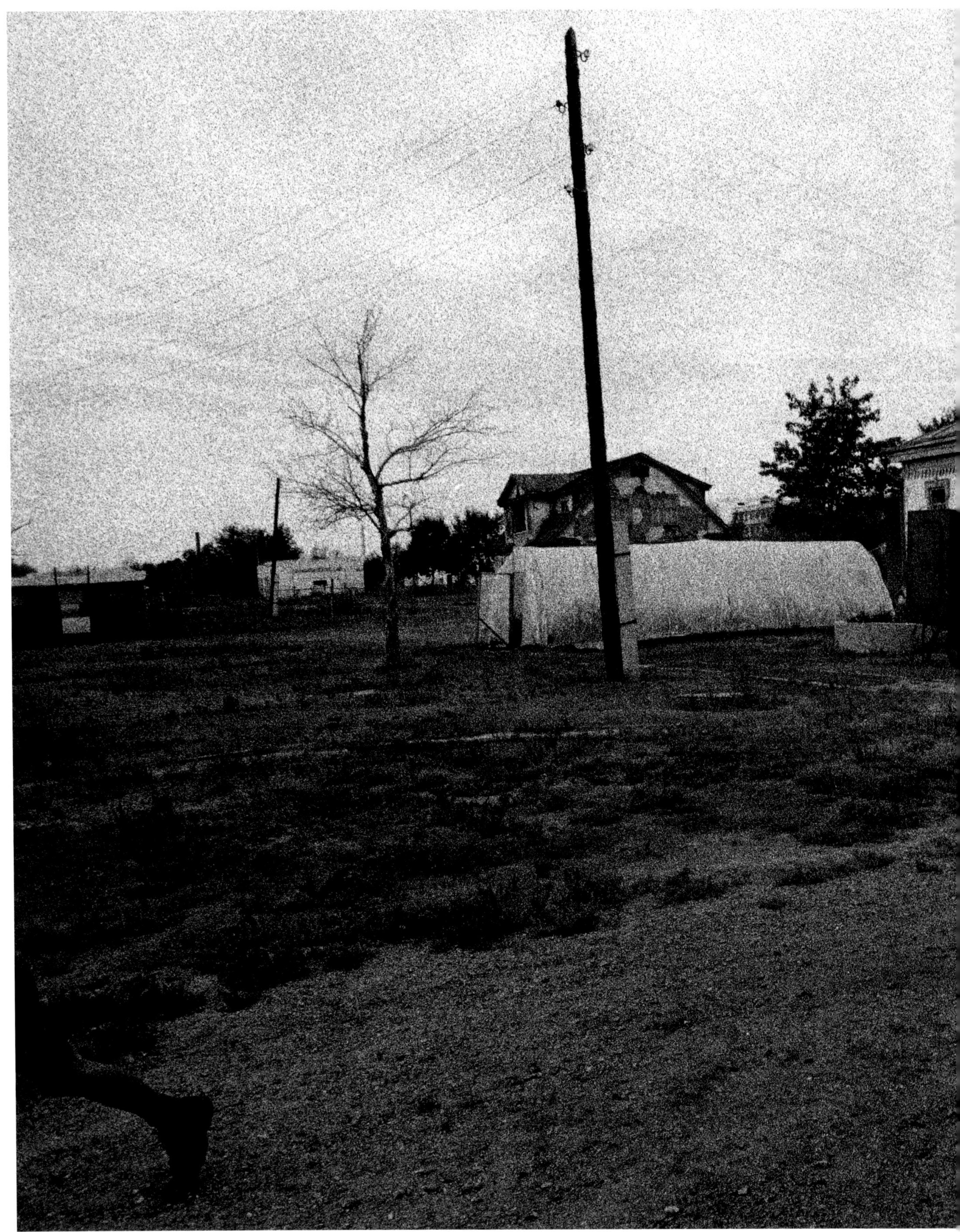

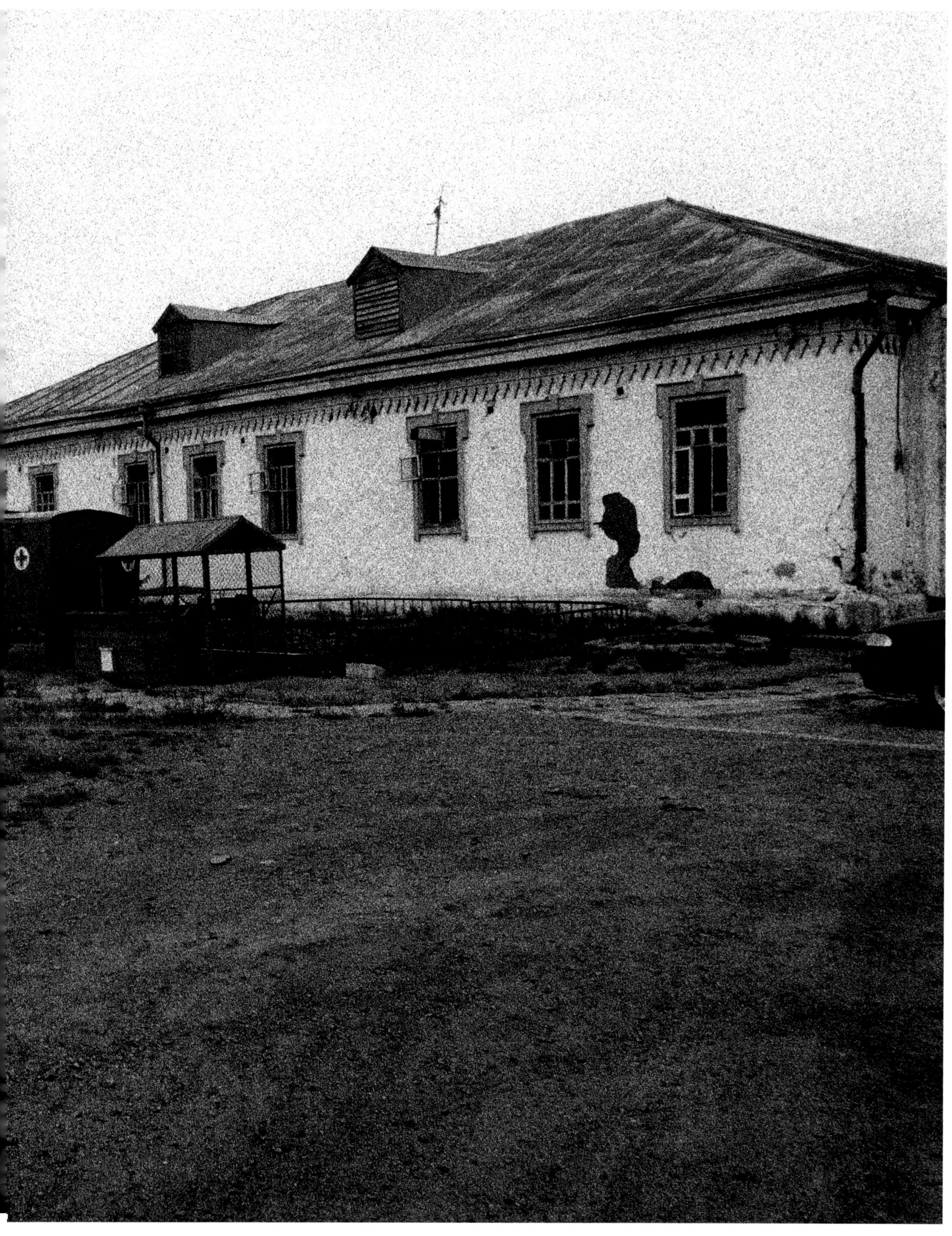

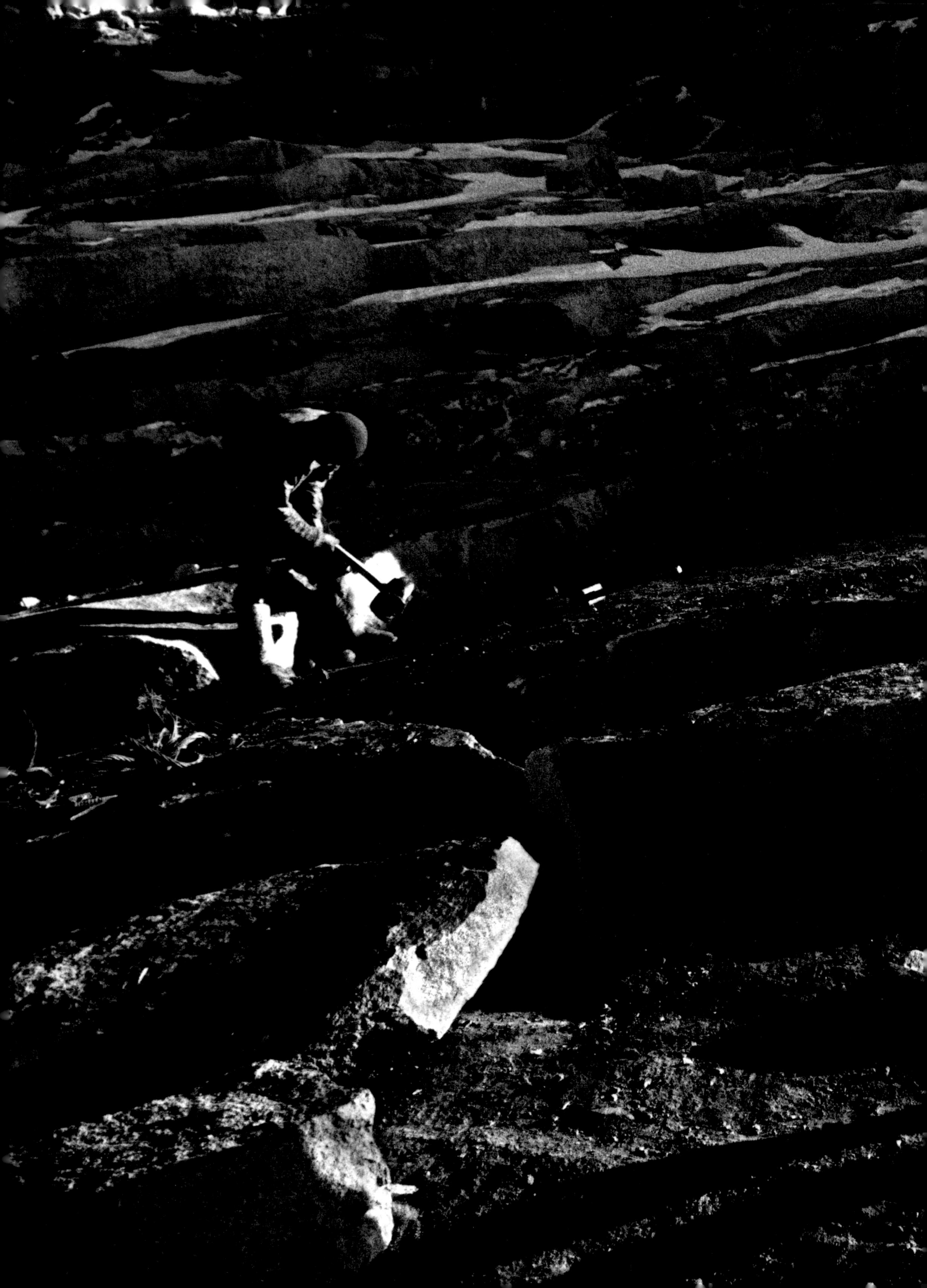

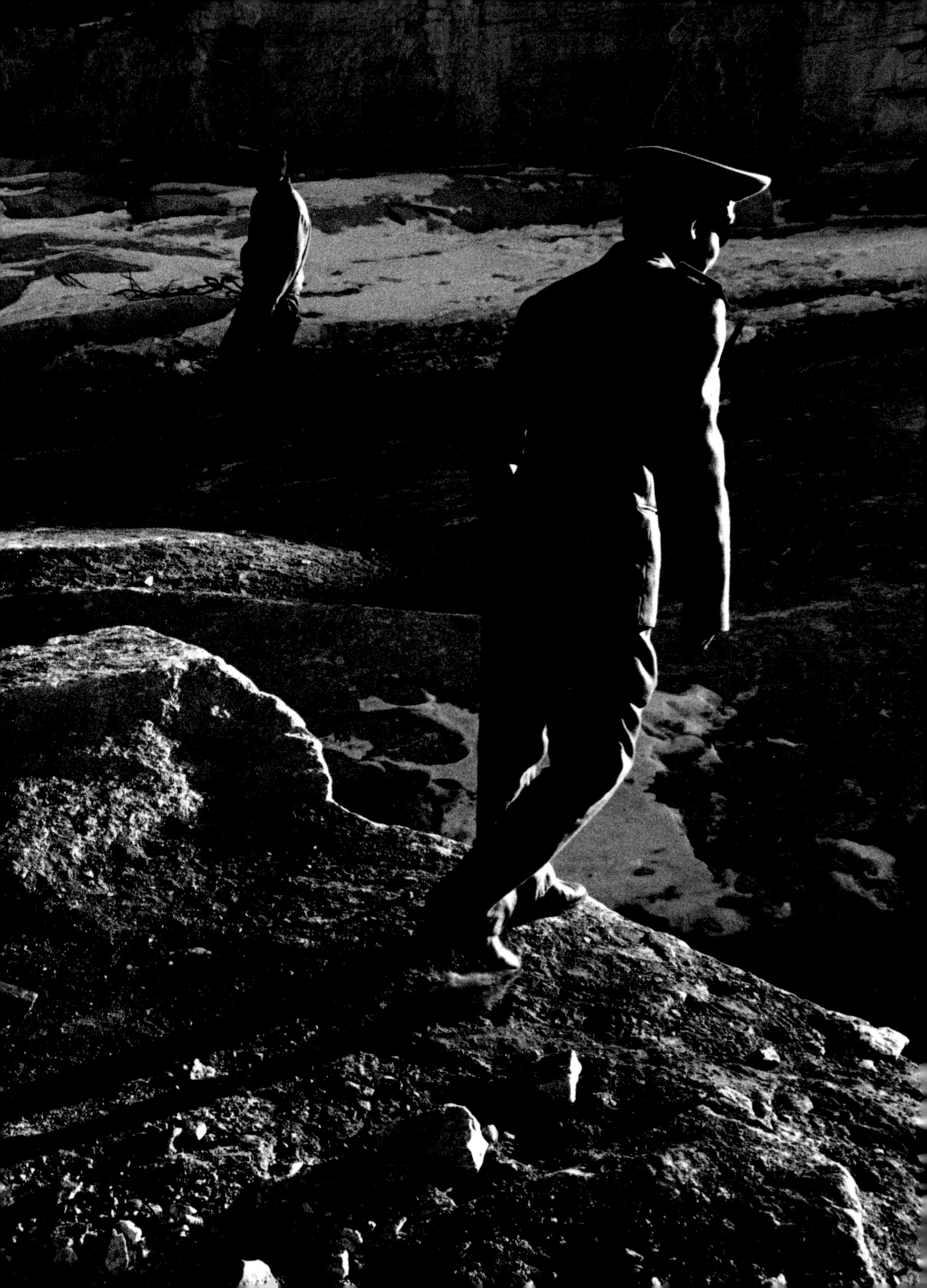

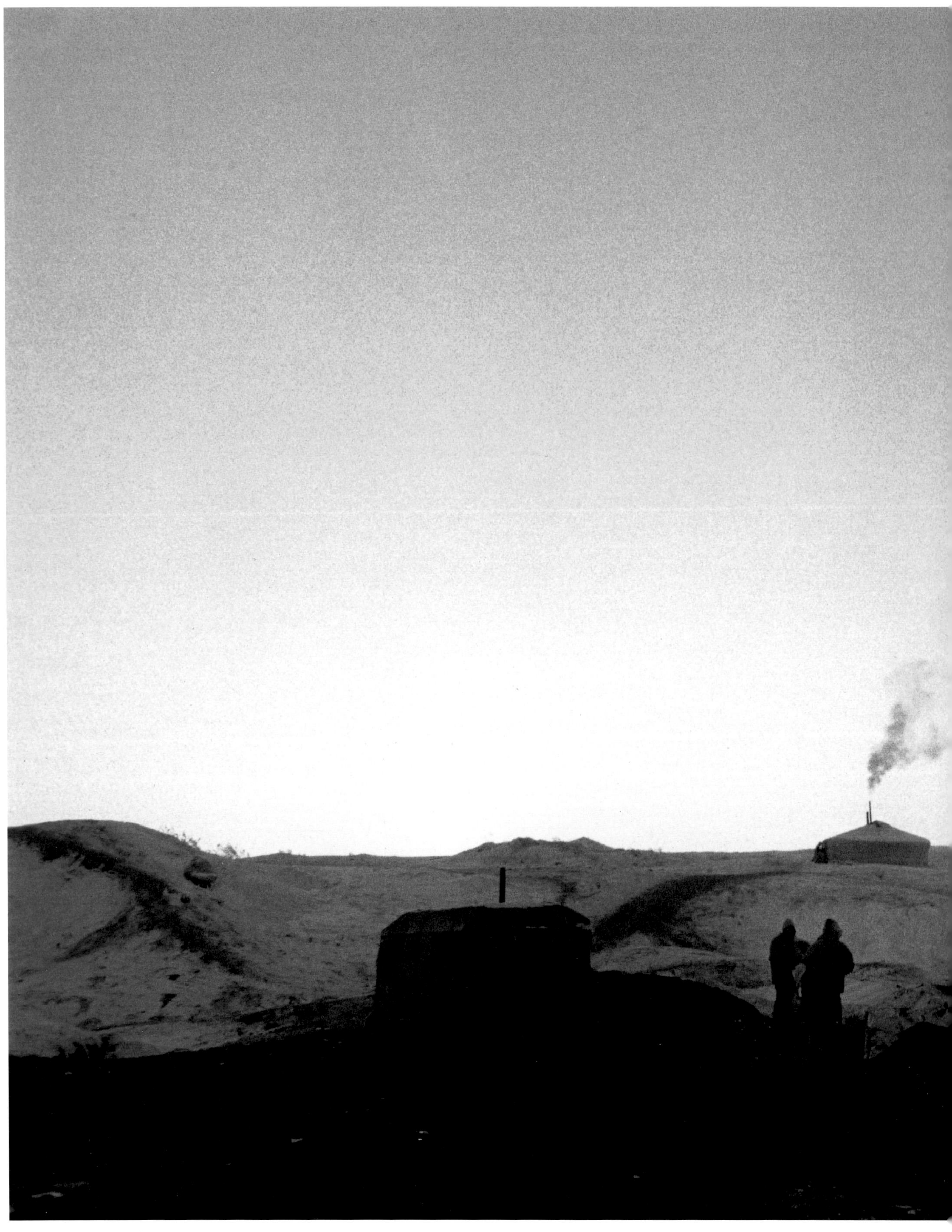

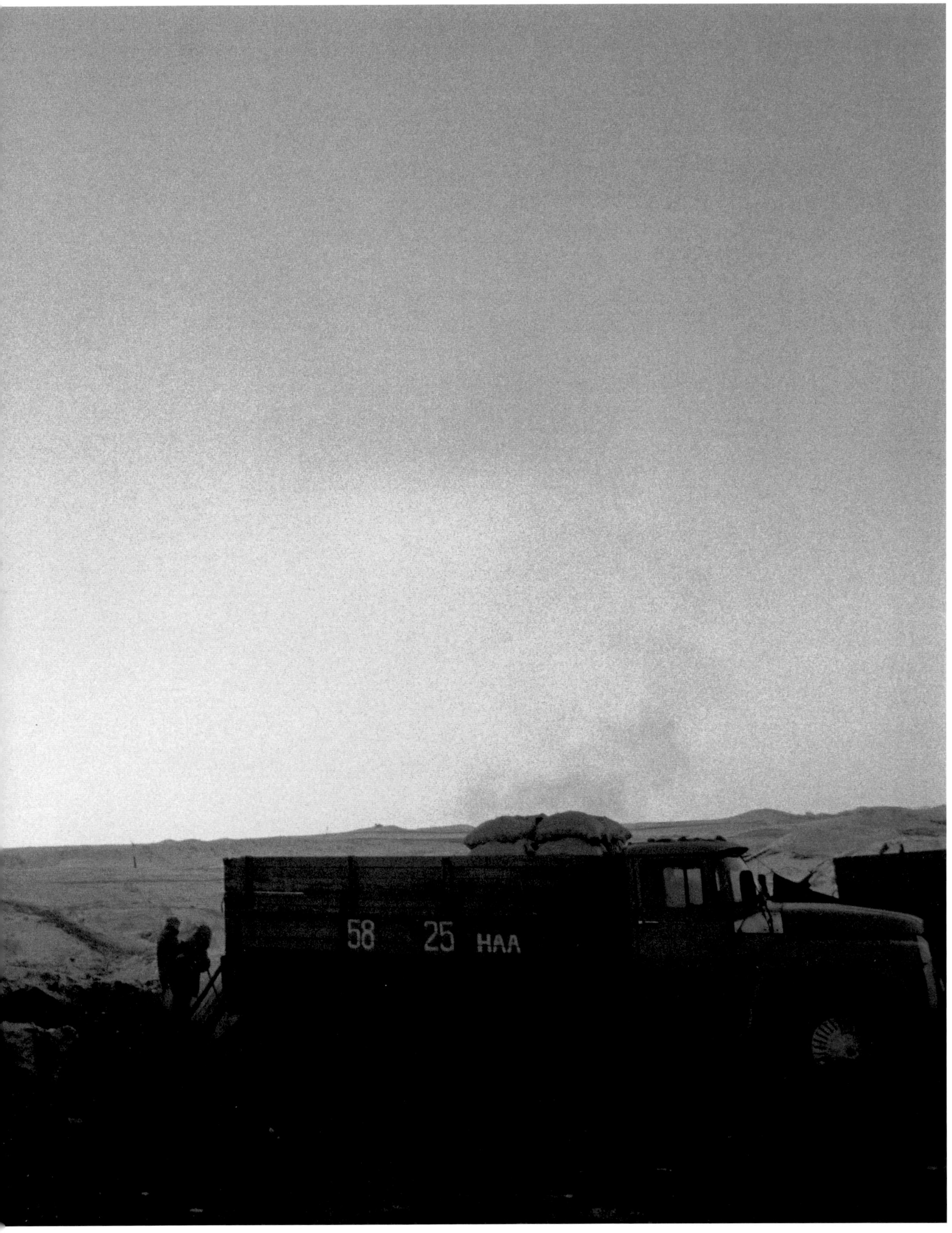
58 25 HAA

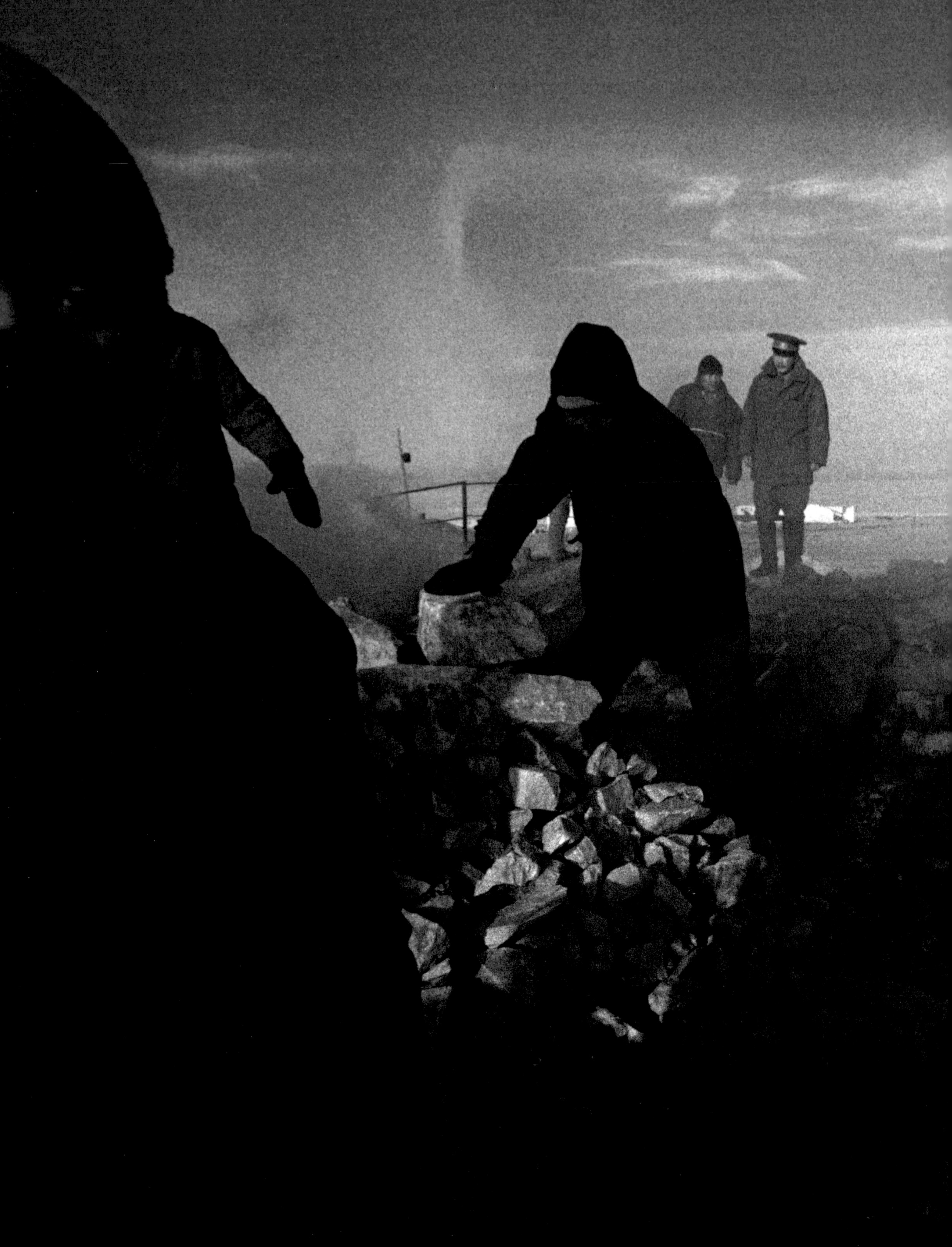

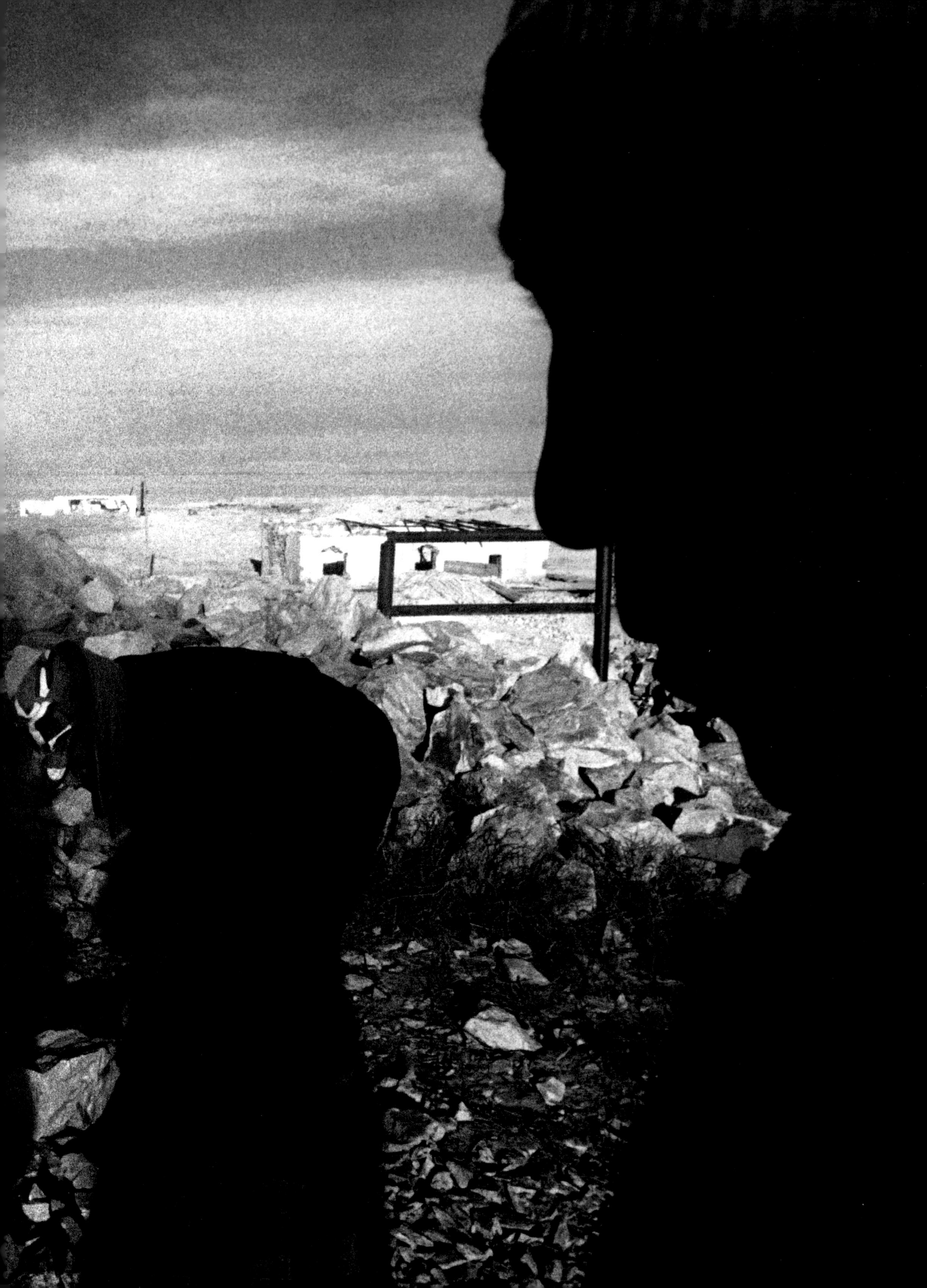

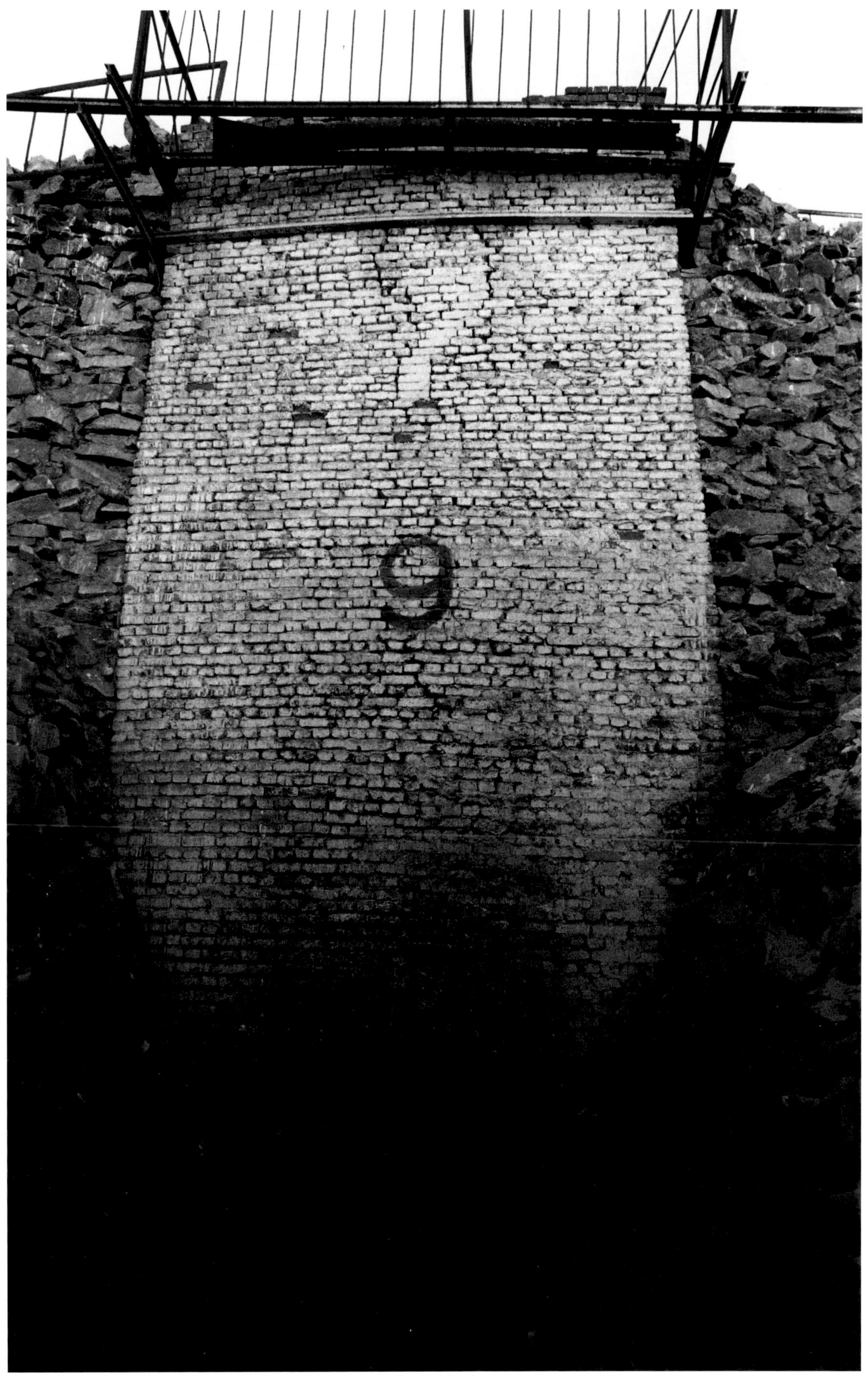
9

These journeys in Mongolia took me 9,000 miles over five years. The common element in all these different voyages, even stronger than the ghosts, were the spirits who live high and free, harmonious with this land where nature still brings mortals to their knees.

Julia Calfee

URBAN SCAPES...

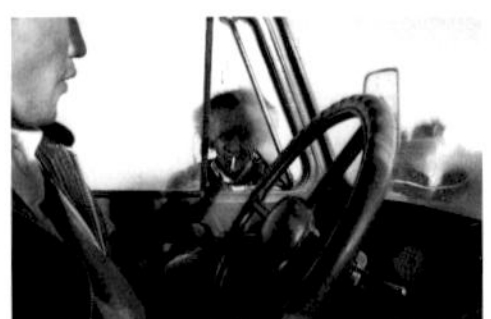
Asking directions on the road from Mantes to Ulaanbaatar.

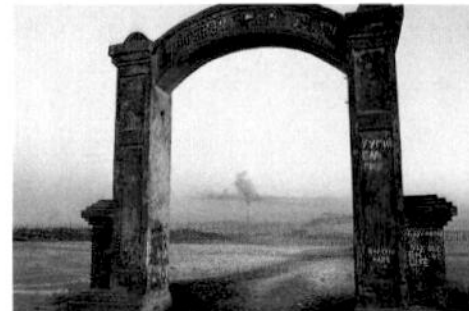
Archway outside Nalaih, an old Russian Communist-era coal-mining town.

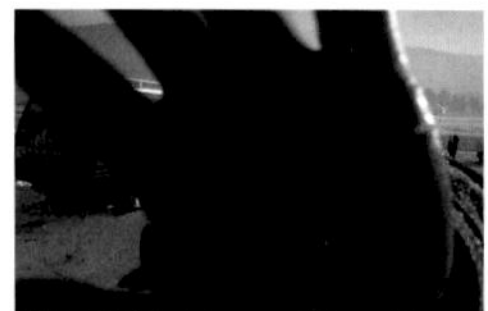
After the strict Communist regime, unease about photography can lead to violence.

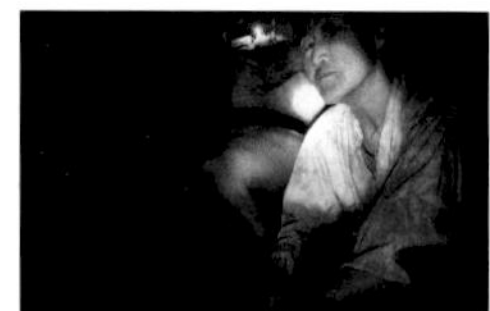
Family living in an underground hot water system.

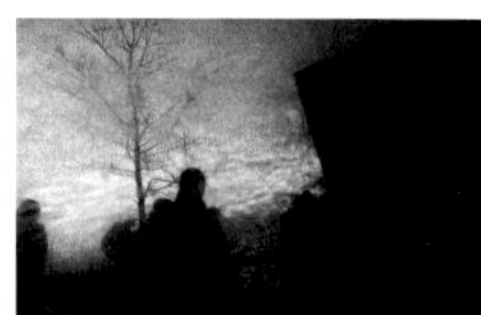
Political rally in the streets of Ulaanbaatar.

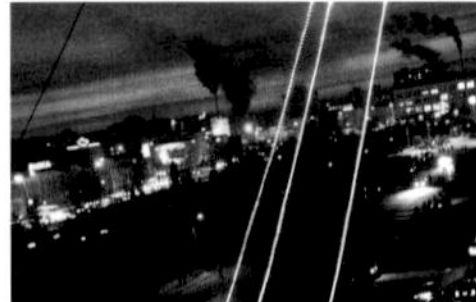
Center of Ulaanbaatar.

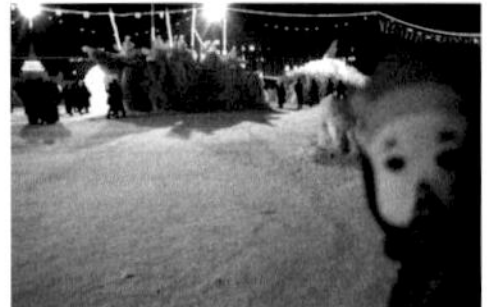
Ice sculptures in Sukhbaatar Square, Ulaanbaatar's central square.

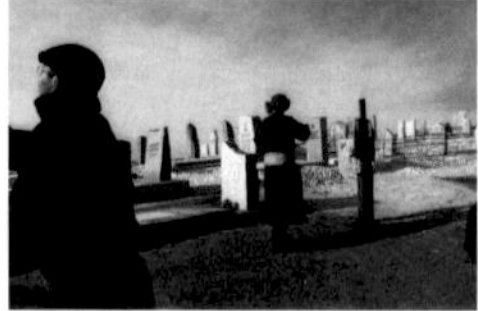
Offerings of fire, food, and vodka being made before a Buddhist funeral.

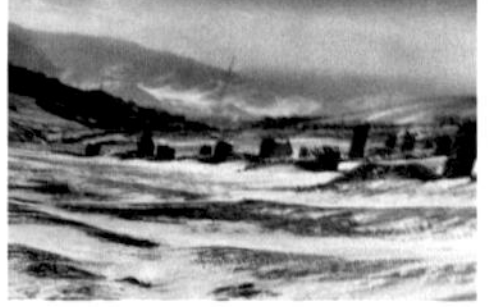
Cemetery on the outskirts of Ulaanbaatar.

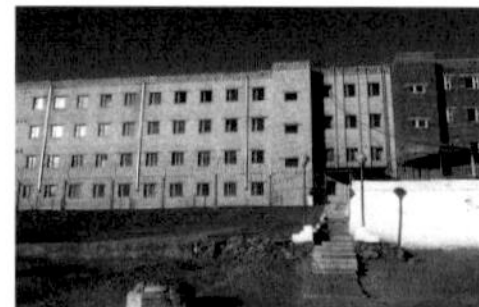
Penitentiary where men, women, and children wait for trial.

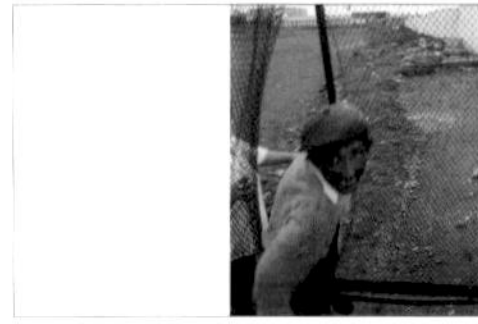
Passing through a black market near Ulaanbaatar.

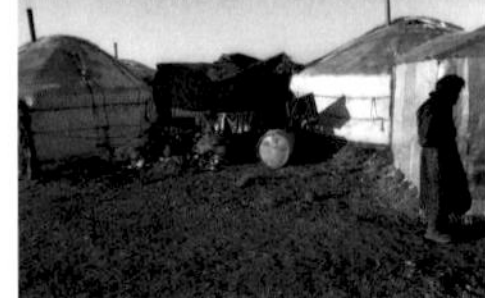
Gers (Mongol traditional felt tents) near the city's garbage dump.

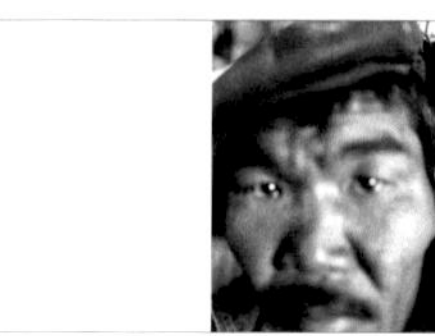
Prisoner convicted of a murder he does not remember.

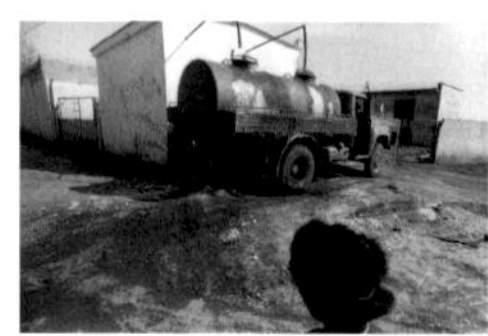
Fuel truck stranded in the frozen mud.

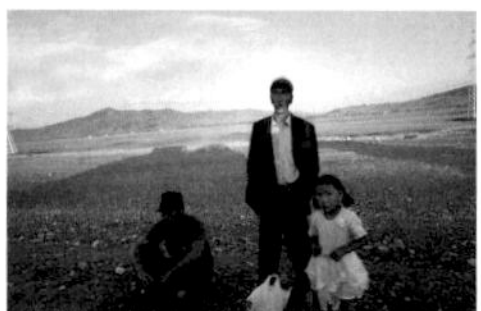
Family waiting beside the road to Gachuurt.

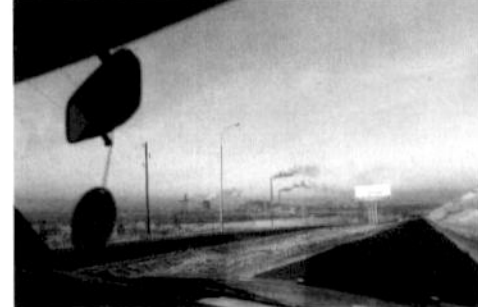
On the road into the city.

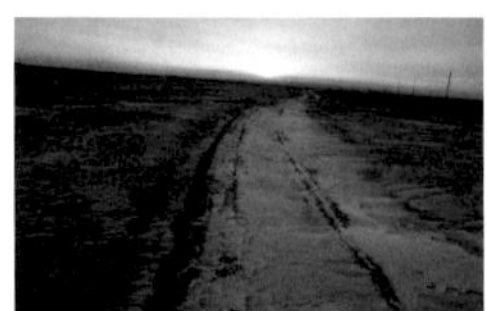
Track leading from the city of Ulaanbaatar to the Eastern provinces.

STEPPES...

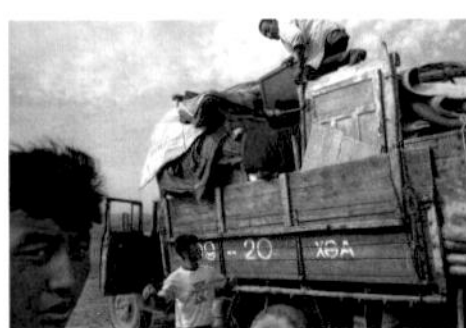
Nomads pack up their gers to move to a new campsite.

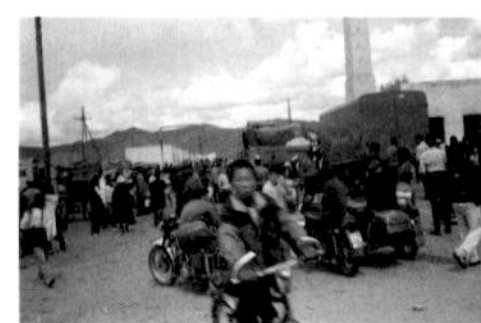
Moron, the economic hub of Northwest Mongolia.

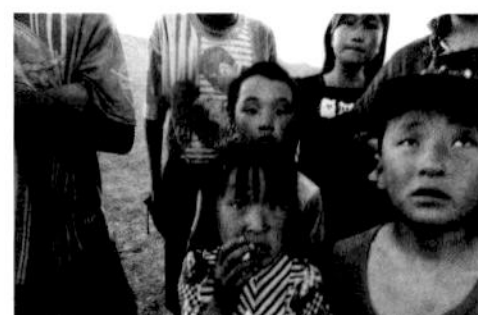
Children watch as campsite disbands.

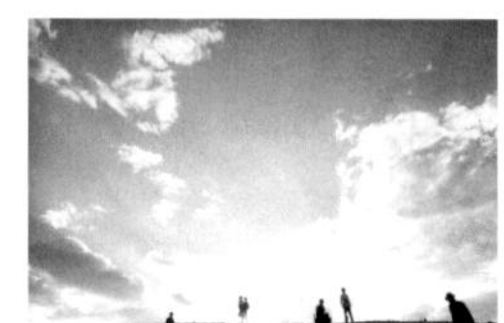
A member of the municipal council makes a routine visit to a nomadic family.

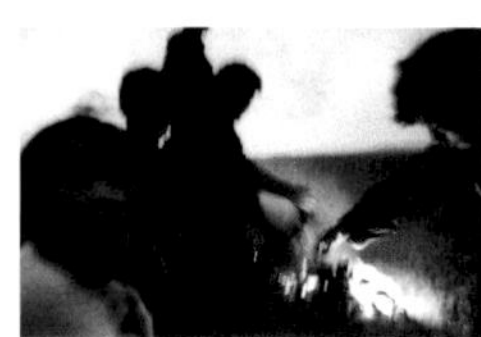
Nomads eat marmots, which may carry the black plague, to conserve meat for the cold winter months.

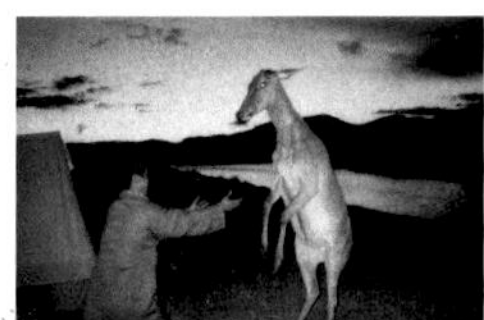
A stag comes down from the mountains to make a rare visit.

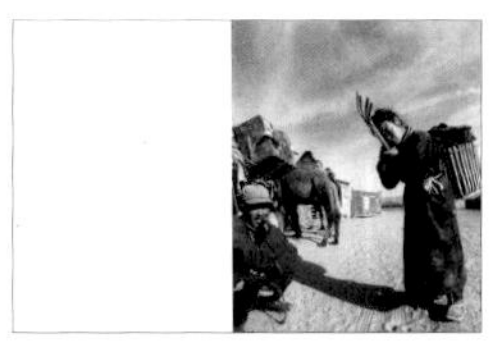
A caravan prepares to depart.

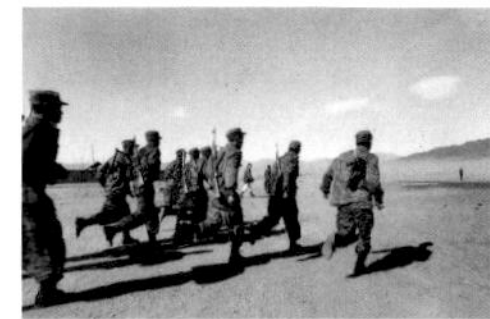
Military exercises in the Steppe.

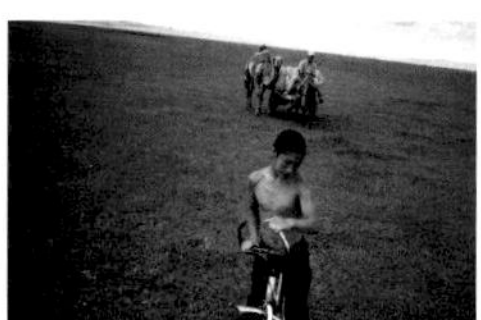
Leading the way to the evening's encampment.

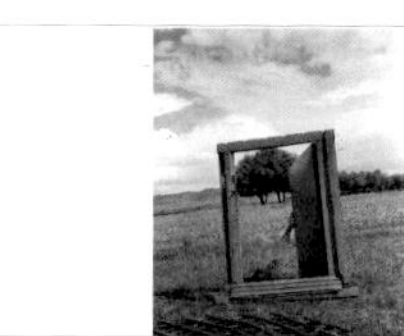
The wooden door of the ger, adorned with a silk scarf to welcome benevolent spirits, is packed up last.

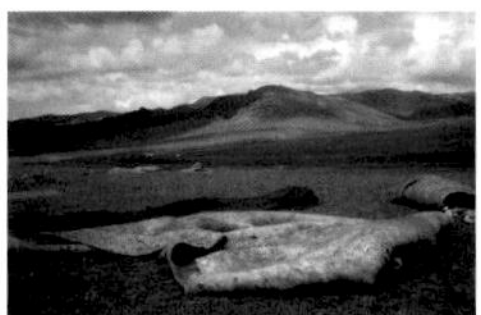
Felt made from sheep and goat's wool, which is used to cover the ger.

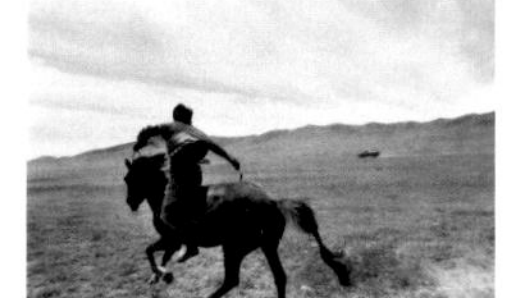
Horse racing in preparation for Nadam, a Mongol national holiday.

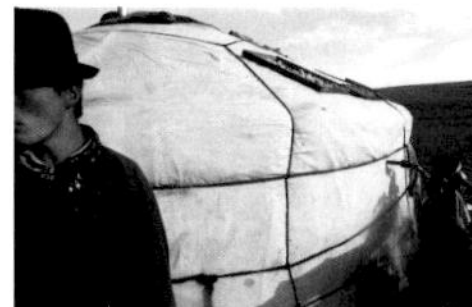
Chunks of yak cheese drying on top of the ger.

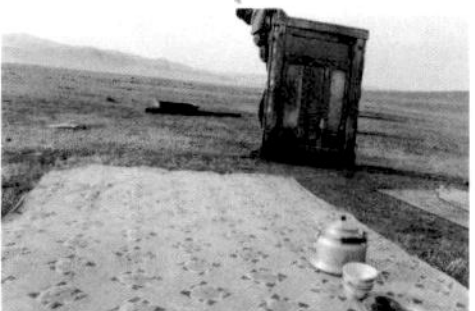
Before removing the door of the ger, tea is served for the last time.

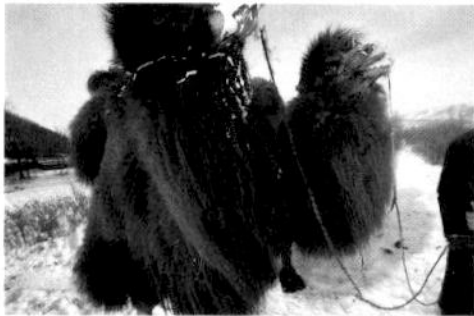
Camels begin the mating season before the end of winter.

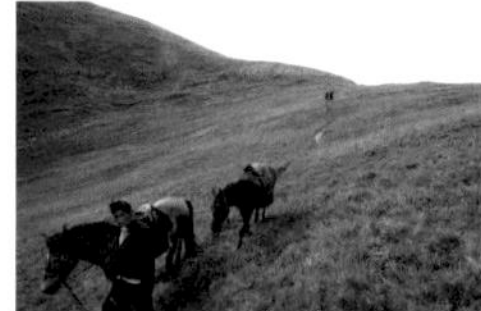
Young nomads searching for berries at summer's end.

JOURNEY WITH A SHAMAN...

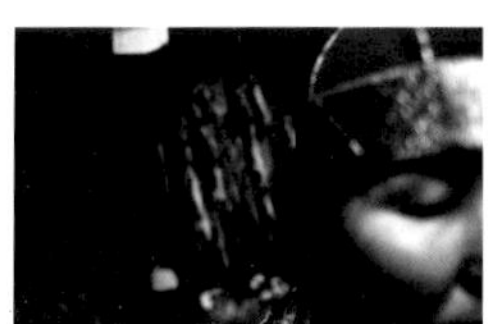
Enktoya, woman shaman and reindeer herder, during a seance.

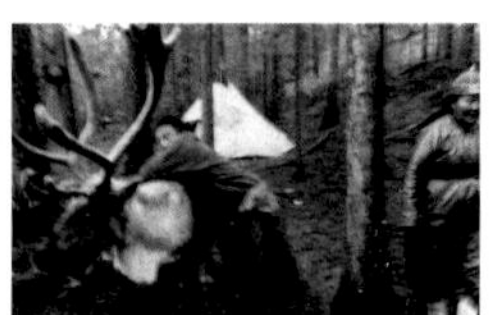
Enktoya preparing to milk her reindeer.

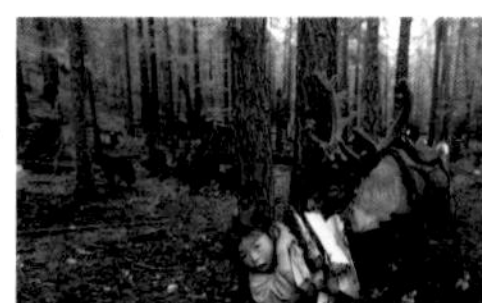
Enktoya's daughter bringing back firewood to the teepee.

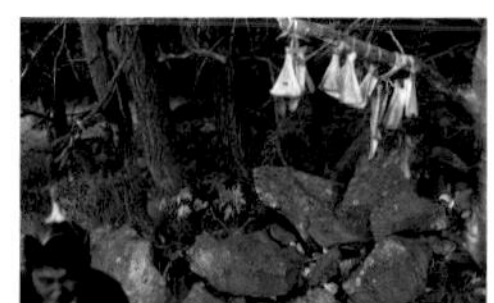
A herder asking for good health and protection by drinking from a sacred spring and listening to shoulder blade bones.

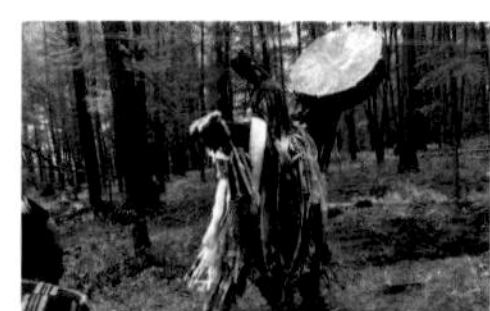
Enktoya dressed in a ceremonial cloak and holding her shaman's drum made from a tree struck by lightning.

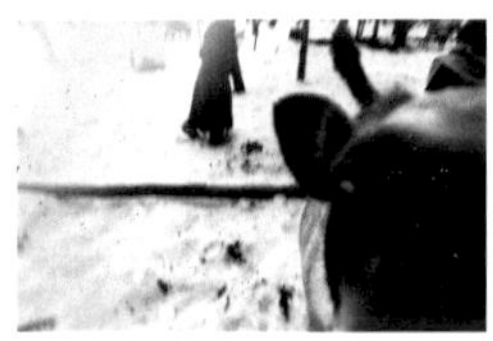
A reindeer believed by the herders to be inhabited by spirits.

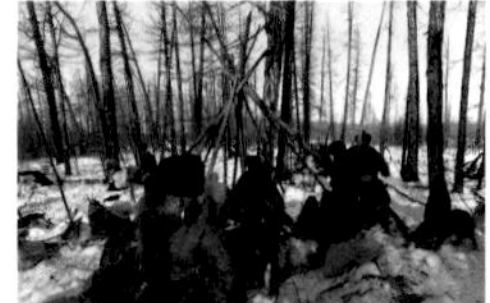
Taking apart the night's teepee.

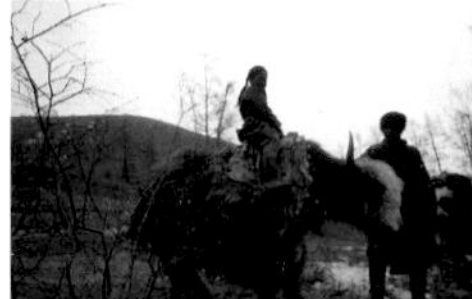
Enktoya's daughter on a yak bringing down big logs from the mountain.

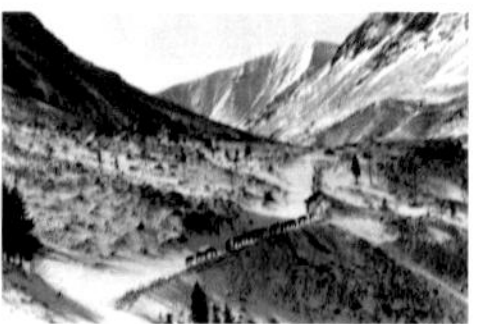
Winter caravan moving over the mountains near the Siberian border.

SPIRITS...

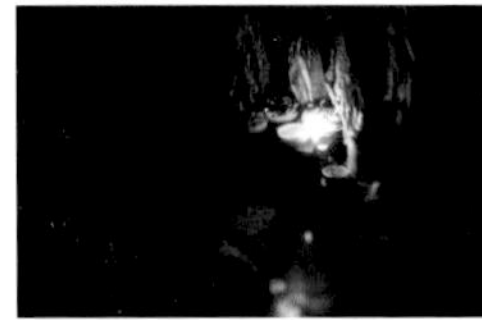
Offerings for the spirits being presented in bowls before the shaman seance.

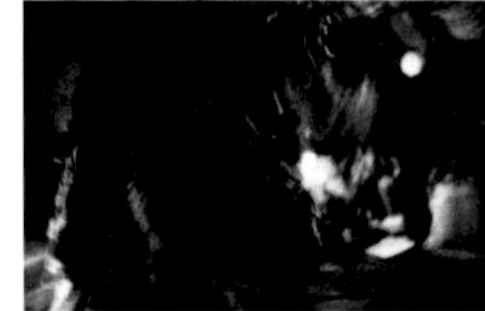
Enktoya dancing during the shaman seance.

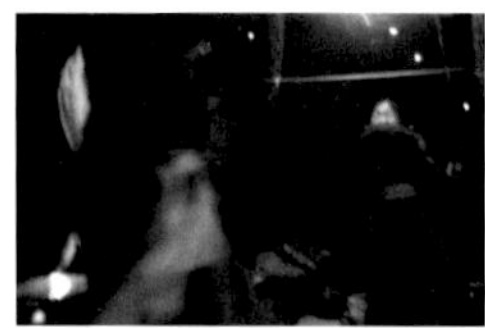
A struggle occurs between the shaman and the spirits who want to possess her.

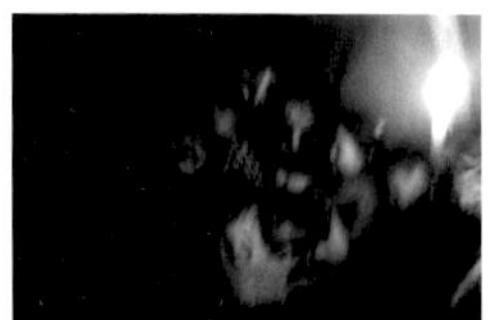
Audience observes seance below burning juniper.

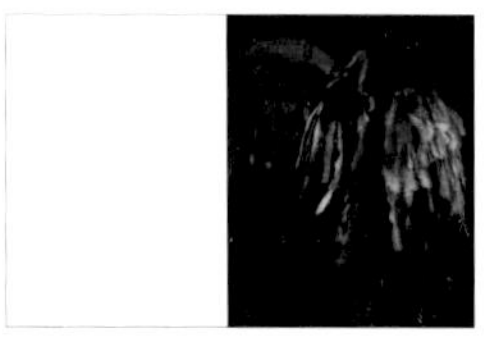
Drumming at the end of the seance.

GOBI DESERT...

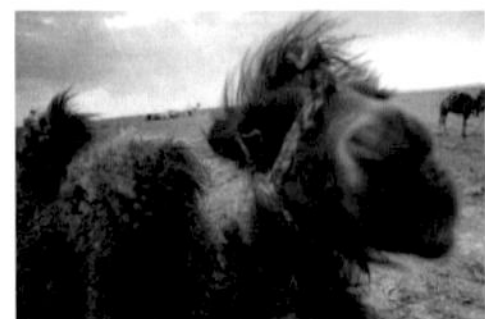
Herding camels in Noyon Soum, near the Mongol-Chinese border.

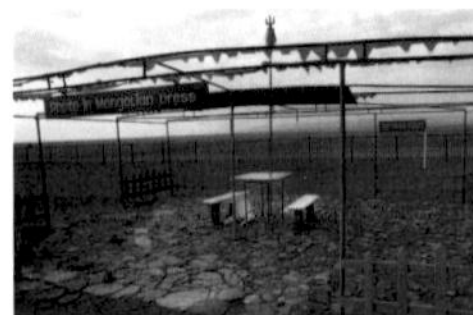
Tourist Camp in South Gobi.

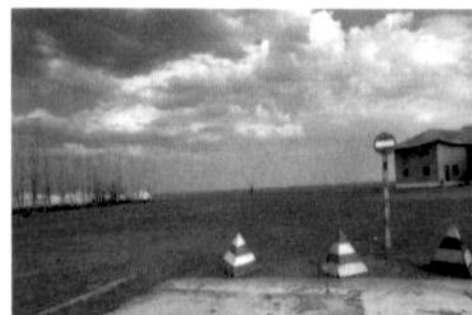
Airport at Juulchin–Gobi.

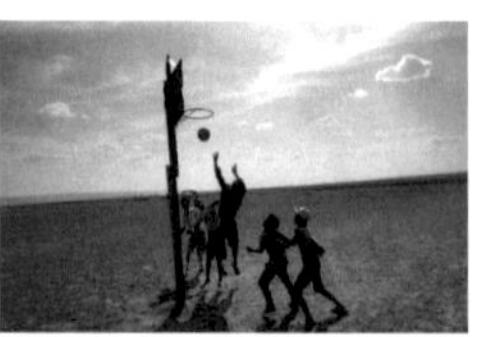
Playing basketball in Southeastern Gobi.

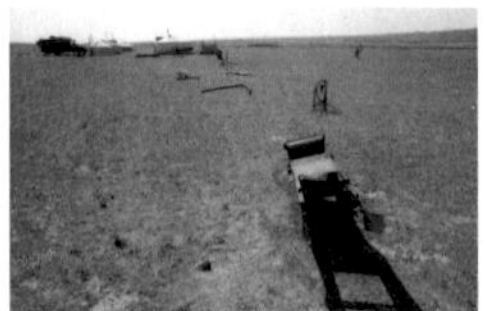
Nomadic settlements near Naran.

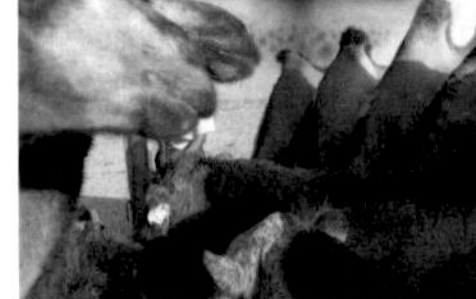
Camels drink from a well.

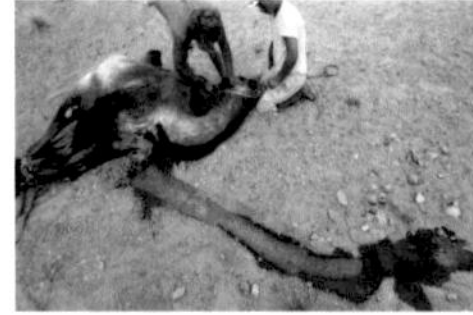
Butchering a camel to sell as meat at the local market.

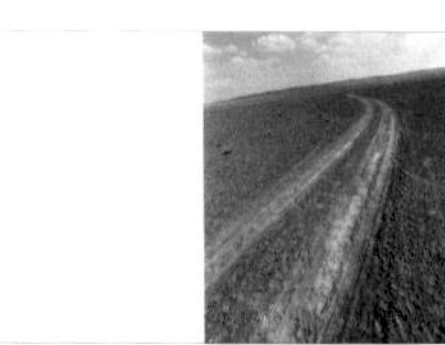
Road to Dalanzadgad.

GHOSTS...

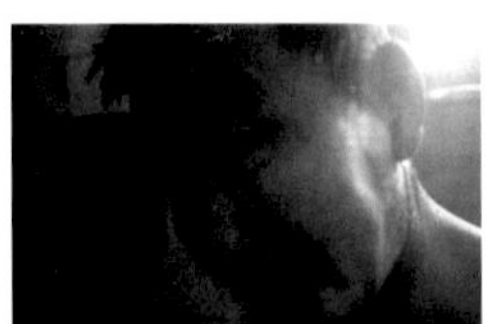
A prisoner in a high-security prison outside Ulaanbaatar.

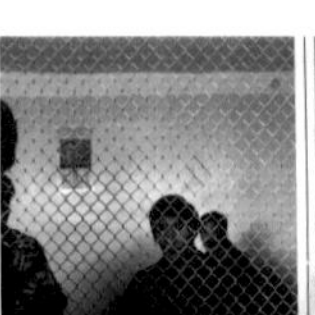
Visitor's room for prisoners and their families inside the Ulaanbaatar penitentiary.

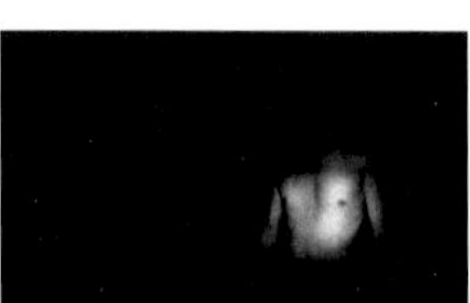
Inside the detention center for drunks, individuals are stripped and left waiting.

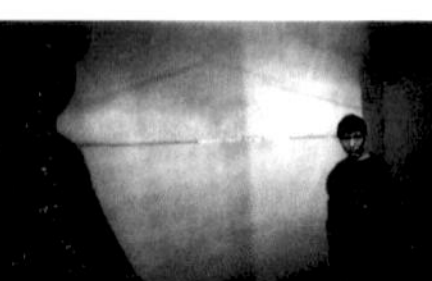
Juvenile section of the penitentiary.

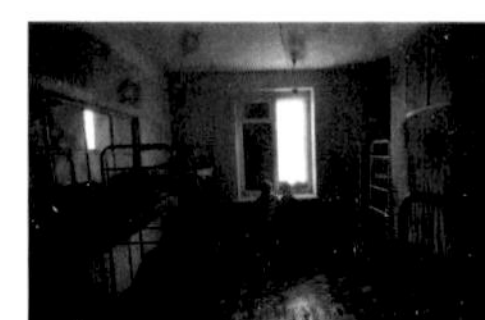
Sleeping quarters in a prison for juveniles.

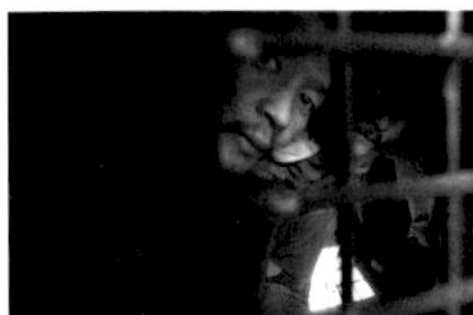
Adult male prisoners in the penitentiary, nine to a cell.

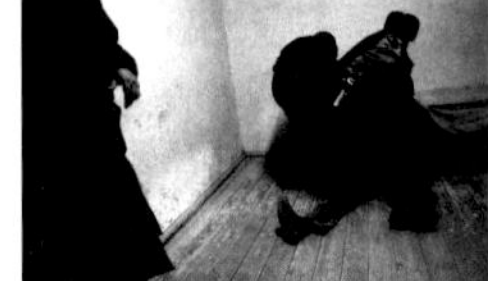
Adult male being stripped for admission to the detention center for drunks.

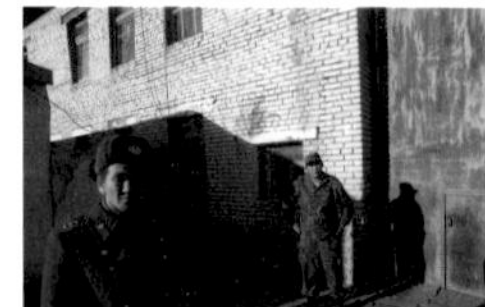
Guards in front of the high-security prison.

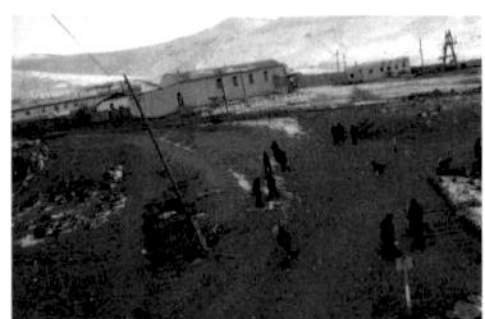
View of maximum-security prison from a watchtower.

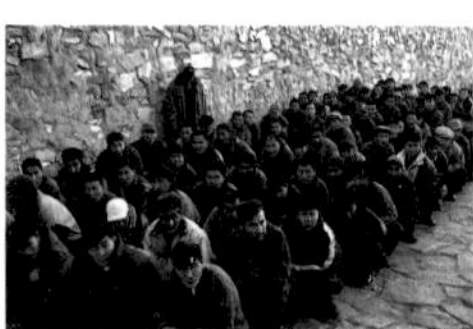
Prisoner counts are made five times a day in the high-security prison.

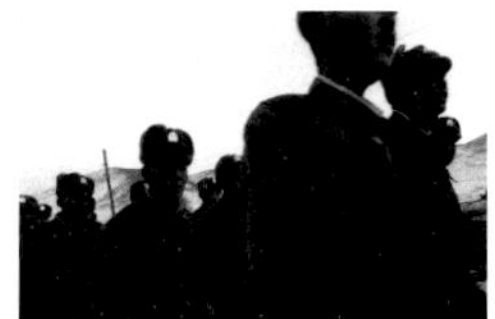

Guards march around a small square evenings and sing military songs.

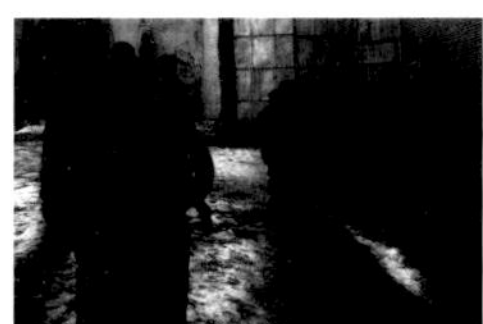

Going to the last prison count of the day.

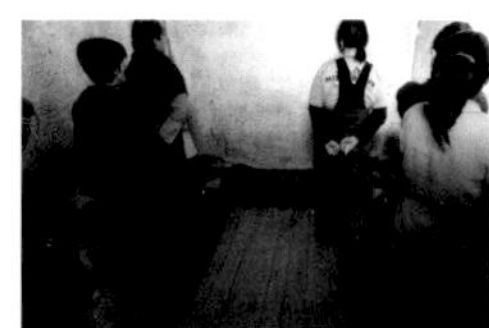

Women's section of the penitentiary.

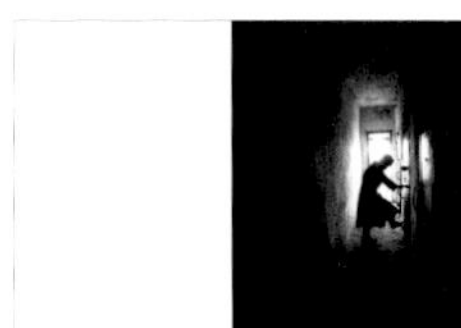

Guard locking the solitary confinement cells.

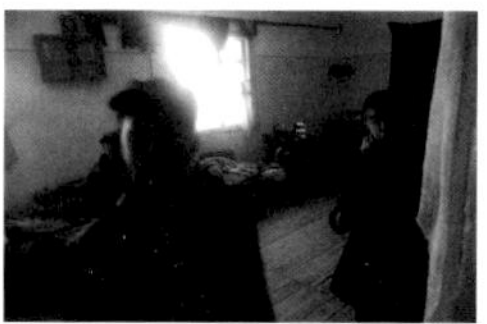

Children's section of the insane asylum.

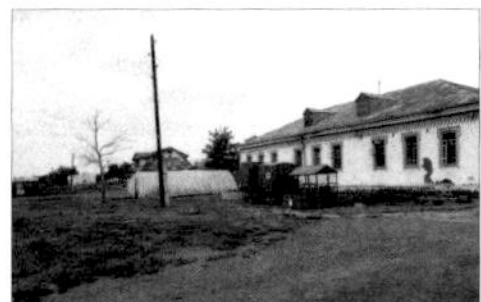

Juvenile prison in Ulaanbaataar.

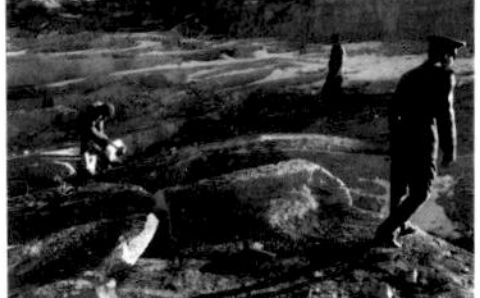

Guard patrolling work camp where prisoners extract hunks of granite for use as gravestones.

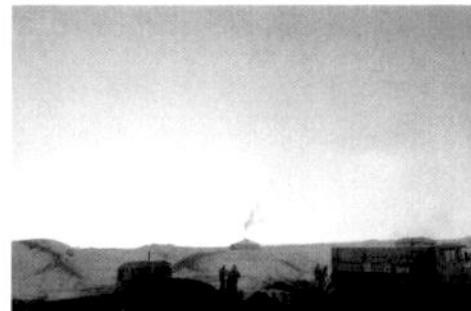

Trucks picking up coal from independent miners for use in work camps.

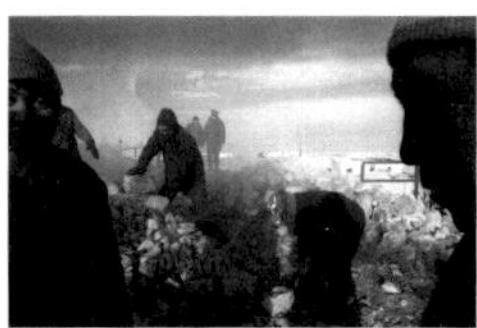

Forced labor processing chalk near the maximum-security prison.

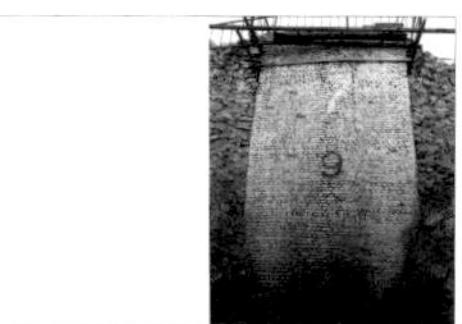

Mine used to extract chalk.

SKYSCAPE...

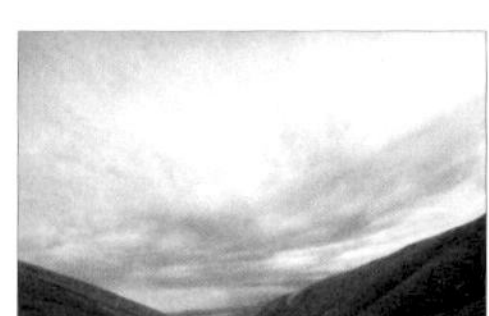

Traveling up over the mountains toward Lake Khosgol.

ACKNOWLEDGEMENTS

Thanks to the following who through their help brought this book into existence:

Antonin Kratochvil, Gabriella Kratochvil, Charles-Guy Le Paul, Daniel Power, Craig Cohen, Jim Megargee, Sendenjav Dulam, Jan Zacharias, and Michael Zacharias.

Special thanks to:

Mark Oppitz, Marcel Hungerbühler, Christopher Gierke, Enke Gierke,Mark Grosset, Pierre Fernandez, Cornelia van der Linde, Walter Brisk, Bryan Smith, Claire Landiss, Doris Elkan, Bruce Stutz, Miltiades Papatheophanes, Grazia Neri, Bum-Ochir Dulam, Erdene Dulam, Mike Persson, Jerome Ruby, Bob Schrei, Philippe Libert, Risa Weber, Martin Colyer, E. Enkhsaikhan, Leos Válka, and Enktuvshin.

SPIRITS AND GHOSTS
Journeys through Mongolia

© 2003 powerHouse Cultural Entertainment, Inc.
Photographs © 2003 Julia Calfee
Introduction © 2003 Antonin Kratochvil

All rights reserved. No part of this book may be reproduced in any manner or transmitted by any means whatsoever, electronic or mechanical (including photocopy, film or video recording, Internet posting, or any other information storage and retrieval system) without the prior written permission of the publisher.

Published in the United States by powerHouse Books,
a division of powerHouse Cultural Entertainment, Inc.
180 Varick Street, Suite 1302, New York, NY 10014-4606
telephone 212 604 9074, fax 212 366 5247
e-mail: spirits@powerHouseBooks.com
web site: www.powerHouseBooks.com

First edition, 2003

Library of Congress Cataloging-in-Publication Data:

Calfee, Julia.
Spirits and ghosts: journeys through Mongolia / Photographs by Julia Calfee; introduction by Antonin Kratochvil.
p. cm
ISBN 1-57687-167-3
1. Calfee, Julia--Journeys--Mongolia. 2. Mongolia--Pictorial works. I. Title: Journeys through Mongolia. II. Title.

DS798.2 .C36 2003

915.17'304--dc21
2002193023

Hardcover ISBN 1-57687-167-3

Separations, printing, and binding by Arti Grafiche Amilcare Pizzi S.p.A., Milan

A complete catalog of powerHouse Books and Limited Editions is available upon request; please call, write, or spirit to our web site.

10 9 8 7 6 5 4 3 2 1

Printed and bound in Italy

Book design by Jan Zacharias, Atelijeur Půda, Prague